Egyptian Colloquial Arabic Vocabulary

Matthew Aldrich

lingualism

Revised edition published 2021

ISBN: 978-0985816087

website: www.lingualism.com

email: contact@lingualism.com

Table of Contents

Introduction

Vocabulary, much more than grammar, is the key to effective communication in Arabic. You need words to speak; you need words to listen and understand.

Knowing grammar inside and out won't save you if you don't have the right word to plug into the structure. You can walk into a shop armed with grammatical structures such as "I would like some __." or "Do you have any __?", but if you don't know the word for the thing you want, you may very well leave the shop empty handed. On the other hand, if you walk into that same shop and simply say "sugar", you're almost certain to get what went there for.

And without an extensive repertoire of vocabulary, you will understand very little of what others are talking about. Spoken Arabic, to your foreign ears, will remain little more than gibberish. But once you can understand the majority of what you hear, something magical happens. The input becomes manageable--you will be able to use contextual clues from what you do understand to guess the meaning of new words and start to make rapid progress in Arabic.

It is therefore very important to build up a large store of words as soon as possible. **Egyptian Colloquial Arabic Vocabulary** is an enormously effective means to this end. By presenting practical words and phrases categorized by topic and arranged with a logical flow, mental connections that assist in vocabulary retention are fostered. The page layout in parallel columns of English translation, phonemic transcription, and Arabic script provides a variety of ways to study the vocabulary by allowing you to cover columns and test yourself.

The accompanying MP3s, free to download from our website at **www.lingualism.com/ecav**, make up an invaluable part of the learning process, allowing you to hear and mimic native speakers' pronunciation, pitch, intonation, and rhythm. Additional study materials (Anki digital flashcards, premium audio, and an e-Book) are available separately from our website and provide even more powerful tools for rapid vocabulary acquisition.

Although extremely important, vocabulary still only makes up one aspect of learning a language. **Egyptian Colloquial Arabic Vocabulary** is the ideal supplementary tool to reinforce vocabulary acquisition. However, it is not meant to be a stand-alone course. It is expected that you have followed, are following, or plan to follow, a course in Egyptian Colloquial Arabic (ECA). Alternatively, you may have studied another dialect of Arabic, or Modern Standard Arabic (MSA), and are curious to learn more about the ECA and tune your ears to the idiosyncrasies of this beautiful dialect.

The author would like to thank Mido Ali, Mostafa Said, and Mostafa El-Kassar for collaborating to provide authentic Egyptian Arabic translations of the items in this book, Lilia Khachroum, and Patrick Baggett for proof-reading the text, and Cameleons Group in Cairo for recording the MP3s.

The accompanying **MP3s** can be downloaded for free at:

www.lingualism.com/ecav

How to Use This Book

Egyptian Colloquial Arabic Vocabulary is made up of 57 thematic sections, each dedicated to a different topic. Each section is numbered to facilitate references from the index and the MP3s.

You may study the sections and individual vocabulary items in any order, or you may work through the book systematically. It is encouraged that you mark up and highlight the book as you use it. Make it your own. There is also a Notebook after the last section where you can add in more words you have learned from other sources.

Many words could logically belong to more than one topic. While some words do appear in more than one section, to avoid superfluous repetition of words, most appear only once. To your surprise, you might not be able to find common animals such as *cow* and *horse* in the section "Animals", for instance. This is because farm animals appear in the section "Agriculture" instead. This might not be entirely intuitive, so to solve this, an index Alphabetical English index can be found at the back of the book.

- For guides to the Lingualism system of orthography (tashkeel rules) and phonemic transcription, see the Resources section on www.lingualism.com/ecav
- For nouns and adjectives having an irregular plural form, the plural appears in parentheses.
- If a noun is listed in its dual or plural ([pl.]) form, this is indicated.
- A noun ending in ـة is feminine, and a noun *not* ending in ـة is masculine. The gender is marked [m.] and [f.] for nouns which do not follow this rule.
- All countries, except those marked [m.] and all cities are feminine. Keep this in mind as countries and cities are not marked [f.].
- Only the masculine version of nouns denoting humans is listed when the feminine equivalent can be formed by adding ـة. For example, مُدرِّس *mudárris* is a male teacher. A female teacher would be مُدرِّسة *mudarrísa.*
- For the sake of consistency and simplicity, the masculine singular form is used in expressions. You will need to use your knowledge of Arabic grammar to produce the feminine or plural equivalents.
- Some nouns are classified as *collective nouns.* An explanation of the usage of collective nouns appears on page 61.

- Some adjectives are invariable and are marked [invar.]. These do not have a feminine or plural form.
- Each verb appears in its base form (its most basic form without any prefixes or suffixes), which is the masculine singular past tense, literally "he did"; however, the English translation appears in its standard citation form: "to do". In order to use a verb in a sentence, it must be conjugated.
- Every verb is followed by small square brackets with a reference to its corresponding table in the book **Egyptian Colloquial Arabic Verbs**, which presents conjugation tables to model all the possible conjugated forms of any verb in ECA.
- The Arabic script reflects common spelling conventions used by Egyptians.
- A few words, which are vulgar or taboo, do not appear on the MP3s because of their sensitive nature. These are marked with an asterisk (*).

1 Life and Death

life	*ḫáya, ḫayā?*	حَياة
to live	*3āš* [1h2]	عاش
I live in Egypt, the mother of the world.	*ána 3āyiš fi maşr, umm iddúnya.*	أنا عايِش في مصْر أُمّ الدُّنْيا.
Long live the king!	*yi3īš ilmálik!*	يِعيش الملِك!
alive	*bi-lḫáya* *3āyiš*	بِالحَياة عايِش
to give birth to	*wílid* [1s5]	وِلِد
to be born	*itwálad* [7s1]	اِتْوَلد
birth	*wilāda*	وِلادة
newborn	*mawlūd (mawalīd)*	مَوْلود (مَوَليد)
baby	*nūnu (nunuhāt)* *bībi (bibihāt)* *3áyyil şuɣáyyar (3iyāl şuɣār)*	نونو (نونوهات) بيبي (بيبيهات) عيِّل صُغيرّ (عِيال صُغار)
infant (who is still being breastfed)	*radī3 (rúda3)*	رضيع (رُضع)
to be breastfed, suckle	*rídi3* [1s4]	رِضِع
to breastfeed	*rádda3* [2s2]	رضّع
toddler	*ţifl*[ə] *şɣáyyar (atfāl şuɣār)*	طِفْل صْغيرّ (أطْفال صُغار)
diaper (UK: nappy)	*ḫafāda*	حفاضة
child (0-17 years old)	*3áyyil (3iyāl)* *ţifl (atfāl)*	عيِّل (عِيال) طِفْل (أطْفال)

well-behaved	*mitrábbi* *muʔáddab*	مِتْربِّي مُؤَدّب
naughty, mischievous	*šáʔi (ašʔíya)*	شقِي (أَشْقِيا)
childish, immature	*3áyyil (fi taşarrufātu)*	عيِّل (في تصرُّفاتُه)
mature(-acting)	*sābiʔ sínnu*	سابِق سِنُّه

The second words listed below for 'boy' and 'girl' may be considered disparaging in many contexts. You are advised only to use the first (standard) words.

boy	*wálad, wād (awlād, wilād)*	وَلد، واد (أَوْلاد، وِلاد)
girl	*bint [f.], bitt [f.] (banāt)*	بِنْت، بِتّ (بنات)
adolescent, teenager	*murāhiq*	مراهِق
to grow up, get older	*kíbir* [1s4]	كِبِر

person	*šaxş (ašxāş)*	شخْص (أَشْخاص)
people	*nās [f. or pl.]*	ناس
young man	*šabb (šubbān)*	شابّ (شُبّان)
young woman	*šábba*	شابّة
man	*rāgil (rigāla)*	راجِل (رِجالة)
woman	*sitt [f.]*	سِتّ
adult	*bāliɣ*	بالِغ
adults, grown-ups	*kubār [pl.]*	كُبار
young people, youth	*šabāb [coll.]*	شباب
young	*şuɣáyyar (şuɣār)*	صُغيِّر (صُغار)

There is no common equivalent in Arabic for 'middle-aged'. Instead, a more precise description, such as 'in one's forties/fifties/sixties' can be used.

in one's fifties, middle-aged	*fi -lxamsiniyāt (min il3úmr)*	في الخمْسينِيات (مِن العُمْر)
old	*kibīr (kubār) fi -ssinn* *3agūz (3awagīz)*	كِبِير (كُبار) في السِّنّ عجوز (عَواجِيز)

old man	*rāgil 3agūz* *rāgil kibīr*	راجِل عجوز راجِل كِبير
old woman	*sitt^ə 3agūza* *sitt^ə kbīra*	سِتّ عجوزة سِتّ كْبيرة
to age, grow old	*3ággiz* [2s1]	عجِّز
Everyone gets old.	*kull innās bit3ággiz.*	كُلّ النّاس بِتْعجِّز.

childhood	*ṭufūla*	طُفولة
in one's childhood	*fi ṭfúltu*	في طْفولْتُه
adolescence	*murāhaqa*	مُراهقة
youth	*šabāb*	شباب
in one's youth	*fi šabābu*	في شبابُه
old age	*sinn^ə kbīr*	سِنّ كْبير

birthday	*3īd milād*	عيد ميلاد
Happy Birthday!	*kull^ə sána w ínta ṭáyyib!* (lit. May you be well every year!)	كُلّ سنة و إنْتَ طيِّب!
Thank you! (response to 'Happy Birthday!'	*w ínta ṭáyyib!* (lit. 'May you too be well!')	و إنْتَ طيِّب!
Happy birthday and may you have many more!, ... and many happy returns!	*kull^ə sána w ínta ṭáyyib wi 3uʔbāl mīt sána, in šāʔ aḷḷāh!* (lit. ... and the same for 100 years, God willing!)	كُلّ سنة و إنْتَ طيِّب و عُقْبال مية سنة إن شاء اللّه!
When is your birthday?	*ímta 3īd milādak?*	إمْتى عيد ميلادك؟
My birthday is in May.	*3īd milādi f māyu.*	عيد ميلادي في مايو.

age, life span	*3umr (a3mār)*	عُمْر (أعْمار)

all one's life	*ṭūl 3úmru*	**طول عُمْرُه**
year	*sána (sinīn)*	**سنة (سِنين)**
How old are you?	*3ándak kam sána?*	عنْدك كام سنة؟
I'm 20 years old.	*3ándi 3išrīn sána.*	عنْدي عِشْرين سنة.
to turn __ years old	*tamm* [1g3] *__ sána*	**تمّ __ سنة**
He's turning ten years old next week.	*haytímmᵊ 3ášar sinīn il?isbū3 ilgáyy.*	هَيْتِمّ عشر سِنين الإسْبوع الجايّ.
I turned thirty last month.	*tammēt talatīn sána -ššahr ílli fāt.*	تمّيْت تلاتين سنة الشّهْر اللي فات.
a ten-year-old boy/child	*wálad/wād/3áyyil/ṭiflᵊ 3ándu 3ášar sinīn*	**وَلد/واد/عيِّل/طِفْل عنْدُه عشر سِنين**
a fifty-year-old woman	*sittᵊ 3andáha xamsīn sána*	**سِتّ عنْدها خمْسين سنة**
When were you born?	*itwaládtᵊ ?ímta?*	اِتْوَلدْت إمْتى؟
What year were you born?	*itwaládtᵊ sánit kām?*	اِتْوَلدْت سنِةْ كام؟
I was born in 1980.	*itwaládtᵊ sánit alfᵊ tús3u míyya w tamanīn.*	اِتْوَلدْت سنِةْ ألْف تُسْعُمية و تمانين.

death	*mōt*	**موْت**
to die	*māt* [1h1]	**مات**
dead	*máyyit (amwāt)*	**ميِّت (أمْوات)**
death, passing	*wafāh (wafiyāt)*	**وَفاة (وَفِيات)**
to pass away	*itwáffa* [5d]	**اِتْوَفّى**
deceased	*mutawáffi*	**مُتَوَفّي**
corpse, body	*gússa (gúsas)*	**جُثّة (جُثث)**
funeral	*ganāza*	**جنازة**
to bury	*dáfan* [1s2]	**دفن**

to be buried	*itdáfan* [7s1]	اِتْدفن
burial	*dáfna*	دفْنة
coffin	*tabūt (tawabīt)*	تابوت (تَوابيت)
cemetary	*mádfan (madāfin)* *maqbára (maqābir)*	مدْفن (مدافِن) مقْبرة (مقابِر)
grave	*qabr (qubūr)*	قبْر (قُبور)
gravestone, headstone	*šāhid (šawāhid) qabr*	شاهِد (شَواهِد) قبْر
to mourn	*ɦízin* [1s4]	حِزِن
mourning	*ɦuzn*	حُزْن
period of mourning	*múddit ɦuzn*	مُدِّةْ حُزْن
to cremate	*ɦáraʔ* [1s1] *gussítu*	حرق جُثِّتُه
cremation	*ɦáraʔ*	حرق

2 Family

(extended) family	*3ēla*	**عايْلة**
(immediate) family	*úsra (úsar)*	**أُسْرة (أُسر)**
relative	*ʔarīb (ʔarāyib)*	**قُريِّب (قرايِب)**
I have some relatives that live in New York.	*ána 3ándi ʔarāyib 3ayšīn fi nyuyōrk.*	أنا عنْدي قرايِب عايْشين في نْيويوْرْك.
to be related to	*yíʔrab* [1s4] *li-*	**يِقْرب لِـ**
Are you two related?	*húwwa -ntu -lʔitnēn tiʔrábu l-ba3ḍ?*	هُوَّ إنْتو الاِتْنينْ تِقْربوا لْبعْض؟
I'm not related to him.	*ána maʔrablūš.*	أنا مقْربْلوش.
father	*abb (abbahāt)* *wālid*	**أبّ (أبّهات)** **والِد**
mother	*umm* [f.] *(ummahāt)* *wālída*	**أمّ (أُمّهات)** **والِدة**

When in a possessive construction, أبّ *abb* becomes أبو *abū*-. But أمّ *umm* is unchanged.

my mother and father	*úmmi w abūya*	**أُمّي و أبويا**
dad	*bāba* [m.]	**بابا**
mom (UK: mum)	*māma* [f.]	**ماما**
my mom and dad	*mámti wi babāya*	**مامْتي و بابايا**
Hi, Dad!	*izzáyyak ya bāba!* *izzáyyak ya ʔábi!*	**إزّيّك يا بابا!** **إزّيّك يا أبي!**
Where are you, Mom?	*fēnik ya māma?* *fēnik ya ʔúmmi?*	فيْنِك يا ماما؟ فيْنِك يا أُمّي؟
parents	*ahl*	**أهْل**

son, (male) child	*ibn (wilād, awlād)*	**إبْن (وِلاد، أَوْلاد)**
daughter, (female) child	*bint* [f.] *(banāt)*	**بِنْت (بنات)**
Do you have any children?	*3ándak awlād?*	عنْدك أَوْلاد؟
How many children do you have?	*3ándak kām wálad?*	عنْدك كام وَلد؟
to have (a child)	*xállif* [1s1]	**خلِّف**
They had triplets.	*xallífu tálat tawāʔim.*	خلِّفوا تلات تَوائِم.

siblings	*ixwāt* [pl.]	**إخْوات**
brother	*axx (ixwāt wilād)*	**أخّ (إخْوات وِلاد)**
When in a possessive construction, أخّ *axx* becomes **أخو** *axū-*.		
My brother and my friend's brother came with me.	*axūya w axū ṣáḥbi gum ma3āya.*	أخويا و أخو صاحْبي جُم معايا.
sister	*uxt* [f.] *(ixwāt banāt)*	**أُخْت (إخْوات بنات)**
older brother	*axx^ə kbīr*	**أخّ كْبير**
younger sister	*uxt^ə ṣɣayyára*	**أُخْت صْغيّرة**
Do you have any brothers or sisters?	*3ándak ixwāt?*	عنْدك إخْوات؟
I have two older sisters and one younger brother.	*3ándi ʔuxtēn ákbar mínni wi ʔaxx^ə ʔáṣɣar mínni.*	عنْدي أُخْتيْن أكْبر مِنّي و أخّ أصْغر مِنّي.
I'm the youngest in my family.	*ána ʔáṣɣar fard^ə fi-lʔúsra.*	أنا أصْغر فرْد في الأُسْرة.
I'm the middle child/son.	*ána -lʔaxx ilʔáwsaṭ.*	أنا الأخّ الأَوْسط.
I'm an only child.	*ma-3andīš ixwāt. (lit. I don't have siblings.)*	معنْديش إخْوات.
twin	*táwʔam (tawāʔim)*	**تَوْأم (توائِم)**
تَوْأم *táwʔam* can refer to siblings in a multiple birth of any number (triplets, quadruplets, etc.)		

Are you two twins?	*húwwa -ntu -lʔitnēn táwʔam?*	هُوَّ إنْتو الاِتْنين تَوْأم ؟
I have a twin brother.	*3ándi ʔaxx^{ə} táwʔam.*	عنْدي أخّ تَوْأم.
half-brother	*axx^{ə} min abb* *axx^{ə} min umm*	أخّ مِن أبّ أخّ مِن أُمّ
half-sister	*uxt^{ə} min abb* *uxt^{ə} min umm*	أُخْت مِن أبّ أُخْت مِن أُمّ
He's my half-brother.	*húwwa (a)xūya min abūya.*	هُوَّ أخويا مِن أبويا.

husband	*gōz (agwāz)* *zōg (azwāg)*	جوْز (أجْواز) زوْج (أزْواج)
wife	*záwga (zawgāt)*	زَوْجة (زَوْجات)
__'s wife	*mirāt-*__ [f.] *issítt^{ə} btā3it*__ [f.]	مِرات __ السِّتّ بِتاعِةْ__
His wife came with him.	*mirātu gat ma3ā.* *issítt^{ə} btá3tu gat ma3ā.*	مِراتُه جت معاه. السِّتّ بِتاعْتُه جت معاه.

Rather than using a single term meaning 'step-' in Arabic, relationships are described.

stepfather	*gōz umm* (lit. mother's husband)	جوْز أُمّ
stepmother	*mirāt abb* (lit. father's wife)	مِرات أبّ
stepbrother	*ibn^{ə} gōz umm* (lit. mother's husband's son) *ibn^{ə} mrāt abb* (lit. father's wife's son)	إبْن جوْز أُمّ إبْن مْرات أبّ
stepsister	*bint^{ə} gōz umm* (lit. mother's husband's daughter) *bint^{ə} mrāt abb* (lit. father's wife's daughter)	بِنْت جوْز أُمّ بِنْت مْرات أبّ

stepson	*ibnᵊ gōz* (lit. husband's son) *ibnᵊ mrāt-* (lit. wife's son)	إبْن جوْز إبْن مْرات
stepdaughter	*bintᵊ gōz* (lit. husband's daughter) *bintᵊ mrāt-* (lit. husband's daughter)	بِنْت جوْز بِنْت مْرات

grandfather	*gidd (gudūd)*	جِدّ (جُدود)
grandmother	*gídda*	جِدّة
my grandparents	*gíddi wi giddíti*	جِدّي و جِدّتي
grandpa	*gíddu*	جِدّو
grandma	*tēta*	تيْتة
great-grandfather	*abū gidd*	أبو جِدّ
grandson	*ɧafīd (aɧfād)*	حفيد (أحْفاد)
granddaughter	*ɧafīda*	حفيدة
grandchildren	*aɧfād* [pl.]	أحْفاد

uncle (father's brother)	*3amm (a3mām, 3imām)*	عمّ (أعْمام ، عِمام)
aunt (father's brother's wife)	*mirāt 3amm*	مِرات عمّ
aunt (father's sister)	*3ámma*	عمّة
uncle (father's sister's husband)	*gōz 3ámma*	جوْز عمّة
uncle (mother's brother)	*xāl (axwāl)*	خال (أخْوال)
aunt (mother's brother's wife)	*mirāt xāl*	مِرات خال
aunt (mother's sister)	*xāla*	خالة
uncle (mother's sister's husband)	*gōz xāla*	جوْز خالة

cousin (father's brother's son)	*ibnᵊ 3amm*	إبْن عمّ

cousin (father's brother's daughter)	*bintᵊ 3amm*	بِنْت عمّ
cousin (father's sister's son)	*ibnᵊ 3ámma*	إبْن عمّة
cousin (father's sister's daughter)	*bintᵊ 3ámma*	بِنْت عمّة
cousin (mother's brother's son)	*ibnᵊ xāl*	إبْن خال
cousin (mother's brother's daughter)	*bintᵊ xāl*	بِنْت خال
cousin (mother's sister's son)	*ibnᵊ xāla*	إبْن خالة
cousin (mother's sister's daughter)	*bintᵊ xāla*	بِنْت خالة
We're cousins.	*íɧna wlād 3amm.*	إحْنا وْلاد عمّ.

The above example refers to two or more men/boys whose fathers are brothers.

orphan	*yatīm (aytām)*	يَتيم (أَيْتام)
orphanage	*málga? (malāgi?) aytām*	ملْجأ (ملاجِئ) أَيْتام
to adopt	*itbánna*	اِتْبنّى
adoption	*tabánni*	تبنّي
to be adopted	*ɧadd itbannā* [5d] (lit. someone adopted him)	حدّ اِتْبنّاه
I was adopted.	*ána mutabánni.*	أنا مُتبنّي.
an adopted son	*ibnᵊ bi-ttabánni*	إبْن بِالتّبنّي
adoptive parents	*ahlᵊ bi-ttabánni*	أهْل بِالتّبنّي
birth parents	*walidēn* [dual]	والِديْن

ancestors, forefathers	*agdād* [pl.]	أجْداد
descendants	*aɧfād* [pl.]	أحْفاد

3 Love, Marriage, and Sex

to love, be in love	*ɧabb* [1g3]	حبّ
love	*ɧubb*	حُبّ
I love you!	*baɧíbbak!*	بحِبّك!
darling	*ɧabīb*	حبيب
romance	*rumansíyya*	رومانْسية
to love passionately	*3íšiʔ* [1s4]	عِشِق
passion	*3ašʔ*	عشْق
lover	*3āšiʔ (3uššāʔ)*	عاشِق (عُشّاق)
date (romantic)	*mí3ād (mawa3īd)*	ميعاد، معاد (مَواعيد)
to go on a date with __	*xárag* [1s3] *má3a __ fi mi3ād*	خرج معَ __ في ميعاد
dating, in a relationship	*fi -rtibāţ* *fi 3alāqit ɧubb*	في ارْتِباط في علاقِةْ حُبّ
a couple; going out, dating	*murtabiţīn* [pl.]	مُرْتبِطين
boyfriend	*şāɧib (aşɧāb, şuɧāb)*	صاحِب (أصْحاب، صُحاب)
girlfriend	*şáɧba*	صاحْبة
to break up	*infáşal* [7s2]	اِنْفصل
to break someone's heart	*kásar* [1s1] *ʔálbu*	كسر قلْبُه

engagement	*xuţūba*	خُطوبة
to get engaged	*itxáţab* [7s1]	اِتْخطب
to ask her father for her hand in marriage	*ţálab* [1s3] *idēha min abūha li-lgawāz*	طلب إيديْها مِن أبوها لِلجَواز

fiancé	*xaṭīb (xuṭṭāb)*	خطيب (خُطّاب)
fiancee	*xaṭība*	خطيبة
Her fiancé works abroad.	*xaṭíbha šaɣɣāl bárra.*	خطيبْها شغّال برّه.
married to	*mitgáwwiz min*	مِتْجوِّز مِن
Are you married?	*ínta mitgáwwiz?*	إنْتَ مِتْجوِّز؟
single, unmarried	*3āzib* *miš mitgáwwiz* [single] [invar.]	عازِب مِش مِتْجوِّز سينْجِل
to get married, marry, wed	*itgáwwiz* [5s1]	اِتْجوِّز
marriage	*gawāz*	جَواز
arranged marriage	*gawāz ṣalunāt* (lit. living room marriage)	جَواز صالونات
They got married last year.	*itgawwízu -ssána -lli fātit.*	اِتْجوِّزوا السّنة اللي فاتِت.
He married her last year.	*itgawwízha -ssána -lli fātit.*	اِتْجوِّزْها السّنة اللي فاتِت.
wedding	*fáraḫ (afrāḫ)*	فرح (أفْراح)
groom	*3arīs (3irsān)*	عريس (عِرْسان)
bride	*3arūs* [f.], *3arūsa (3arāyis)*	عروس، عروسة (عرايِس)
honeymoon	*šahr^{ə} 3ásal*	شهْر عسل
newlyweds	*líssa mitgawwizīn* [pl.]	لِسّه مِتْجوِّزين
(wedding) anniversary	*3īd gawāz*	عيد جَواز
They celebrated their tenth anniversary.	*iḫtáfalu bi-3īd gawázhum il3āšir.*	اِحْتفلوا بِعيد جَوازْهُم العاشِر.

divorce	*ṭalāʔ*	**طلاق**
to get divorced	*itṭállaʔ* [5s2]	**اِتْطلّق**
divorcee	*muṭállaq*	**مُطلّق**
to remarry	*itgáwwiz* [5s1] *tāni*	**اِتْجوِّز تاني**
My father remarried last year.	*abūya -tgáwwiz tāni -ssána -lli fātit.*	أبويا اتْجوِّز تاني السّنة اللي فاتِت.
to be widowed	*itrámmil* [5s1]	**اِتْرمِّل**
widower	*ármil (arāmil)*	**أرْمِل (أرامِل)**
widow	*armíla (arāmil)*	**أرْمِلة (أرامِل)**

to cheat on __ with, have an affair with	*xān* [1h1] __ *má3a*	**خان __ معَ**
He was cheating on his wife with his secretary.	*kān biyxūn mirātu má3a -ssikirtēra.*	كان بِيْخون مِراتُه معَ السِّكِرْتيرْة.

kiss	*bōsa*	**بوْسة**
to kiss	*bās* [1h1]	**باس**
sex	*gins*	**جِنْس**
The following do not appear on the audio tracks due to their sensitive nature:		
to have sex	*māris* [3s] *ilgíns**	**مارِس الجِنْس**
to sleep with	*nām* [1h3] *má3a**	**نام معَ**
to sleep together	*nām* [1h3] *má3a ba3ḍ**	**نام معَ بعْض**
to fuck	*nāk** [1h2] [vulgar]	**ناك**

4 Names and Addressing People

name; first name	*ism (asmāʔ, asāmi)*	**إسْم (أسْماء، أسامي)**
What's your name?	*ísmak ʔē?*	إسْمك أيْه؟
My name is __.	*ísmi __.*	إسْمي.__
last name (UK: surname)	*ism^{ə} 3ēla*	**إسْم عايْلة**
full name	*ism^{ə} kāmil*	**إسْم كامِل**
to name	*sámma* [2d]	**سمّى**
to be called, named	*itsámma* [5d]	**اِتْسمّى**
to call	*nāda* [3d]	**نادى**
How should I address you?	*tiɧíbb anadīk bi-ʔē?*	تِحِبّ أناديك بِأيْه؟
Just call me __.	*nadīni __.* *ʔúlli __.*	نادِيني __. قولّي.__
title; nickname	*láqab (alqāb)*	**لقب (ألْقاب)**
There's no need for titles.	*ma-fīš dā3i l-ʔalqāb.*	مفيش داعي لِلألْقاب.
I don't have a nickname.	*ma-3andīš láqab.*	معنْديش لقب.
alias, pseudonym	*ism^{ə} šúhra*	**إسْم شُهْرة**

A teknonym is an epithet used in Arab culture to show familiarity and respect. It consists of the word **أبو** *abū* for a man and **أُمّ** *umm* for a woman followed by the name of his or her eldest son, or, if there is no son, eldest daughter.

teknonym	*kúnya*	**كُنْية**
Abu Khaled	*abū xālid* (lit. father of Khaled)	أبو خالِد
Umm Ali	*umm^{ə} 3áli* (lit. mother of Ali)	أُمّ علي

Sir!, Ma'am!, Miss!	*ya-fándim!*	يافنْدِم!
Sir!	*ya ʔustāz!*	يا أُسْتاذ!
Ma'am! (UK: Madam)	*ya madām!*	يا مدام!
Miss!	*ya ʔānísa!*	يا آنِسة

The following are titles that precede someone's name. Unlike English, titles usually precede one's given (first) name.		
Mr. __	*ustāz __*	أُسْتاذ__
Mrs. __, Ms. __	*madām __*	مدام__
Miss __	*ānisa __*	آنِسة__
Dr. (medical or Ph.D.)	*duktūr __*	دُكْتور__
architect	*bašmuhándis __*	باشْمُهنْدِس__

Yes? (response to someone calling your name)	*afándim?*	أفنْدِم؟

5 The Human Body & Describing People

body	*gism (agsām)*	جِسْم (أجْسام)
head	*rās* [f.] *(rūs)*	راس (روس)
brain, mind	*dimāɣ* *muxx (amxāx)*	دِماغ مُخّ (أمْخاخ)
skull	*gumgúma (gamāgim)*	جُمْجُمة (جماجِم)
face	*wišš (wušūš)*	وِشّ (وُشوش)
He has a round face.	*wíššu mdáwwar.*	وِشُّه مْدوّر.
She has an oblong face.	*wiššáha ṭawīl.*	وِشّها طَويل
I have a square face.	*wíšši mrábba3.*	وِشّي مْربّع.
You have an oval face.	*wíššak bayḍāwi.*	وِشّك بَيْضاوي.
to wash one's face	*ɣásal* [1s2] *wíššu*	غسل وِشُّه
forehead	*ʔūra (ʔíwar)*	قورة (قِوَر)
He has a big forehead.	*3ándu ʔūra kbīra.*	عنْدُه قورة كْبيرة.
brow	*gibīn (agbína)*	جبين (أجِبْنة)
to frown, knit one's brow, scowl	*káffar* [2s2]	كفّر
cheek	*xadd (xudūd)*	خدّ (خُدود)
chin	*daʔn* [f.] *(duʔūn)*	دقْن (دُقون)
jaw	*fakk (fukūk)*	فكّ (فُكوك)
eye	*3ēn* [f.] *(3iyūn, 3inēn)*	عيْن (عِيون، عِنيْن)

The dual and plural becomes عِنيْـ 3inē- when taking a pronoun suffix. The singular, dual, or plural may be used when referring to a person's eyes.

My eyes itch.	*3ēni btakúlni.*	عيْني بِتاكُلْني.
blue eyes	*3iyūn zárʔa*	**عِيون زرْقا**
green eyes	*3iyūn xáḑra*	**عِيون خضْرا**
brown eyes	*3iyūn búnni*	**عِيون بُنّي**
She has beautiful brown eyes.	*3inēha ḩílwa wi lúnhum búnni.*	عِنيْها حِلْوَة و لونْهُم بُنّي.
What color are his eyes?	*lōn 3inē ʔē?*	لوْن عِنيْه أيْه؟
His eyes are green.	*3inē xáḑra.*	عِنيْه خضْرا.
eyebrow	*ḩāgib (ḩawāgib)*	**حاجِب (حَواجِب)**
eyelid	*gifn (gufūn)*	**جِفْن (جُفون)**
eyelash	*rimš (rumūš)*	**رِمْش (رُموش)**
She has long eyelashes.	*rumúšha ţawīla.*	رُموشْها طَويلة.
to have thick eyelashes	*rumūšu kasīfa*	**رُموشُه كثيفة**
sclera, the white of one's eyes	*bayāḑ 3ēn*	**بَياض عيْن**
iris	*nínni 3ēn*	**نِنّي عيْن**
pupil	*ḩádaqa*	**حدقة**
to blink	*rámaš*	**رمش**
to wink	*ɣámaz*	**غمز**
to close one's eyes	*ɣámmaḑ* [2s2] *3ēnu*	**غمّض عيْنُه**
to open one's eyes	*fátaḩ* [1s1] *3inē*	**فتح عِنيْه**

to have dark circles under one's eyes	*3inē taḥtáha ʔíswid*	عِنيه تَحْتها إسْوِد
cross-eyed	*áḥwal* [m.]*, ḥōla* [f.] *(ḥūl)*	أحْوَل، حوْلا (حول)
blind	*3áma* [m.]*, 3ámya* [f.] *(3umy)*	عمى، عمْيا (عُمْى)
to see	*šāf* [1h1]	شاف
I can't see the clock from here.	*miš šāyif issā3a min hína.*	مِش شايِف السّاعة مِن هِنا.
eyesight, vision	*náẓar*	نظر
I have perfect eyesight.	*náẓari ʔáwi.*	نظري قَوِي.
to wear glasses	*líbis* [1s5] *naḍḍāra*	لِبِس نضّارة
I think you need glasses.	*ána šāyif ínnak miḥtāg naḍḍāra.*	أنا شايِف إنّك مِحْتاج نضّارة.
to cry	*3áyyaṭ* [2s2]	عيّط
a tear	*dám3a (dimū3)*	دمْعة (دِموع)
Why are your eyes red? Have you been crying?	*3ēnak ḥámra lē? kunt⁹ bit3áyyaṭ?*	عيْنك حمْرا ليْه؟ كُنْت بِتْعيّط؟
nose	*manaxīr* [pl.]	مناخير

مناخير *manaxīr* is always plural, whether talking about one nose or more. This is because the singular originally referred to a 'nostril.'

nostril	*fátḥit manaxīr*	فتْحِةُ مناخير
big/pronounced nose	*manaxīr kibīra*	مناخير كِبيرة
petite nose	*manaxīr ṣuɣayyára*	مناخير صُغيّرة
straight/sharp/pointy nose	*manaxīr mudabbába*	مناخير مُدبّبة

hook/crooked nose	*manaxīr ma3ʔūfa*	مناخير معْقوفة
to sneeze	*3áṭas* [1s1]	عطس
snot	*barbūr (barabīr)*	برْبور (برابير)
to have a runny nose	*bárbar* [11s2]	برْبر
to blow one's nose	*naff* [1g3]	نفّ
to pick one's nose	*lí3ib* [1s4] *fi manaxīru*	لِعِب في مناخيرُه
to smell	*šamm* [1g2]	شمّ
sense of smell	*ḫássit šamm*	حاسّةْ شمّ
I don't have a very good sense of smell.	*ḫássit šámmi miš ʔawíyya.* *miš bá3raf ašímmᵊ kwáyyis.*	حاسّةْ شمّي مِش قَوية. مِش بعْرف أشِمّ كُوَيِّس.
I think I smell smoke.	*ána ḫāsis ínni šāmim rīḫit duxxān.*	أنا حاسِس إنّي شامِم ريحِةْ دُخّان.

ear	*widn* [f.] *(widān)*	وِدْن (وِدان)
earlobe	*šáḫmit widn*	شحْمِةْ وِدْن
to cup one's ear (put one's hand up to one's ear to hear better)	*ḫaṭṭ* [1g2] *īdu wára wídnu*	حطّ إيدُه وَرا وِدْنُه
to hear	*sími3* [1s4]	سِمِع
Do you hear that noise?	*sāmi3 iddáwša di?*	سامِع الدَّوْشة دي؟
to have ringing in one's ear	*wídnu bitṣáffar*	وِدْنُه بِتْصفّر
to be hard of hearing	*sám3u taʔīl*	سمْعُه تقيل

deaf	*áṭraš* [m.], *ṭárša* [f.] *(ṭurš)*	أطْرش، طرْشا (طُرْش)
to wear a hearing aid	*líbis* [1s5] *sammā3a*	لِبِس سمّاعة
to have pierced ears	*wídnu maxrūma*	وِدْنُه مخْرومة
ear wax	*šam3ᵊ widn*	شمْع وِدْن
mouth	*buʔʔ (biʔāʔ)*	بُقّ (بِقاق)
to smile	*ibtásam* [8s1]	اِبْتسم
to open one's mouth	*fátaɧ* [1s1] *búʔʔu*	فتح بُقُّه
to close one's mouth	*ʔáfal* [1s2] *búʔʔu*	قفل بُقُّه
tongue	*lisān (alsína)*	لِسان (ألْسِنة)
to taste	*dāʔ* [1h1]	داق
Can you taste the mint in this dessert?	*ɧāsis bi-ṭá3mᵊ ni3nā3 fi -lɧalawiyyāt di?*	حاسِس بِطعْم نِعْناع في الحلَويات دي؟
lip	*šíffa (šafāyif)*	شِفّة (شفايِف)
upper lip	*iššíffa -lli fōʔ*	الشِّفّة اللي فوْق
lower lip	*iššíffa -lli taɧt*	الشِّفّة اللي تحْت
to have thin lips	*3ándu šafāyif ṣuɣayyára*	عنْدُه شفايِف صُغيرّة
full lips	*šafāyif milyāna*	شفايِف مِلْيانة
chapped (dry) lips	*šafāyif nášfa*	شفايِف ناشْفة
tooth	*sinn, sínna (sinān)*	سِنّ، سِنّة (سِنان)
gums	*lísa*	لِثة
to brush one's teeth	*ɣásal* [1s2] *sinānu*	غسل سِنانُه

to floss one's teeth	*náddaf* [2s2] *sinānu bi-lxēt*	نضّف سِنانُه بِالخيْط
front teeth	*sinā n ʔuddamaníyya* [pl.]	سِنان قُدّمانية
to bite	*3add* [1g2]	عضّ
molar	*dirs (durūs)*	ضِرْس (ضُروس)
to chew	*nádaɣ* [1s3]	نضغ
to spit	*taff* [1g3]	تفّ
spit, spittle	*tifāfa*	تِفافة
saliva	*rīʔ* *lu3āb*	ريق لُعاب
to yawn	*ittāwib* [6s]	اِتّاوِب
to cough	*kaħħ* [1g2]	كحّ
to burp, belch	*itkárra3* [5s2]	اِتْكرّع
to have bad breath	*rīħit búʔʔu wíħša*	ريحِةْ بُقُّه وِحْشة
tonsils	*lōza (líwaz)*	لوْزة (لِوَز)

neck	*ráʔaba (riʔāb)*	رقبة (رِقاب)
nape of the neck	*ʔáfa (ʔafawāt)*	قفا (قفَوات)
throat	*zūr (zuwār)*	زور (زُوار)
larynx	*ħangára (ħanāgir)*	حنْجرة (حناجِر)
to breathe	*itnáffis* [5s1]	اِتْنفِّس
to take a deep breath	*itnáffis* [5s1] *bi-3úmq*	اِتْنفِّس بِعُمْق
breath	*náfas (anfās)*	نفس (أنْفاس)
to swallow	*bála3* [1s1]	بلع

to choke on	*šíri? [1s4] fi*	**شِرِق في**
He started choking on a piece of food.	*šíri? fi ɧíttit akl.*	شِرِق في حِتِّةْ أكْل.

hair	*ša3r* [coll.]	**شعْر**
dark brown hair	*ša3rᵊ búnni ɣāmi?*	**شعْر بُنّي غامِق**
light brown hair	*ša3rᵊ búnni fātiɧ*	**شعْر بُنّي فاتح**
blond hair	*ša3r áşfar*	**شعْر أصْفر**
She's blond.	*ša3ráha ?áşfar.*	شعْرها أصْفر.
black hair	*ša3r íswid*	**شعْر إسْوِد**
red hair	*ša3r áɧmar*	**شعْر أحْمر**
gray hair	*ša3rᵊ ruşāşi*	**شعْر رُصاصي**
white hair	*ša3r ábyaḑ*	**شعْر أبْيَض**
to dye one's hair	*şábaɣ [1s3] šá3ru*	**صبغ شعْرُه**
She dyes her hair blond.	*bitúşbuɣ ša3ráha ?áşfar.*	بِتُصْبُغ شعْرها أصْفر.
She's a natural blond.	*ša3ráha ?áşfar ţabī3i.*	شعْرها أصْفر طبيعي.
long hair	*ša3rᵊ ţawīl*	**شعْر طَويل**
short hair	*ša3rᵊ ?uşáyyar*	**شعْر قُصيّر**
shoulder-length hair	*ša3rᵊ l-ɧadd ilkítf*	**شعْر لِحدّ الكِتْف**
straight hair	*ša3rᵊ nā3im*	**شعْر ناعِم**
curly hair	*ša3rᵊ kírli*	**شعْر كيرْلي**
wavy hair	*ša3rᵊ mumáwwag*	**شعْر مُموّج**
She has long, beautiful straight brown hair.	*ša3ráha ţawīl wi ɧilwᵊ w nā3im wi búnni.*	شعْرها طَويل و حِلْو و ناعِم و بُنّي.

to comb/brush one's hair	*máššaṭ* [2s2] *šá3ru*	مشّط شعْرُه
to get a haircut	*ʔaṣṣᵊ* [1g2] *šá3ru*	قصّ شعْرُه
bald	*áṣla3* [m.], *ṣál3a* [f.] *(ṣul3)*	أصْلع، صلْعا (صُلْع)
to go bald	*iṣlá33* [9s] *báʔa* [1d1] *áṣla3*	أصْلع بقى أصْلع
sideburns	*sawālif* [pl.]	سَوالِف
pony-tail	*dēl ɧusān*	ديْل حُصان
braids	*ḍafāyir* [pl.]	ضفايِر
She wears her hair in braids.	*bití3mil ša3ráha ḍafāyir.*	بِتِعْمِل شعْرها ضفايِر.
bun	*káɧka*	كحْكة
She usually wears her hair in a bun.	*híyya dáyman bitlímmᵊ ša3ráha káɧka.*	هِيَّ دايْماً بِتْلِمّ شعْرها كحْكة.
bangs (UK: fringe)	*ʔúṣṣa (ʔúṣaṣ)*	قُصّة (قُصص)
You look good with bangs.	*šáklak ɧilw bi-lʔúṣṣa.*	شكْلك حِلْو بِالقُصّة.
wig, toupee	*barūka*	باروكة
You can tell he wears a toupee.	*šáklu lābis barūka.*	شكْلُه لابِس باروكة.
beard	*daʔn* [f.] *(duʔūn)*	دقْن (دُقون)
mustache	*šánab*	شنب
He has a beard and mustache.	*3ándu šánab wi daʔn*	عنْدُه شنب و دقْن.
goatee	*saksūka*	سكْسوكة
to trim one's beard	*házzib* [2s1] *dáʔnu*	هذِّب دقْنُه

to shave	*ɧála?* [1s1]	**حلق**
I shave every morning.	*báɧla? kullᵊ yōm iṣṣúbɧ.*	بحْلق كُلّ يوْم الصُّبْح.
clean-shaven	*ɧalī? iddá?n*	**حليق الدّقْن**
stubble	*da?nᵊ xafīfa*	**دقْن خفيفة**

skin	*gild* *bášra*	**جِلْد** **بشْرة**
pimple, blemish (UK: spot)	*fasfūsa (fasafīs)*	**فسْفوسة (فسافيس)**
I have a huge pimple on my chin!	*3ándi fasfūsa kbīra fi dá?ni.*	عنْدي فسْفوسة كْبيرة في دقْني.
acne	*ɧabb iššabāb*	**حبّ الشّباب**
As a teenager, he had a lot of acne.	*kān 3ándu ɧabb iššabāb wi húwwa šabb.*	كان عنْدُه حبّ الشّباب و هُوَّ شاب.
to have bad skin	*wíššu mɧábbib*	**وِشُّه مْحبِّب**
to have a good complexion	*bašrítu ṣáfya*	**بشْرِتُه صافْيَة**
fair-skinned	*ábyaḍ* [m.], *bēḍa* [f.] *(bēḍ)*	**أبْيَض، بيْضا (بيْض)**
dark-skinned	*?ásmar* [m.], *sámra* [f.] *(sumr)*	**أسْمر، سمْرا (سُمْر)**
to have an olive complexion	*bašrítu ?ámɧi*	**بشْرِتُه قمْحي**
to have dry skin	*bašrítu gáffa*	**بشْرِتُه جافّة**
to put on lotion	*ɧattᵊ* [1g2] [lotion]	**حطّ لوْشِن**

to put on sunscreen	*ɧaʈʈᵊ* [1g2] *wāqi šams* *ɧaʈʈᵊ* [1g2] [sun block]	**حطّ واقي شمْس** **حطّ صن بْلوك**
freckles	*námaš* [coll.]	**نمش**
She has a lot of freckles.	*3andáha námaš kitīr.*	عنْدها نمش كِتير.
mole, birthmark	*wáɧma*	**وَحْمة**
wrinkles	*taga3īd* [pl.]	**تجاعيد**
You get wrinkles as you get older.	*kullᵊ ma tíkbar bitgīlak taga3īd.*	كُلّ ما تِكْبر بِتْجيلك تجاعيد.
scar	*nádba*	**ندْبة**
tattoo	*tatū* *wašm* [coll.]	**تاتو** **وَشْم**
He has a tattoo on his left arm.	*húwwa 3ándu tatū 3ála drā3u -ššimāl.*	هُوَّ عنْدُه تاتو على دْراعُه الشِّمال.
Do you have any tattoos?	*ínta rāsim wašm?*	إنْتَ راسِم وَشْم؟

arm	*dirā3*	**دِراع**
elbow	*kū3 (ki3ān)*	**كوع (كِعان)**
armpit	*bāʈ* *taɧt ilbāʈ*	**باط** **تحْت الباط**
sweat	*3ára?*	**عرق**
to sweat	*3íri?* [1s4]	**عِرِق**
sweaty	*3ar?ān*	**عرْقان**

He was very sweaty after playing soccer.	*húwwa kān 3arʔān áwi ba3dᵊ li3bᵊ kōra.*	هُوَّ كان عرْقان أَوي بعْد لِعْب كوْرة.
hand, wrist	*īd* [f.] *(idēn, ayādi)*	**إيد (إيديْن، إيادى)**
What's in your hand?	*fī ʔē f- īdak?*	فيه أيْه في إيدك؟
The plural becomes إيديـْ *idē-* when taking a pronoun suffix.		
They're all wearing watches on their wrists.	*kullúhum labsīn sa3āt fi ʔidēhum.*	كُلُّهُم لابْسين ساعات في إيديْهُم.
finger	*ṣubā3 (ṣawābi3)*	**صُباع (صَوابِع)**
fingerprint	*báṣmit ṣubā3*	**بصْمِةْ صُباع**
thumb	*ṣubā3 kibīr*	**صُباع كِبير**
index finger	*ṣubā3 tāni*	**صُباع تاني**
middle finger	*ṣubā3 wisṭāni* *sabbāba*	**الصُّباع وِسْطاني** **سبّابة**
ring finger	*ṣubā3 xātim*	**صُباع خاتِم**
little finger, pinky	*ṣubā3 ṣuɣáyyar*	**صُباع صُغيرّ**
fingertip	*ṭáraf ṣubā3*	**طرف صُباع**
fingernail	*ḍufr (ḍawāfir)*	**ضُفْر (ضَوافِر)**
palm	*kaff (kufūf)*	**كفّ (كُفوف)**
back of the hand	*ḍahrᵊ ʔīd (ḍuhūr idēn)*	**ضهْر إيد (ضُهور إيديْن)**
ball of the hand	*bāṭin īd (bawāṭin idēn)*	**باطِن إيد (بَواطِن إيديْن)**
knuckles	*máfṣal ṣubā3 (mafāṣil ṣawābi3)*	**مفْصل صُباع) مفاصِل صَوابِع)**

wrist	*máfṣal īd (mafāṣil idēn)*	**مفْصل إيد (مفاصِل إيديْن)**
to make a fist	*káwwar* [2s2] *īdu*	**كوّر إيدُه**
to extend one's fingers	*madd*[a] [1g3] *ṣawáb3u*	**مدّ صَوابْعُه**
to hold, grip	*mísik* [1s5]	**مِسِك**
to point to	*šāwir* [3s] *3ála*	**شاوِر على**
He pointed at the clock.	*šāwir 3ála -ssā3a.*	شاوِر على السّاعة.

leg, foot	*rigl* [f.] *(riglēn)*	**رِجْل (رِجْليْن)**
The plural becomes رجليـ *riglē-* when taking a pronoun suffix.		
thigh	*faxd (fixād)*	**فخْد (فِخاد)**
shin	*ʔáṣabit rigl*	**قصبِةْ رِجْل**
calf	*sammāna*	**سمّانة**
knee	*rúkba (rúkab)*	**رُكْبة (رُكب)**
ankle	*máfṣal rigl (mafāṣil riglēn)*	**مفْصل رِجْل (مفاصِل رِجْليْن)**
sole	*bāṭin rigl (bawāṭin riglēn)*	**باطِن رِجْل (بَواطِن رِجْليْن)**
heel	*ka3b (ku3ūb)*	**كعْب (كُعوب)**
toe	*ṣubā3 rigl (ṣawābi3 riglēn)*	**صُباع رِجْل (صَوابِع رِجْليْن)**

shoulder	*kitf (kitāf)*	**كِتْف (كِتاف)**

to have broad shoulders	*kitāfu 3arīḍa*	كِتافُه عريضة
chest, bosom	*ṣadr (ṣudūr)*	صدْر (صُدور)
to be flat chested	*ma-3andahāš ṣadr** (lit. she doesn't have a bosom)	معنْدهاش صدْر
breast, boob	*bizz (bizāz)**	بِزّ (بِزاز)
nipple	*ḫálama*	حلمة
abdomen, belly, stomach	*baṭn* [f.] *(buṭūn)*	بطْن (بُطون)
back	*ḍahr (ḍuhūr)*	ضهْر (ضُهور)
waist, hips	*wisṭ*	وِسْط
navel, belly button	*súrra (súrar)*	سُرّة (سُرر)

internal organs	*aḫšāʔ* [pl.]	أحْشاء
stomach	*mí3da (mí3ad)*	مِعْدة (مِعد)
intestines, bowels	*maṣarīn* [pl.]	مصارين
lung	*ríʔa (riʔtēn)*	رِئة (رِئْتينْ)
heart	*ʔalb (ʔulūb)*	قلْب (قُلوب)
to beat, palpitate	*daʔʔ* [1g2] *nábaḍ* [1s3]	دقّ نبض
heartbeat, pulse	*dáʔʔit ʔalb* *nábḍit ʔalb*	دقّةْ قلْب نبْضِةْ قلْب
liver	*kibd (akbād)*	كِبْد (أكْباد)
kidney	*kílya*	كِلْيَة
bladder	*masāna*	مثانة

gall-bladder	*marāra*	مرارة
gland	*ɣúdda (ɣúdad)*	غُدّة (غُدد)
thyroid gland	*ɣúdda daraqíyya*	غُدّة درقية

bone	*3áḑma*	عضْمة
skeleton	*háykal 3áẓmi (hayākil 3azmíyya)*	هَيْكل عظْمي (هَياكِل عظْمية)
spine	*3amūd fáʔri (3awamīd faʔríyya)*	عمود فقْري (عَواميد فقْرية)
rib	*ḑil3 (ḑulū3)*	ضِلْع (ضُلوع)
muscle	*3áḑala*	عضلة
vein	*warīd (awrída)*	وَريد (أَوْرِدة)
artery	*širyān (šarayīn)*	شِرْيان (شرايين)
blood	*damm*	دمّ
nerve	*3áşab (a3şāb)*	عصب (أَعْصاب)

sexual organs, private parts	*a3ḑāʔ tanasulíyya*	أعْضاء تناسُلية

Needless to say, caution should be exercised when talking about 'private parts.' There are numerous synonyms (and euphemisms) for these, but each is appropriate only in certain social contexts. There are medical terms that can be used when necessary to mention 'private parts,' such as when speaking to a doctor. There are also euphemisms used with small [children]. And of course, there are [vulgar] terms which should only be used among close friends who are not offended by such vulgarities. As a non-native speaker, you are advised to avoid using vulgar terms altogether, as they will tend to get you into trouble; nonetheless, they have been included here for recognition purposes.

However, due to their sensitive nature, they (and related words) do not appear on the MP3s.

penis	*ʔaḑīb (ʔuḑbān)**	قضيب (قُضْبان)
pee-pee (penis)	*ɧamāma** [children]	حمامة
dick, cock	*zibb (azbāb)** [vulgar] *zubr (azbār)** [vulgar]	زِبّ (أزْباب) زُبْر (أزْبار)
to get an erection	*intáşab**	اِنْتصب
erection	*intişāb**	اِنْتِصاب
to get a boner	*zíbbu wíʔif** [i5] [vulgar]	زِبُّه وِقِف
boner, hard-on	*zibbᵊ wāʔif** [vulgar]	زِبّ واقِف
testicle	*xáşya**	خصْيَة
scrotum, testicles	*kīs şáfan (ikyās aşfān)**	كيس صفن (إكْياس أصْفان)
balls, nuts (scrotum)	*xaşyitēn** [dual] *biḑān** [vulgar]	خصْيِتيْن بيضان
vagina	*míhbal (mahābil)**	مِهْبل (مهابِل)
'girl parts'	*ilɧítta -lli min ʔuddām** [children]	الحِتّة اللي مِن قُدّام
pussy	*kuss (iksās)** [vulgar]	كُسّ (إكْساس)
naked, bare	*3iryān (3arāya)**	عِرْيان (عرايا)
buttocks, bottom, posterior	*máʔ3ad (maʔā3id)** *muʔaxxíra**	مقْعد (مقاعِد) مُؤخِّرة
bottom	*ilɧítta -lli wára** [children]	الحِتّة اللي وَرا

ass, butt (UK: arse, bum)	*ṭīz* [f.] (tiyāz)* [vulgar]	طيز (طِياز)
anus	*šárag**	شرج
ass hole	*xurm ṭīz (xurūm ṭiyāz)** [vulgar]	خُرْم طيز (خُروم طِياز)
to urinate	*itbáwwil** [5s1]	اِتْبوّل
urine	*bōl**	بوْل
to pee	*3ámal* [1s2] *bībi**	عمل بيبى
pee	*bībi**	بيبى
to piss, take a piss	*šaxx** [1g2] [vulgar]	شخّ
There was a man peeing on the side of the road.	*kān fī rāgil biyšúxxᵊ 3ála gamb iṭṭarīʔ.**	كان فيه راجِل بيْشُخّ على جنْب الطّريق.
to pee (while standing)	*ṭárṭar** [11s2] [vulgar]	طرْطر
to defecate	*itbárriz** [5s1]	اِتْبرّز
excrement, feces	*burāz**	بُراز
Careful! Don't step in the dog poo!	*xálli bālak! ma-tdússšᵊ 3ála brāz ilkálb!**	خلّي بالك !متْدوسْش على بْراز الكلِب!
to poo, poop	*3ámal* [1s2] *kāka** [children]	عمل كاكا
poo, poop	*kāka** [children]	كاكا
to shit	*xíri** [1d5] [vulgar]	خِري
shit	*xára** [coll.; vulgar]	خرى
to fart	*ḍárraṭ** [2s2]	ضرّط
fart	*ḍárṭa**	ضرْطة
to pass gas, break wind	*ṭálla3* [2s2] *rīḥ*	طلّع ريح

to go to the bathroom (UK: to go to the loo)	*rāḫ* [1h1] *ilḫammām* *rāḫ* [1h1] *ittuwalítt*	راح الحمّام راح التُّواليتّ
I need to go to the bathroom.	*3āyiz arūḫ ilḫammām.*	عايِز أروح الحمّام.

height	*ṭūl (aṭwāl)*	طول (أطْوال)
tall	*ṭawīl (ṭuwāl)*	طَويل (طُوال)
average height	*mutawássiṭ iṭṭūl*	مُتَوَسِّط الطّول
short	*ʔuṣáyyar (ʔuṣār)*	قُصيرّ (قُصار)
How tall are you?	*ṭūlak ʔaddᵊ ʔē?*	طولك أدّ أيْه؟
I'm 1.75 meters tall.	*ṭūli míyya xámsa wi sab3īn sánti. (lit. My height is 175 centimeters.)*	طولي ميّة خمْسة و سبْعين سنْتي.

weight	*wazn (awzān)*	وَزْن (أَوْزان)
How much do you weigh?	*wáznak kam kīlu?*	وَزْنك كام كيلو؟
I weigh 70 kg.	*wázni sab3īn kīlu.*	وَزْني سبْعين كيلو.
one's build, body shape	*šaklᵊ gism*	شكْل جِسْم
fat	*tixīn (tuxān)*	تِخين (تُخان)
to get fat	*tíxin* [1s4]	تِخِن
Don't overeat, so you don't get fat.	*ma-takúlšᵊ b-ziyāda 3ašān ma-titxánš.*	متاكُلْش بِزِيادة عشان متِتْخنْش.
overweight	*wáznu zāyid*	وَزْنُه زايِد
chubby	*mikálbaẓ*	مِكلْبظ

plump, stout	*malyān*	ملْيان
average weight	*wáznu kwáyyis* *gísmu kwáyyis*	وَزْنه كْوَيِّس جِسْمُه كْوَيِّس
thin	*rufáyya3*	رُفيّع
skinny	*gild[ə] 3ála 3aḍm* (lit. skin on bones)	جِلْد على عضْم

one's looks	*šáklu*	شكْلُه
handsome; beautiful	*gamīl (gumāl)*	جميل (جُمال)
good-looking, handsome, pretty	*ḫilw* *wasīm*	حِلْو وَسيم
cute	[cute] [invar.]	كْيوت
My God, those girls are so cute!	*wallāhi, ilbanāt dōl kyūt xāliṣ!*	واللّهِ البنات دوْل كْيوت خالِص!
ugly	*wíḫiš*	وِحِش
average-looking	*šáklu 3ādi*	شكْلُه عادي

6 Clothing, Jewelry, and Accessories

clothing	*hudūm* [pl.] *malābis* [pl.]	هُدوم ملابِس
men's clothing	*hudūm rigāli*	هُدوم رِجالي
women's clothing	*hudūm ħarīmi*	هُدوم حريمي

underwear (UK: pants)	*hudūm daxlíyya*	هُدوم داخلية
long johns	*kalsōn*	كلْسوْن
undershirt (also: T-shirt, soccer jersey; UK: vest)	*fanílla* *falínna*	فانِلّة فالِنّة
panties	*kulútt*	كُلوتّ
pantyhose, tights	*kulōn*	كولوْن
bra	*sutyān* *sintiyān*	سوتْيان سِنْتِيان

shirt	*ʔamīş (ʔumşān)*	قميص (قُمْصان)
collar	*yāʔa*	ياقة
sleeve	*kumm (kimām)*	كُمّ (كِمام)
a long-sleeved shirt	*ʔamīş bi-kúmm^{ə} ţawīl*	قميص بِكُمّ طَويل
short-sleeved	*bi-núşş^{ə} kumm* *bi-kúmm^{ə} ʔuşáyyar*	بِنُصّ كُمّ بِكُمّ قُصيّر
t-shirt	*tī širt*	تي شيرْت
polo shirt	*tī širt^{ə} pōlu*	تي شيرْت بوْلو
blouse	*bilūza*	بِلوزة

(pair of) pants (UK: trousers)	*banṭalōn*	بنْطلوْن
pant leg	*rigl ilbanṭalōn*	رِجْل البنْطلوْن
jeans	*žins, žīnz*	چينْز
shorts	*šōrt*	شوْرْت
belt	*ḫizām (ḫizíma)*	حِزام (حِزِمة)
(belt) buckle	*tōkit ḫizām*	توْكِةْ حِزام

suit	*bádla (bídal)*	بدْلة (بِدل)
suit jacket	*žākit bádla*	چاكيت بدْلة
uniform	*yunifōrm* *ziyy (azyāʔ)*	يونيفوْرْم زِيّ (أزْياء)
galabeya (traditional Egyptian garment)	*gallabíyya (galalīb)*	جلّابية (جلاليب)

necktie	*garafátta*	كرافتّة
to tie one's necktie	*rábaṭ* [1s3] *garafattítu*	ربط كرافتِّتُه
watch	*sā3a*	ساعة
wallet	*maḫfáẓa (maḫāfiz)*	محْفظة (محافِظ)
bag, briefcase	*šánṭa (šúnaṭ)*	شنْطة (شُنط)
courier bag	*šánṭa rigāli*	شنْطة رِجالي
handbag, purse	*šánṭit īd*	شنْطِةْ إيد

dress	*fustān*	فُسْتان
skirt	*žība*	چيبة
hijab, headscarf	*ḫigāb [no pl.]*	حِجاب
niqab	*niqāb [no pl.]*	نِقاب
(women's) scarf	*išārb*	إشارْب

hair ribbon	*širīṭit (šarāyiṭ) ša3r*	شِرِيطِةْ (شرايِط) شعْر
barette, hair clip	*tōka*	توْكة
hat	*burnēṭa (baranīṭ)*	بُرْنيْطة (برنيط)
(baseball) cap	*kāb*	كاب
skull cap, (knit) beanie	*ṭaʔíyya (ṭawāʔi)*	طاقية (طَواقي)
turban	*3imāma (3amāyim)*	عِمامة (عمايِم)
jacket	*žākit (žawākit)* *žakítta (žakittāt)*	چاكيت (چَواكِت) چاكِتّة (چاكِتّات)
coat	*bálṭu (balāṭi)*	بالْطو (بلاطي)
sweater	*bulōvar*	بُلوْڤر
zip-up sweater	*swītar*	سْويتر
sweatshirt	*swīt širt*	سْويت شيرْت
scarf	*skarf*	سْكارْف
glove	*fárdit guwánti*	فرْدِةْ جُوانْتي
a pair of gloves	*guwánti*	جُوانْتي
bathrobe (UK: dressing gown)	*búrnuṣ (barāniṣ)* *rōb (arwāb) ḥammām*	بُرْنُص (برانِص) روْب (أرْواب) حمّام
pajamas (UK: pyjamas)	*bižāma (bažāyim, bižamāt)*	بيچامة (بچايِم، بيچامات)
nightgown, teddy	*ʔamīṣ nōm*	قميص نوْم
swimsuit, bathing suit	*mayōh*	مايوْه
bikini	*bikīni*	بيكيني

pocket	*gēb (giyūb)*	جيْب (جيوب)
to put __ in one's pocket	*ħaṭṭ* [1g2] *__ fi gēbu*	حطّ __ في جيْبُه
to take __ out of one's pocket	*šāl* [1h2] *__ min gēbu*	شال __ مِن جيْبُه
button	*zurār (zarāyir)*	زُرار (زرايِر)
to button up	*zárrar* [2s2]	زرّر
to unbutton	*fátaħ* [1s1] *izzarāyir* *fakk izzarāyir*	فتح الزّرايِر فكّ الزّرايِر
zipper	*sústa (súsat)*	سوسْتة (سوست)
to zip up	*ʔáfal* [1s2] *issústa*	قفل السّوسْتة
to unzip	*fátaħ* [1s1] *issústa* *fakk* [1g2] *issústa*	فتح السّوسْتة فكّ السّوسْتة

(pair of) shoes	*gázma (gízam)*	جزْمة (جِزم)
shoe	*fárdit gázma*	فرْدِةْ جزْمة
(pair of) boots	*būt*	بوت
(pair of) sandals	*ṣándal, sándal (ṣanādil)*	صنْدل (صنادِل)
(pair of) high heels	*gázma ka3b 3āli*	جزْمة كعْب عالي
(pair of) slippers	*šíbšib (šabāšib)*	شِبْشِب (شباشِب)
shoelaces	*rubāṭ gázma*	رُباط جزْمة
to tie one's shoes	*rábaṭ* [1s3] *rubāṭ ilgázma*	ربط رُباط الجزْمة
to untie one's shoes	*fakk*ᵊ [1g2] *rubāṭ ilgázma*	فكّ رُباط الجزْمة
Your shoelaces have come undone.	*irrubāṭ bitā3 gazmítak itfákk.* *irrubāṭ bitā3 gazmítak mafkūk.*	الرُّباط بِتاع جزْمِتك اتْفكّ. الرُّباط بِتاع جزْمِتك مفْكوك.
shoe polish	*warnīš*	وَرْنيش
to polish one's shoes	*lámma3* [2s2] *gazmítu*	لمّع جزْمِتُه

shoe size	*maʔās gázma*	**مقاس جزْمة**
What size shoes do you wear?	*ʔē maʔās gazmítak?*	أيْه مقاس جزْمِتك؟
I wear size 40.	*bálbis maʔās arbi3īn.*	بلْبِس مقاس أرْبِعين.
I'm not sure about my size.	*ma-3ráfš maʔāsi.* *miš mutaʔákkid maʔāsi kām.*	معْرفْش مقاسي. مِش مُتأكِّد مقاسي كام.
(pair of) socks	*šarāb*	**شراب**

to wear, to get dressed, to put on	*líbis* [1s5]	**لِبس**
What are you going to wear today?	*ínta hatílbis ʔē innahárda?*	إنْتَ هتِلْبِس أيْه النّهارْده؟
He took a shower, got dressed, and left for work.	*istaḫámma, líbis, wi rāḫ iššúɣl.*	اِسْتحمّى، لِبس و راح الشُّغْل.

Like the English verbs 'put on' and 'wear', لِبس *líbis* can take a variety of complements: shirt, pants, hat, belt, shoes, glasses, jewelry, etc. But it is not used with perfume, lotion, etc.

to get undressed	*ʔála3* [1s1] *hudūmu*	**قلع هُدومُه**
to take off	*ʔála3* [1s1]	**قلع**
I took off my jacket.	*ʔalá3t ižžākit.*	قلعْت الجاكيت.
to change one's clothes	*ɣáyyar* [2s2] *hudūmu*	**غيّر هُدومُه**

(clothing) size	*maʔās*	**مقاس**
small (S)	*smōl*	**سْموْل**
medium (M)	*mīdiyam*	**ميدِيَم**
large (L)	*larž*	**لارْج**
extra-large (XL)	*eks larž*	**إكْس لارْج**
loose	*wāsi3*	**واسِع**
tight	*ḑáyyaʔ*	**ضيّق**

just right (not too loose or tight)	*mazbūt*	مظْبوط
Does the shirt fit you?	*maʔās ilʔamīṣ mazbūt?*	مقاس القميص مظْبوط؟
It fits just right.	*mazbūt.*	مظْبوط.
It doesn't fit.	*miš mazbūt.*	مِش مظْبوط.
It's a little big.	*kibīr šuwáyya*	كِبير شُوَيَّة.
It's too tight.	*ḍáyyaʔ áwi*	ضيّق أَوي.
I think I need the next size up.	*3āyiz ilmaʔās ilʔákbar.*	عايِز المقاس الأكْبر.

to do the laundry	*ɣásal* [1s2] *ilɣasīl*	غسل الغسيل
to hang out the laundry	*náššar* [2s2] *ilɣasīl*	نشّر الغسيل
to dry the laundry	*náššif* [2s1] *ilɣasīl*	نشِّف الغسيل
washing machine	*ɣassāla*	غسّالة
(clothes) dryer	*migáffif*	مِجفِّف
clothesline	*ḥabl (ḥibāl) ɣasīl*	حبْل (حِبال) غسيل
laundry basket	*sállit (sílal) ɣasīl*	سلِّةْ (سِلل) غسيل
to iron	*káwa* [1d2]	كَوى
iron	*mákwa (makāwi)*	مكْوى (مكاوي)
ironing board	*ṭarabēzit mákwa*	طرابيْزِةْ مكْوى
wrinkled	*mikármiš*	مِكرْمِش
This shirt is wrinkled. I need to iron it.	*ilʔamīṣ mikármiš. 3āyiz akwī.*	القميص مِكرْمِش .عايِز أكْويه.

cloth, fabric	*ʔumāš (aʔmíša)*	قُماش (أقْمِشة)
cotton	*ʔuṭn*	قُطْن
wool	*ṣūf*	صوف

silk	*ɦarīr*	**حرير**
nylon	*naylōn*	**نايْلوْن**
linen	*kittān*	**كِتّان**
Is this t-shirt cotton?	*ittī širtᵊ di ʔuṭn?*	التّي شيرْت دي قُطْن؟
This blouse is silk.	*ilbilūza di ɦarīr.*	البِلوزة دي حرير.
leather	*gild*	**جِلْد**

glasses	*naḍḍāra*	**نضّارة**
contact lenses	*3adasāt* [pl.]	**عدسات**
Do you wear glasses?	*ínta btílbis naḍḍāra?*	إنْتَ بْتِلْبِس نضّارة؟
Oh, you're wearing glasses today!	*ʔē da, ínta lābis naḍḍāra -nnahárda!*	**أيْه ده، إنْتَ لابِس نضّارة النّهارْده!**
I usually wear contacts.	*ána fi -ṭṭabī3i bálbis 3adasāt.*	أنا في الطّبيعي بلْبِس عدسات.
sunglasses	*naḍḍārit šams*	**نضّارةْ شمْس**
reading glasses	*naḍḍārit ʔirāya*	**نضّارةْ قِرايَة**
I can't find my glasses!	*miš lāʔi -nnaḍḍāra btá3ti.*	مِش لاقي النّضّارة بْتاعْتي.

jewelry	*migawharāt* [pl.]	**مِجَوْهرات**
ring	*xātim (xawātim)*	**خاتِم (خَواتِم)**
wedding ring	*díbla (díbal), díblit gawāz*	**دِبْلة (دِبل)، دِبْلِةْ جَواز**
engagement ring	*díblit xuṭūba*	**دِبْلِةْ خُطوبة**
bracelet	*ɣiwēša (ɣawāyiš)* *iswíra (asāwir)*	**غويْشة (غَوايِش)** **إسْوِرة (أساوِر)**
earring	*ɦálaʔ (ɦilʔān)*	**حلق (حِلْقان)**
I lost my earring.	*ḍā3 mínni -lɦálaʔ bitā3i.*	ضاع مِنّي الحلق بِتاعي.

a pair of earrings	*ɦilʔān*	حِلْقان
necklace	*3uʔd (3uʔūd)*	عقد (عُقود)
brooch	*burōš*	بُروْش
diamonds	*almāz̧*	ألْماظ
ruby	*yaʔūt*	ياقوت
topaz	*yaʔūt áṣfar*	ياقوت أصْفر
emeralds	*zumúrrud*	زُمُرُّد
gold	*dáhab*	دهب
silver	*fáḍḍa*	فضّة
a diamond ring, gold bracelet, and silver necklace	*xāṭim almāz̧, ɣiwēša dáhab, wi 3uʔdᵊ fáḍḍa*	خاتِم ألْماظ، غِويْشة دهب و عُقْد فضّة

7 The House

house	*bēt (biyūt)*	بيْت (بِيوت)
apartment (UK: flat)	*šáʔʔa (šúʔaʔ)*	شقّة (شُقق)
two-story apartment	*vílla* [f.] *(vílal)*	ڤيلّا (ڤِلل)
penthouse apartment	*vílla rūf*	ڤيلّا روف
story, floor	*dōr (adwār)*	دوْر (أدْوار)
two-story house for sale	*li-lbē3 bēt durēn*	لِلبيْع بيْت دوريْن
The apartment is on the fourth floor.	*iššáʔʔa fi -ddōr irrābi3.*	الشّقّة في الدّوْر الرّابِع.

to rent an apartment	*ʔággar* [2s2] *šáʔʔa*	أجّر شقّة
rent	*ʔigār*	إيجار
How much is the rent?	*ilʔigār kām?*	الإيجار كام؟
How much do you pay in rent?	*bitídfa3 kām lilʔigār?*	بِتِدْفع كام لِلإيجار؟
tenant, renter	*muʔággir*	مُؤجِّر
landlord **landlady**	*ṣāḫib šáʔʔa* *ṣáḫbit šáʔʔa*	صاحِب شقّة صاحْبِةْ شقّة
to rent an apartment to	*ʔággar* [2s2] *šáʔʔa li-*	أجّر شقّة لِـ

roof	*saṭḫ (suṭūḫ)* *rūf*	سطْح (سُطوح) روف
The plural سُطوح *suṭūḫ* is commonly used instead of the singular.		
fence	*sūr (aswār)*	سور (أسْوار)
gate	*bawwāba*	بوّابة
gardener	*ganáyni*	جنايْني

The gardener comes once a week.	*ilganáyni biyīgi márra fi -lʔisbū3*	الجنايْني بِيِيجي مرّة في الإسْبوع.
housekeeper, maid	*šaɣɣāla*	**شغّالة**
doorman	*bawwāb*	**بوّاب**
Ask the doorman to wash our car this afternoon.	*xálli -lbawwāb yímsaḫ il3arabíyya ba3d iḍḍúhr.*	خلّي البَوّاب يِمْسح العربية بعْد الضُّهْر.

room	*ōḍa (úwaḍ)*	**أوْضة (أُوَض)**
furniture	*3afš* [coll.] *asās*	**عفْش** **أثاث**
furnished	*mafrūš* *bi-l3áfš*	**مفْروش** **بِالعفْش**
chair	*kúrsi (karāsi)*	**كُرْسي (كراسي)**
table	*ṭarabēza, tarabēza*	**طرابيْزة**
door	*bāb (abwāb)*	**باب (أبْواب)**
front door	*bāb amāmi*	**باب أمامي**
key	*muftāḫ (mafatīḫ)*	**مُفْتاح (مفاتيح)**

floor	*arḍíyya*	**أرْضية**
ceiling	*saʔf (suʔūf)*	**سقْف (سُقوف)**
carpet	*siggāda (sagagīd)*	**سِجّادة (سجاجيد)**
tiles	*balāṭ* [coll.]	**بلاط**
hardwood floor	*parkēh*	**پرکيْه**
window	*šubbāk (šababīk)*	**شُبّاك (شبابيك)**
curtain, blinds	*sitāra (satāyir)*	**سِتارة (ستايِر)**
shutters	*šīš* [coll.]	**شيش**
shelf	*raff (rufūf)*	**رفّ (رُفوف)**

wall	*ḫēṭa (ḫiṭān)*	**حيْطة (حيطان)**
wall clock	*sā3it ḫēṭa*	**ساعِةْ حيْطة**
painting, picture	*ṣūra (ṣíwar)* *lōḫa*	**صورة (صِوَر)** **لوْحة**
to hang a picture on the wall	*3álla?* [2s2] *ṣūra 3ála -lḫēṭa*	**علّق صورة على الحيْطة**
I love that painting hanging over the sofa.	*3agbāni -ṣṣūra -lmit3allá ?a fō? ilkánaba.*	عاجْباني الصّورة المِتْعلّقة فوْق الكنبة.
poster	[poster]	**پوْسْترِ**

to do housework	*3ámal* [1s2] *šuɣl ilbēt*	**عمل شُغْل البيْت**
to clean, tidy up	*náḍḍaf* [2s2]	**نضّف**
to wash the windows	*ɣásal* [1s2] *iššababīk*	**غسل الشّبابيك**
broom	*mi?áššša*	**مِقشّة**
to sweep	*kánas*	**كنس**
mop	*mamsáḫa (mamāsiḫ)*	**ممْسحة (مماسِح)**
to mop	*másaḫ* [1s1] *(bi-lmamsáḫa)*	**مسح (بِالممْسحة)**
vacuum cleaner (UK: hoover)	*maknása (makānis) kahraba?íyya*	**مكْنسة (مكانِس) كهْربائية**
to vacuum the carpet	*kánas* [1s2] *issiggāda (bi-lmaknása -lkahraba ?íyya)*	**كنس السِّجادة (بِالمكْنسة الكهْربائية)**
to dust	*náffaḍ* [2s2]	**نفّض**
dust	*turāb*	**تُراب**
dusty	*mittárrab*	**مِترّب**
to beat the dust out of a carpet	*náffaḍ* [2s2] *issiggāda min itturāb*	**نفّض السِّجّادة مِن التُّراب**

light	*nūr (anwār)*	**نور (أنْوار)**
lamp	*lámba*	**لمْبة**
to turn on the light	*wálla3* [2s2] *innūr* *náwwar* [2s2] *innūr*	**وَلّع النّور** **نوّر النّور**
to turn off the light	*ṭáfa* [1d2] *-nnūr*	**طفى النّور**
Could you turn off the light in the kitchen, please?	*múmkin tíṭfi -nnūr fi -lmáṭbax, law samáħt?*	مُمْكِن تِطْفي النّور في المطْبخ لَوْ سمحْت؟
light switch	*kubs^{ə} (ikbās) nūr* *muftāħ (mafatīħ) nūr*	**كُبْس (إكْباس) نور** **مُفْتاح (مفاتيح) نور**
electrical outlet, socket	*barīza (barāyiz)*	**بريزة (برايِز)**
plug	*fīša*	**فيشة**
to plug in	*ħaṭṭ^{ə}* [1g2] *fīša*	**حطّ فيشة**
to unplug	*šāl* [1h2] *fīša*	**شال فيشة**
extension cord, adapter	*muštárak*	**مُشْترك**
fuse box	*tablō kahrába*	**تابْلوْه كهْربا**
fuse	*fiyūz*	**فِيوز**
A fuse has blown.	*fī fyūz ḍárab.*	فيه فِيوز ضرب.
the power went out	*ilkahrába ʔáṭa3it* *innūr ʔáṭa3*	**الكهْربا قطعِت** **النّور قطع**
The power went out for an hour this afternoon.	*ilkahrába ʔáṭa3it sā3a -ḍḍuhr.*	الكهْربا قطعِت ساعة الضُّهْر.
candle	*šám3a*	**شمْعة**
heater	*daffāya*	**دفّايَة**
air-conditioner	*takyīf háwa*	**تكْييف هَوا**

living room	*ōḍit ma3īša* *antirēh*	أوْضِةْ معيشة أنْترِيْه
formal sitting room (for entertaining guests)	*ṣalōn*	صالوْن
sofa, couch	*kánaba*	كنبة
armchair	*futēh*	فوتيْه
television	*tilivizyōn*	تِليفِزْيوْن
to watch TV	*itfárrag* [5s2] *3ála -ttilivizyōn*	اِتْفرّج على التّليفِزْيوْن
The only thing I want to do this evening is sit on the couch and watch TV.	*3āyiz ma-3mílš*[ə] *ḥāga bi-llēl ɣēr ínni áʔ3ud 3ála -lkánaba w- atfárrag 3ála -tilivizyōn.*	عايِز معْمِلْش حاجة بِاللّيْل غيرْ إنيّ أقْعُد على الكنبة و أتْفرّج على التّليفِزْيوْن.
dining room	*ōḍit súfra*	أوْضِةْ سُفْرة
dining table	*ṭarabēzit súfra*	طرابيْزِةْ سُفْرة
to set the table	*gáhhiz* [5s1] *iṭṭarabēza*	جهِّز الطّرابيْزة
to clear the table	*náḍḍaf* [5s2] *iṭṭarabēza*	نضّف الطّرابيْزة
to sit at the table	*ʔá3ad* [1s3] *3ála -ṭṭarabēza*	قعد على الطّرابيْزة
Dinner's ready! Come to the table!	*il3áša gāhiz! ta3ālu 3and iṭṭarabēza!*	العشا جاهِز !تعالوا عنْد الطّرابيْزة!
(flower) vase	*fāza*	فازة
plate, dish	*ṭábaʔ (aṭbāʔ)*	طبق (أطْباق)
spoon	*ma3láʔa (ma3āliʔ)*	معْلقة (معالِق)
fork	*šūka (šíwak)*	شوكة (شِوَك)
knife	*sikkīna (sakakīn)*	سِكّينة (سكاكين)

bowl	*sulṭaníyya* *zibdíyya*	سُلْطانية زِبْدية
napkin	*mandīl (manadīl)*	منْديل (مناديل)

kitchen	*máṭbax (maṭābix)*	مطْبخ (مطابِخ)
cupboard, cabinet	*dulāb (dawalīb)*	دولاب (دَواليب)
counter	*ruxāmit máṭbax*	رُخامِةْ مطْبخ
refrigerator	*talāga*	تلاجة
freezer	[freezer]	فْريزِر
stove (UK: cooker)	*butagāz*	بوتاجاز
oven	*furn (afrān)*	فُرْن (أفْران)
microwave (oven)	[microwave]	مَيْكروْويْڤ
to microwave	*ṭábax* [1s3] *fi -l*[microwave]	طبخ في المَيْكروْويْڤ
Just put it in the microwave for two minutes.	*ḫúṭṭu bass^{ə}* *fi -l*[microwave] *li-múddit diʔiʔtēn.*	حُطُّه بسّ في المَيْكروْويْڤ لِمُدِّةْ دِقيقْتينْ.
to heat up	*sáxxan* [2s2]	سخّن
I heated up the soup in the microwave.	*ána saxxánt iššúrba* *fi -l*[microwave].	أنا سخّنِت الشّورْبة في المَيْكروْويْڤ.
cooking	*ṭabx*	طبْخ
to make dinner	*3ámal* [1s2] *il3áša*	عمل العشا
to cut	*ʔáṭa3* [1s1]	قطع
to dice	*ʔáṭa3* [1s1] *ḫítat ṣuɣayyára*	قطع حِتت صُغيّرة
to slice	*ʔáṭa3* [1s1] *šarāyiḫ*	قطع شرايِح
to chop (up)	*xárraṭ* [2s2]	خرّط
to cut in half	*ʔáṭa3* [1s1] *nuṣṣēn*	قطع نُصّينْ
to cook (on the stove)	*ṭábax* [1s3]	طبخ

to bake (bread)	*xábaz* [1s2]	خبز
to boil	*sálaʔ* [1s3]	سلق
to fry	*ʔála* [1d2]	قلى
pot	*ɧálla (ɧílal)*	حلّة (حِلل)
pan	*ţāsa*	طاسة
tray, casserole dish	*şiníyya (şawāni)*	صينية (صَوانى)
recipe	*wáşfa*	وَصْفة
to follow a recipe	*míši ɧasb ilwáşfa*	مِشي حسْب الوَصْفة
cookbook	*kitāb (kútub) ţabx*	كِتاب (كُتُب) طبْخ
blender	*xallāţ*	خلّاط
mixer	*xallāţ yádawi*	خلّاط يَدَوي
toaster	*tústir*	توسْترِ
sink	*ɧōḑ (aɧwāḑ)*	حوْض (أحْواض)
faucet (UK: tap)	*ɧanafíyya*	حنفية
to do the dishes (UK: do the washing up)	*ɣásal* [1s2] *ilʔaţbāʔ*	غسل الأطْباق
dishwashing liquid	*sāyil ɣasīl ilʔaţbāʔ*	سايِل غسيل الأطْباق
to make tea	*3ámal* [1s2] *šāy*	عمل شايْ
kettle	*ɣallāya* [kettle]	غلّايَة كيْتِل
to make coffee	*3ámal* [1s2] *ʔáhwa*	عمل قهْوَة
coffee maker	[coffee maker] *mákanit ʔáhwa*	كوْفي ميْكِر مكنِةْ قهْوَة
garbage (UK: rubbish)	*zibāla*	زِبالة

garbage can (UK: dustbin)	*şafīĥit zibāla*	صفيحِةْ زِبالة
to throw away	*ráma* [1d2]	رمى
to take out the garbage	*xárrag* [2s2] *izzibāla*	خرّج الزِّبالة

bedroom	*ōḍit nōm*	أوْضِةْ نوْم
bed	*sirīr (sarāyir)*	سِرير (سرايِر)
single bed, twin bed	*sirīr suɣáyyar* *sirīr li-šáxş*	سِرير صُغيّر سِرير لِشخْص
double bed, queen bed, king bed	*sirīr kibīr* *sirīr li-šaxşēn*	سِرير كِبير سِرير لِشخْصينْ
headboard	*rās sirīr* [f.] *(rūs sarāyir)*	راس سِرير (روس سرايِر)
mattress	*martába (marātib)*	مرْتبة (مراتِب)
blanket	*baṭṭaníyya (baṭaṭīn, baṭaniyyāt)*	بطّانية (بطاطين، بطانِيّات)
duvet, quilt	*liĥāf (ilĥífa)*	لِحاف (إلْحِفة)
bedsheet	*milāya*	مِلايَة
pillow, cushion	*maxádda*	مخدّة
pillowcase	*kīs maxádda (akyās maxaddāt)*	كيس مخدّة (أكْياس مخدّات)
to make one's bed	*ráwwaʔ* [2s2] *sirīru*	روّق سِريرُه

sleep	*nōm*	نوْم
to sleep, fall asleep, go to sleep, go to bed	*nām* [1h3]	نام
I only got four or five hours' sleep last night.	*nimt imbāriĥ bi-llēl árba3 aw xámas sa3āt bass.*	نِمْت إمْبارِح بِاللّيْل أرْبع أَوْ خمْس ساعات بسّ.
What time did you go to bed?	*ínta nimt issā3a kām?*	إنْتَ نِمْت السّاعة كام؟

asleep	*nāyim*	نايِم
sleepy, drowsy	*na3sān*	نعْسان
to be sleepy	*kābis* [3s] *3alēh innōm*	كابِس عليْه النّوْم
to doze off	*nām* [1h3] *3ála rōḫu*	نام على روْحُه
to take a nap	*xad* [i3] *ʔaylūla* *nām* [1h3] *šuwáyya suɣayyarīn*	خد قَيْلولة نام شُوَيَّة صُغيّرين
I was feeling sleepy, so I took a short nap.	*kān kābis 3aláyya -nnōm fa ʔaxádtᵊ ʔaylūla.*	كان كابِس عليّا النّوْم فا أخدْت قَيْلولة.
to dream	*ḫílim* [1s4]	حِلِم
a dream	*ḫilm (aḫlām)*	حِلْم (أحْلام)
a nightmare	*kabūs (kawabīs)*	كابوس (كَوابيس)
to have a nightmare	*ḫílim* [1s4] *bi-kabūs*	حِلِم بِكابوس
to snore	*šáxxar* [2s2]	شخّر
to talk in one's sleep	*itkállim* [5s1] *wi húwwa nāyim*	اِتْكلِّم و هُوَّ نايِم
to sleepwalk	*míši* [1d5] *w húwwa nāyim*	مِشي و هُوَّ نايِم
to be unable to get to sleep, have a restless night's sleep	*miš 3ārif yinām kuwáyyis*	مِش عارِف يِنام كُوَيِّس
You don't look like you slept well.	*šáklak ma-nímtiš kuwáyyis.*	شكْلك منِمْتِش كُوَيِّس.
to have insomnia	*3ándu áraq*	عنْدُه أرق
to be a light sleeper	*nōmu xafīf*	نوْمُه خفيف
to be in a deep sleep	*nām* [1h3] *bi-3úmq*	نام بِعُمْق
to be a deep sleeper	*nōmu tʔīl*	نوْمُه تْقيل
to stay up late	*síhir* [1s4]	سِهِر
to stay up all night	*síhir* [1s4] *ṭūl illēl*	سِهِر طول اللّيْل
to wake (up), rouse	*ṣáḫḫa* [2d]	صحّى

My mom woke me up.	*úmmi ʂaɦɦítni min innōm.*	أُمّي صحِّتْني مِن النّوْم.
to wake up	*ʂíɦi* [1d4]	**صِحى**
I woke up at six o'clock in the morning.	*ʂiɦīt issā3a sítta -ʂʂubɦ.*	صِحيت السّاعة سِتّة الصُّبْح.
A loud noise woke me up.	*ʂiɦīt min iddáwša. (lit. I woke up because of the noise.)*	صِحيت مِن الدَّوْشة.
to get up, get out of bed	*ʔām* [1h1] *min issirīr*	**قام مِن السِّرير**

wardrobe	*dulāb (dawalīb)*	**دولاب (دَواليب)**
hanger	*šammā3a*	**شمّاعة**
dresser	*šufunīra*	**شوفُنيرة**
drawer	*durg (adrāg)*	**دُرْج (أدْراج)**
bedside table	*kōmudīnu*	**كوْمودينو**
alarm clock	*minábbih*	**مِنبِّهْ**
I set my alarm for six in the morning.	*ʐabáʈʈ ilminábbih 3ála (-ssā3a) sítta -ʂʂubɦ.*	ظبطْت المِنبِّهْ على (ألسّاعة) سِتّة الصُّبْح.
bookcase	*maktába*	**مكْتبة**
desk	*ʈarabēza*	**طرابيْزة**

bathroom	*ɦammām*	**حمّام**
bathtub	*bányu (banyuhāt)*	**بانْيو (بانْيوهات)**
to take a bath	*istaɦámma* [10.2d]	**اِسْتحمّى**
shower	*dušš* *šāwir*	**دُشّ** **شاوِر**
to take a shower	*ʔáxad* [i3] *dušš* *áxad* [i3] *šāwir*	**أخد دُشّ** **أخد شاوِر**

sponge, loofah	*līfa*	ليفة
shampoo	[shampoo]	شامْپو
to dry off, towel oneself off	*náššif* [2s1] *náfsu*	نشِّف نفْسُه
towel	*fūṭa (fúwaṭ)*	فوطة (فُوَط)
towel rack	*fawāṭa*	فَواطة
hairdryer	*sišwār*	سِشْوار

toilet (bowl)	*tawalítt*	تَواليتّ
toilet seat	*ʔá3dit tawalítt*	قعدِةْ تَواليتّ
to flush the toilet	*šadd* [1g3] *issifōn*	شدّ السّيفوْن
toilet paper	*mandīl ɦammām*	منْديل حمّام

sink	*ɦōḍ (aɦwāḍ)*	حوْض (أحْواض)
hot water	*máyya súxna* [f.]	ميّة سُخْنة
cold water	*máyya sáʔ3a* [f.]	ميّة ساقْعة
(gas) water heater	*saxxān*	سخّان
mirror	*mirāya*	مِرايَة
to brush one's teeth	*ɣásal* [1s2] *sinānu*	غسل سِنانُه
toothbrush	*fúršit (fúraš) sinān*	فُرْشِةْ (فُرش) سِنان
toothpaste	*ma3gūn sinān*	معْجون سِنان
dental floss	*xēṭ ilʔasnān*	خيْط الأسْنان
to floss (teeth)	*náḍḍaf* [2s2] *sinānu bi-lxēṭ*	نضّف سِنانُه بِالخيْط
mouth wash	*ɣasūl ilfám*	غسول الفم
to gargle	*ɣárɣar* [11s2]	غرْغر
to wash one's face	*ɣásal* [1s2] *wíššu*	غسل وِشُّه
(bar of) soap	*ṣabūna*	صابونة

to shave	*ħálaʔ* [1s1]	حلق
razor (blade)	*mūs (amwās)*	موس (أمْواس)
electric razor	*mákanit ħilāʔa*	مكنِةْ حِلاقة
shaving cream	*ráɣwit ħilāʔa*	رغْوِةْ حِلاقة

lawn	*3ušb* [coll.]	عُشْب
to mow the lawn	*ʔaşş* [1g2] *il3úšb*	قصّ العُشْب
courtyard	*ħōš (aħwāš)*	حوْش (أحْواش)
garden, yard	*ginēna (ganāyin)*	جِنيْنة (جنايِن)
to garden	*ištáɣal* [8s2] *fi -lginēna*	اِشْتغل في الجِنيْنة
shovel	*garūf (gawarīf)*	جاروف (جَواريف)
to dig	*ħáfar* [1s3]	حفر
(garden) hose	*xarţūm (xaraţīm)*	خرْطوم (خراطيم)

tool	*adāh (adawāt)*	أداهْ (أدَوات)
saw	*munšār (manašīr)*	مُنْشار (منشير)
to saw	*ʔáţa3* [1s1] *bi-lmunšār*	قطع بِالمُنْشار
hammer	*šakūš (šawakīš)*	شاكوش (شَواكيش)
to hammer	*daʔʔ^{ə}* [1g2] *bi-ššakūš*	دقّ بِالشّاكوش
nail, screw	*musmárr (masamīr)*	مُسْمارّ (مسامير)
screwdriver	*mafákk*	مفكّ
ax	*fās* [f.] *(fūs)*	فاس (فوس)
to chop wood	*ʔáţţa3* [2s2] *xášab*	قطّع خشب
wrench (UK: spanner)	*muftāħ (mafatīħ) ingilīzi*	مُفْتاح (مفاتيح) إنْجِليزي

8 Food and Drink

to eat	*ʔákal* [i3] *kal* [i3]	أكل كل
What do you feel like eating?	*tiђíbbᵊ tākul ʔē?*	تِحِبّ تاكُل أيْه؟
food	*akl*	أكْل
to drink	*šírib* [1s4]	شِرِب
drink, beverage	*mašrūb*	مشْروب
a bite	*ʔáṭma* *ђítta (ђítat)*	قطْمة حِتّة (حِتت)
to take a bite of	*xad* [i3] *ʔáṭma min* *xad* [i3] *ђítta min*	خد قطْمة مِن خد حِتّة مِن
He took a bite of the hamburger and put it down.	*ʔáṭam ʔáṭma min ilhambúrgur wi sābu.*	قطم قطْمة مِن الهمْبرْجُر و سابُه.
a sip	*šáfṭa*	شفْطة
to take a drink/sip (of)	*xad* [i3] *šáfṭa min*	خد شفْطة مِن
mouthful	*buʔʔ*	بُقّ
to take a bite of, take a sip of	*xad* [i3] *buʔʔᵊ min*	خد بُقّ مِن
She took a sip of water and put the glass down.	*xádit šáfṭit máyya wi sābit ilkubbāya.* *xádit buʔʔᵊ máyya wi sābit ilkubbāya.*	خدِت شفْطِةْ ميّة و سابِت الكوبّاية. خدِت بُقّ ميّة و سابِت الكوبّاية.
to chew	*náday* [1s3] *máḍay* [1s3]	ندغ مضغ
to swallow	*bála3* [1s1]	بلع

to choke on	*šíri? [1s4] min*	**شِرِق مِن**
Chew carefully. You don't want to choke on a fishbone.	*úmḍuɣ bi-rāḫa 3ašān ma-tišrá?š^{ə} min šōk issámak.*	أُمْضُغ بِراحة عشان متِشرْقْش مِن شوْك السّمك.

hungry	*ga3ān*	**جعان**
to get hungry	*gā3 [1h1]*	**جاع**
hunger	*gū3*	**جوع**
thirsty	*3aṭšān*	**عطْشان**
I'm so thirsty. Could I have some water?	*ána 3aṭšān áwi. múmkin tiddīni šwáyyit máyya?*	أنا عطْشان أوي .مُمْكِن تِدّيني شُوَيِّةْ ميّة؟
to become thirsty	*3íṭiš [1s4]*	**عِطِش**
thirst	*3áṭaš*	**عطش**
full, satiated	*šab3ān*	**شبْعان**
to become full	*šíbi3 [1s4]*	**شِبِع**
Thanks, I'm full.	*šúkran, ána šbí3t.*	شُكْراً، أنا شْبِعْت.

to taste	*dā? [1h1]*	**داق**
Taste the soup. Does it need salt?	*dū? iššúrba. 3áyza milḫ?*	دوق الشّورْبة .عايْزة مِلْح؟
delicious, tasty	*lazīz (luzāz)*	**لذيذ (لُذاذ)**
taste	*ṭa3m*	**طعْم**
I don't like how it tastes.	*miš 3agíbni ṭá3mu.*	مِش عاجِبْني طعْمُه.
The milk tastes funny.	*ṭa3m illában ɣarīb.*	طعم اللّبن غريب.
to go bad	*bāẓ [1h1]*	**باظ**
The milk has gone bad.	*illában bāẓ.*	اللّبن باظ.
expiration date	*tarīx intihā? iṣṣalaḫíyya*	**تاريخ اِنْتِهاء الصّلاحية**

The milk is past its expiration date.	*illában tarīxu xíliṣ.*	اللّبن تاريخه خِلِص.
to rot	*3áffin* [2s1]	عفِّن
fresh	*ṭāza* [invar.]	طازة
stale	*bāyit*	بايِت

bland	*xafīf*	خفيف
salty	*māliɧ*	مالِح
How does the soup taste? It's a little salty.	*ʔē ráʔyak fi -ššúrba?* *málɧa šwáyya.*	أيْه رأْيَك في الشّورْبة؟ مالْحة شْوَيَّة.
sweet	*ɧilw* *misákkar*	حِلْو مِسكّر
sour	*míziz*	مِزِز
bitter	*murr*	مُرّ
spicy	*ɧarrāʔ*	حرّاق
I don't like spicy food.	*ma-baɧíbbiš ilʔákl ilɧarrāʔ.*	مبحِبِّش الأكْل الحرّاق.
pungent	*ɧāmi*	حامي

healthy, healthful	*ṣíɧɧi* *mufīd*	صِحّي مُفيد
good for you	*mufīd li-ṣiɧɧítak*	مُفيد لِصِحِّتك
unhealthy	*muḍírr* *miš ṣíɧɧi*	مُضِرّ مِش صِحّي
bad for you	*muḍírr li-ṣiɧɧítak*	مُضِرّ لِصِحِّتك
Potato chips are really bad for you.	*iššíbsi muḍírrᵊ áwi.*	الشّيبْسي مُضِرّ أوي.

meal	*wágba*	وَجْبة

breakfast	*fiṭār*	فِطار
to have breakfast	*fíṭir* [1s4]	فِطِر
lunch	*ɣáda*	غدا
to have lunch	*itɣádda* [5d]	اِتْغدّى
dinner	*3áša*	عشا
to have dinner	*it3ášša* [5d]	اِتْعشّى
a snack	*wágba xafīfa* *taşbīra* *ʔazʔáza* [snack]	وَجْبة خفيفة تصْبيرة قزْقزة سْناك
to have a snack	*ʔázʔaz* [11s2] *xad* [i3] *taşbīra*	قزْقز خد تصْبيرة
If I feel hungry, I just have a small snack.	*lámma -ħiss ínni ga3ān, baʔázʔaz ʔayyᵊ ħāga xafīfa.*	لمّا أحِسّ إنّي جعان، بقزْقز أيّ حاجة خفيفة.

water	*máyya*	ميّة
ice	*talg*	تلْج
Can I have a glass of water, please?	*múmkin kubbāyit máyya, law samáħt?*	مُمْكِن كوبّايةْ ميّة لَوْ سمحْت؟
mineral water	*máyya ma3daníyya*	ميّة معْدنية
juice	*3aşīr*	عصير
orange juice	*3aşīr burtuʔān*	عصير بُرْتُقان
soda, carbonated drink	*mašrūb ɣāzi*	مشْروب غازي
cola	*kōla*	كوْلا
Would you like some cola?	*tiħíbbᵊ tāxud šuwáyyit kōla?*	تِحِبّ تاخُد شُوَيّةْ كوْلا؟

Colas are commonly referred to as 'Pepsi' in Egypt, regardless of the actual brand.		
Pepsi	[Pepsi]	پيْپْسى
Diet Pepsi	[Pepsi] *dāyit*	پيْپْسي دايِت
Coke, Coca Cola	*kōka kōla*	كوْكا كوْلا
Diet Coke	*kōka kōla dāyit*	كوْكا كوْلا دايِت
can	*3ílba (3ílab)* *kān* *kanzāya*	عِلْبة (عِلب) كان كنْزايَة
There's a can of cola in the fridge.	*fī kān* [Pepsi] *fi -ttalāga.*	فيه كان پيْپْسي في التّلاجة.
bottle	*izāza (azāyiz)*	إزازة (أزايِز)
glass	*kubbāya*	كوبّايَة
cup	*fingāl (fanagīl)*	فِنْجال (فناجيل)
mug	*kubbāya* [mug]	كوبّايَة مج
coffee	*ʔáhwa*	قهْوَة
espresso	[espresso]	إسْپْرِيْسو
Turkish coffee	*ʔáhwa túrki* *ʔáhwa 3árabi*	قهْوَة تُرْكي قهْوَة عربي
How would you like your (Turkish) coffee?	*tiђíbbᵊ ʔahwítak ʔē?*	تِحِبّ قهْوِتك أيْه؟
without sugar	*sāda*	سادة
with little sugar	*3ála -rrīђa*	على الرّيحة
medium-sweet	*mazbūṭ*	مظْبوط
sweet	*súkkar ziyāda*	سُكّر زِيادة

coffee beans	*bunn* [coll.] *ḫubūb ʔáhwa* [pl.]	بُنّ حُبوب قهْوَة
instant coffee	*ʔáhwa fawríyya*	قهْوَة فَوْرية
tea	*šāy*	شايْ

alcohol	*kuḫūl*	كُحول
beer	*bīra*	بيرة
wine	*nibīt* *xamr* [coll.]	نِبيت خمْر
red wine	*nibīt áḫmar*	نِبيت أحْمر
white wine	*nibīt ábyaḍ*	نِبيت أبْيَض
liquor	*xamr* [coll.]	خمْر
drunk	*sakrān* *šārib*	سكْران شارِب
to get drunk	*síkir* [1s4]	سِكِر
tipsy	*sakrān šuwáyya*	سكْران شُوَيَّة
to drink and drive	*sāʔ* [1h1] *wi húwwa sakrān*	ساق و هُوَّ سكْران
Cheers!	*bi-ṣiḫḫítak*	بِصِحِّتك

dairy products	*muntagāt ilʔalbān* [coll.]	مُنْتجات الألْبان
milk	*lában*	لبن
yogurt	*zabādi*	زبادي
butter	*zíbda*	زِبْدة
Egyptian ghee (made from water buffalo milk)	*sámna báladi*	سمْنة بلدي
ice cream	*āys krīm*	آيْس كْريم
Eat your ice cream before it melts.	*kul ilʔāys krīm bitā3ak ʔablᵊ ma ydūb.*	كُلّ الآيس كْريم بِتاعك قبْل ما يْدوب.

cream	*ʔíšṭa* *krīma*	قِشْطة كْريمة
margarine	*samn*ᵊ *nabāti*	سمْن نباتي
cheese	*gíbna (gíban)*	جِبْنة (جِبن)
Areesh cheese (similar to cottage cheese or Ricotta)	*gíbna ʔarīš*	جِبْنة قريش
Cheddar cheese (semi-hard, sharp, yellow cheese)	*gíbna šēdar*	جِبْنة شيْدر
Domiati cheese (soft, white, salty cheese)	*gíbna dumyāṭi* *gíbna bēḍa*	جِبْنة دُمْياطي جِبْنة بيْضا
Halloumi cheese (semi-hard, unripened cheese made from goat milk)	*gíbna ɧallūm*	جِبْنة حلّوم
Istanbuli cheese (feta cheese)	*gíbna -sṭanbūli*	جِبْنة إسْطنْبولي
Romy cheese (a sharp, pungent, hard cheese)	*gíbna rūmi*	جِبْنة رومي

junk food, fast food	*akl*ᵊ *sarī3*	أكْل سريع
pizza	*pítsa*	پيتْزا
hamburger	*hambúrgur*	همْبُرْجُر
chewing gum	*libān* [coll.]	لِبان
to chew gum	*máḍaɣ* [1s3] *libāna*	مضغ لِبانة
chocolate	*šukulāta*	شوكولاتة
Dark chocolate is better for you than milk chocolate.	*iššukulāta -lɣámʔa ʔaɧsánlak min iššukulāta bi-llában.*	الشّوكولاتة الغامْقة أحْسنْلك مِن الشّوكولاتة بِاللبن.
potato chips (UK: crisps)	*šíbsi*	شيبْسي
pastries, sweets	*ɧalawiyyāt* [pl.]	حَلَويات

candy (UK: sweets)	*bimbōni* [coll.]	بِنْبوْنى
cotton candy	*ɣazl ilbanāt*	غزْل البنات
cookie	[cookies]	كوكيز
wafer, cracker, cookie UK: biscuit)	*bask(a)wīt*	بسْكَويت
cake	*kēka*	كيْكة
pie	*fiṭīra*	فِطيرة
baklava (syrupy layers of phyllo pastry)	*baʔlāwa*	بقْلاوَة
basboosa (syrupy semolina cake)	*basbūsa*	بسْبوسة
fateer meshaltet (layered pastry)	*faṭīr mišáltit*	فطير مِشلْتِت
kahk (shortbread stuffed with dates and nuts)	*kaɦk*	كحْك
kunafeh (syrupy fried cheese pastry)	*kunāfa*	كُنافة
luqmat al-qadi (syrupy deep-fried dough balls)	*lúʔmit ilʔāḍi*	لُقْمِةْ القاضي
om ali (a very popular sweet bread pudding)	*umm^ə 3áli*	أُمّ علي
qatayef (sweet dumpling with nuts and cream)	*ʔaṭāyif*	قطايِف
rice pudding	*ruzz^ə b-lában*	رُزّ بِلبن

Most fruit and vegetables are ***collective nouns***. These are used with a plural meaning, although they are grammatically singular. Collective forms have singular and plural forms, but these are only used with numbers. The plural is formed with the familiar ـات *-āt*. The singular is formed by adding ـة *-a*, resulting in a feminine noun. For collective nouns that already end in ـة *-a* (and sometimes even for those that do not), this ending is changed to ايَة *-āya*. The dual is formed by adding ـيْن *-ēn* to the singular.

coll.	bananas *mōz* موْز	tomatoes *ʔūṭa* قوطة
sing.	one banana *mōza wáɦda* موْزة واحْدة	one tomato *ʔuṭāya wáɦda* قوطايَة واحْدة
dual	two bananas *muztēn* موزْتيْن	two tomatoes *ʔuṭaytēn* قوطايْتيْن
pl.	*talat muzāt* تلات موزات three bananas	*xámas ʔuṭayāt* خمس قوطايات five tomatoes

vegetable	*xuḑār (xaḑrawāt)*	خُضار (خضْرَوات)
asparagus	*hilyōn* [coll.]	هِلْيوْن
bean, green bean	*faşúlya* [coll.]	فاصولْيا
beet(root)	*bángar* [coll.]	بنْجر
broad bean, fava bean	*fūl* [coll.]	فول
broccoli	*brōkuli*	بْروكُلي
cabbage	*kurúmb* [coll.]	كُرُنْب
capsicum, sweet pepper, bell pepper	*fílfil rūmi* [coll.]	فِلْفِل رومي
carrot	*gázar* [coll.]	جزر
cauliflower	*ʔarnabīţ* [coll.]	قرْنبيط
celery	*karáfs*	كرفْس
chickpea	*ɧúmmuş* [coll.]	حُمُّص
chili pepper	*fílfil ɧarrāʔ* [coll.]	فِلْفِل حرّاق
cucumber	*xiyār* [coll.]	خِيار
eggplant (UK: aubergine)	*bitingān* [coll.]	بِتِنْجان
garlic	*tūm* [coll.]	توم
green onion	*báşal áxḑar* [coll.]	بصل أخْضر
mushroom	*māšrum* *3išš^{ə} ɣurāb* [coll.]	مشْروم عيشّ غُراب
okra	*bámya*	بامْيَة
olive	*zatūn* [coll.]	زتون
onion	*báşal* [coll.]	بصل
pea	*bisílla* [coll.]	بِسِلّة
potato	*baţāţis* [coll.]	بطاطِس
radish	*figl* [coll.]	فِجْل
spinach	*sabānix*	سبانِخ

sweet potato	*baṭāṭa* [coll.]	بطاطا
tomato	*ṭamāṭim* [coll.] *ʔūṭa* [coll.]	طماطم قوطة
turnip	*lift* [coll.]	لِفْت
zucchini (UK: courgette)	*kōsa* [coll.]	كوْسة

salad	*sálaṭa*	سلطة
salad dressing	*ṣōṣ sálaṭa* *tatbīlit sálaṭa*	صوْص سلطة تتْبيلِةْ سلطة
Caesar salad	*sálaṭa sīzar*	سلطة سيزر
chickpea salad	*sálaṭit ḥúmmuṣ*	سلطِةْ حُمُّص
green salad	*sálaṭa xáḍra*	سلطة خضْرا
potato salad	*sálaṭit baṭāṭis*	سلطِةْ بطاطِس
tahini salad	*sálaṭit ṭiḥīna*	سلطِةْ طِحينة

fruit	*fákha (fawākih)*	فاكْهة (فَواكِهْ)
apple	*tuffāḥ* [coll.]	تُفّاح
apricot	*míšmiš* [coll.]	مِشْمِش
banana	*mōz* [coll.]	موْز
berry	*tūt* [coll.]	توت
blueberry	*tūt ázraʔ* [coll.]	توت أزْرق
cherry	*kirēz* [coll.]	كِريْز
date	*bálaḥ* [coll.]	بلح
fig	*tīn* [coll.]	تين
grape	*3ínab* [coll.]	عِنب
grapefruit	*grēp frūt*	جْريْپ فْروت
lemon	*lamūn* [coll.]	لمون

mango	*mánga* [coll.]	منْجة
orange	*burtuʔān* [coll.]	بُرْتُقان
peach	*xūx* [coll.]	خوخ
pear	*kummítra* [coll.]	كُمِّتْرى
pineapple	*ananās* [coll.]	أناناس
plum	*barʔūʔ* [coll.]	برْقوق
pomegranate	*rummān* [coll.]	رُمّان
raspberry	*tūt áɧmar* [coll.]	توت أحْمر
strawberry	*faráwla* [coll.]	فراوْلة
tangerine	*yustafándi* [coll.]	يوسْتفنْدى
nut, hazelnut	*búnduʔ* [coll.]	بُنْدُق
almond	*lōz* [coll.]	لوْز
coconut	*gōz hind* [coll.] (lit. Indian walnut)	جوْز هِنْد
peanut	*(fūl) sudāni* [coll.] (lit. Sudanese (bean)*)*	)فول) سوداني
peanut butter	*zíbdit fūl sudāni*	زِبْدِةْ فول سوداني
walnut	*gōz* [coll.] *3ēn gámal*	جوْز عينْ جمل
mixed nuts	*makassarāt* [pl.]	مكسّرات
fresh herbs	*á3šāb* [pl.]	أعْشاب
dry herbs, spices, condiments	*tawābil* [pl.] *buharāt* [pl.]	توابِل بُهارات
aniseed	*yansūn*	ينْسون
basil	*riɧān*	ريحان
black pepper	*fílfil íswid*	فِلْفِل إسْوِد

chives	*tūm mi3ámmar*	توم مِعمّر
cinnamon	*ʔírfa*	قِرْفة
clove	*ʔurúnful mugáffaf*	قُرُنْفُل مُجفّف
cumin	*kammūn*	كمّون
curry (powder)	*kāri*	كاري
ginger	*ganzabīl*	جنْزبيل
nutmeg	*gōz ṭīb*	جوْز طيب
oregano	*ur(e)gānu*	أوريْجانو
parsley	*baʔdūnis*	بقْدونِس
peppermint, spearmint	*ni3nā3*	نِعْناع
rosemary	*rōz mēri*	روْز ميْري
sage	*marmaríyya*	مرْمرية
salt	*milḥ*	مِلْح
sugar	*súkkar*	سُكّر
thyme	*zá3tar*	زعْتر
vanilla	*vanílya*	ڤانيلْيا

sauce	*ṣōṣ*	صوْص
gravy	*ṣálṣit láḥma*	صلْصِةْ لحْمة
ketchup	*kétšab*	كاتْشب
mayonnaise	*mayunēz*	مايونيْز
mustard	*mastárda*	مسْترْدة
salsa, tomato puree	*ṣálṣa*	صلْصة
soy sauce	*ṣōya ṣōṣ*	صوْيا صوْص
tomato sauce	*ṣálṣit ṭamāṭim*	صلصِةْ طماطِم
vinegar	*xall*	خلّ

rice	*ruzz* [coll.]	رُزّ
pasta	*makarōna* *pásta*	مكروْنة پاسْتا
bread	*3ēš*	عيْش
loaf of bread	*riɣīf (arɣífit) 3ēš*	رِغيف (أرْغِفِةْ) عيْش
slice of bread	*šarīħit (sarāyiħ) 3ēš*	شريحِةْ (شرايح) عيْش
piece of bread	*ħíttit (ħítat) 3ēš*	حِتِّةْ (حِتت) عيْش
sliced bread; toast	*3ēš tust*	عيْش توسْت
baguette, sandwich roll	*3ēš fīnu*	عيْش فينو
pita bread (white flour)	*3ēš šāmi*	عيْش شامي
pita bread (whole wheat)	*3ēš báladi*	عيْش بلدي
aysh dora (corn "tortilla")	*3ēš dúra*	عيْش دُرة

yeast	*xamīra*	خميرة
flour	*diʔīʔ*	دِقيق
toast	*tust*	توسْت
jam	*mirábba*	مِربّى
honey	*3ásal*	عسل

protein	*brutīn*	بْروتين
egg	*bēḍ* [coll.]	بيْض
yolk	*ṣafār bēḍ*	صفار بيْض
egg white	*bayāḍ bēḍ*	بَياض بيْض
fried egg	*bēḍ máʔli*	بيْض مقْلي
boiled egg	*bēḍ maslūʔ*	بيْض مسْلوق
scrambled egg	*bēḍ maxfūʔ*	بيْض مخْفوق

omelet	umlétt	أوْمْليتّ
meat	laḥm [coll.]	لحْم
	láḥma	لحْمة
beef	láḥma (báʔari)	لحْمة (بقري)

When the type of meat is unspecified, لحْمة láḥma is understood to mean 'beef.'

I don't feel like chicken. Let's have beef.	miš 3āyiz ākul firāx. ta3āl nigīb láḥma.	مِش عايِز آكُل فِراخ . تعال نِجيب لحْمة.
(beef) steak	[steak]	سْتيْك
	buftēk	بُفْتيْك
pastrami	bastírma	بسْطِرْمة
minced meat	láḥma mafrūma	لحْمة مفْرومة
chicken	firāx	فِراخ
chicken filet	firāx filēh	فِراخ فيليْهْ
lamb	laḥmᵃ xirfān	لحْمر خِرْفان
pork	(laḥme) xanzīr	(لحْمر) خنْزير
ham	hām	هام
sausage	sugúʔʔ	سُجُقّ
hot dog	susīs	سوسيس

fish	sámak [coll.]	سمك
fishbone	šōk sámak	شوْك سمك
Bolti (Nile perch)	sámak búlṭi [coll.]	سمك بُلْطي
lethrinus nebulosus (Red Sea fish)	šu3ūr [coll.]	شُعور
meagre (Mediterranean fish)	lūṭ [coll.]	لوط

mullet (Mediterranean fish)	*būri* [coll.]	بوري
salmon	*sálamun*	سلمون
shark	*sámak ʔirš*	سمك قِرْش
tuna	*tūna*	تونا، تونة

seafood	*maʔkulāt baɧríyya* [pl.]	مأْكولات بحْرية
crab	*kabúrya*	كابورْيا
lobster	*astakōza*	أسْتاكوْزا
mussel	*bálaɧ baɧr*	بلح بحْر
octopus	*ixtabūʈ*	إخْطبوط
oyster	*maɧār*	محار
shellfish	*umm^ə xlūl*	أُمّ خْلول
shrimp	*gambári*	جمْبري
squid, cuttlefish	*ɧabbār*	حبّار

fat	*dihn (duhūn)*	دِهْن (دُهون)
This meat has a lot of fat on it.	*illáɧma malyāna dihn.* *illáɧma di fīha dihn^ə ktīr.*	اللّحمة ملْيانة دِهْن. اللّحْمة دي فيها دِهْن كِتير.
greasy, oily	*midáhnin* *simīn*	مِدهْنِن سِمين
This dish is quite greasy.	*iʈʈábaʔ da smīn šuwáyya.*	الطّبق ده سِمين شُوَيّة.

soup	*šúrba*	شورْبة
to eat soup	*šírib* [1s4] *šúrba*	شِرِب شورْبة
to sip	*šáfaʈ* [1s3]	شفط
to slurp soup	*šáfaʈ* [1s3] *šúrba b-ʂōt*	شفط شورْبة بِصوْت

cream soup	*šúrbit krīma*	شورْبِةْ كْريمة
Jew's mallow (slimy green soup)	*muluxíyya*	مُلوخية
orzo soup	*súrbit lisān 3aşfūr*	شورْبِةْ لِسان عصْفور
tomato soup	*šúrbit ţamāţim*	شورْبِةْ طماطِم
vegetable soup	*šúrbit xuḍār*	شورْبِةْ خُضار

fried	*máʔli* *miђámmar*	مقْلي مِحمّر
(vegetable) oil	*zēt*	زيْت
baked (bread)	*maxbūz*	مخْبوز
baked, roast	*fi furn*	في فُرْن
boiled	*máɣli* *maslūʔ*	مغْلي مسْلوق
grilled, roast	*mášwi*	مشْوي

carton	*kartōna*	كرْتوْنة
bag	*kīs (akyās)*	كيس (أكْياس)
jar	*barţamān*	برْطمان

brain sandwich	*sandiwítšᵊ muxx*	سنْدِوِتْش مُخّ
falafel	*ţa3míyya*	طعْمية
fateer (Egyptian pizza)	*faţīr*	فطير
ful (refried fava beans)	*fūl*	فول
ful medames (boiled fava beans)	*fūl midámmis*	فول مِدمِّس
koshari (lentils, rice, and macaroni)	*kúšari*	كُشري
liver sandwich	*sandiwítšᵊ kíbda*	سنْدِوِتْش كِبْدة

pickled vegetables	*mixállil* *ṭúrši*	مِخلِّل طُرْشي
table manners	*adāb issúfra*	آداب السُّفْرة
Thank you for the meal! (said to host(ess) after having tried the food)	*tíslam īdak!*	تِسْلم إيدك.
to talk with one's mouth full	*itkállim* [5s1] *wi f búʔʔu akl*	اِتْكلِّم و في بُقُّه أكْل
Don't talk with your mouth full!	*ma-titkallímšᵊ w fi búʔʔak akl!*	متِتْكلِّمْش و في بُقّك أكْل!
Could you pass the salt, please?	*múmkin tiddīni -lmilḫ?*	مُمْكِن تِدّيني المِلْح؟
Excuse me for a moment. (when excusing oneself from the table)	*ba3dᵊ íznak.*	بعْد إذْنك.
Thank you for the meal. (said after finishing a meal in someone's home)	*dáyman 3āmir*	دايْماً عامِر.
You're welcome. (response)	*dāmit ḫayātak.*	دامِت حَياتك.

9 Work

work, job	*šuɣl (ašɣāl)* *waẓīfa (waẓāyif)*	شُغْل (أشْغال) وَظيفة (وَظايِف)
to work, be employed	*ištáɣal* [8s2]	اِشْتغل
She works as a teacher.	*híyya btištáɣal mudarrísa.*	هِيَّ بِتِشْتغل مُدرِّسة.
She works in (the field of) teaching.	*híyya btištáɣal fi (magāl) ittadrīs.*	هِيَّ بِتِشْتغل في مجال التّدريس.
I work five days a week.	*baštáɣal xámas tiyyām fi -lʔisbū3.*	بشْتغل خمس تيّام في الإسْبوع.
job, task	*šúɣla* *šuɣlāna*	شُغْلة شغْلانة
full-time	*dawām kāmil* [full time]	دَوام كامِل فول تايْم
I work full-time.	*baštáɣal* [full time].	بشْتغل فول تايْم.
part-time	*dawām guzʔi* *nuṣṣᵊ yōm* [part time]	دَوام جُزْئي نُصّ يوْم پارْت تايْم
I want a part-time job.	*3āyiz šuɣlᵊ dawām gúzʔi.*	عايِز شُغْل دَوام جُزْئي.
the private sector	*ilqitā3 ilxāṣṣ*	القِطاع الخاصّ
the public sector	*ilqiṭā3 il3āmm*	القِطاع العامّ
civil servant	*muwáẓẓaf ḫukūmi*	مُوَظّف حُكومي

to look for a job	*dáwwar* [2s2] *3ála šuɣl*	دوّر على شُغْل
to apply for a job	*ʔáddim* [2s1] *3ála šuɣl*	قدِّم على شُغْل
applicant, candidate	*mitʔáddim*	مِتْقدِّم

experience	*xíbra*	خِبْرة
to have a job interview	*3ándu muʔáblit šuɣl*	عَنْدُه مُقابْلِةْ شُغْل
to interview	*3ámal* [1s2] *muʔábla*	عمل مُقابْلة
to get a job	*gālu* [i1] *šuɣl*	جالُه شُغْل

to find a job	*láʔa* [i4] *šugl*	لقى شُغْل
to obtain employment	*itwáẓẓaf* [5s2]	اِتْوَظّف
Have you found a job yet?	*laʔēt šuɣlᵊ wálla líssa?*	لقيْت شُغْل وَلّا لِسّه؟
to employ	*wáẓẓaf* [2s2] *3áyyin* [2s1] *šáɣɣal* [2s2]	وَظّف عيِّن شغّل
employee	*muwáẓẓaf*	مُوَظّف
employer	*ṣāħib (aṣħāb) šuɣl*	صاحِب (أصْحاب) شُغْل
boss, manager	*mudīr*	مُدير
colleague, coworker	*zimīl (zamāyil)*	زِميل (زمايِل)
company	*šírka*	شِرْكة

to start work	*bádaʔ* [1s1] *šúɣlu*	بدأ شُغْلُه
to take a break	*ʔáxad* [i3] *istirāħa*	أخد اِسْتِراحة
lunch break	*istirāħit ɣáda*	اِسْتِراحِةْ غدا
to finish work, get off work	*xállaṣ* [2s2] *iššúɣl*	خلّص الشُّغْل
to work overtime	*ištáɣal* [8s2] [overtime]	اِشْتغل أوْفر تايْم
working hours	*dawām*	دَوام
I work eight hours a day.	*ána baštáɣal dawām táman sa3āt yumíyyan.*	أنا بشْتغل دَوام تمان ساعات يوميّاً.

day shift	*šift[ə] bi-nnahār* *wardíyyit innahār*	شِفْت بِالنّهار وَرْديةْ النّهار
night shift, graveyard shift	*šift[ə] bi-llēl* *wardíyyit illēl*	شِفْت بِاللّيْل وَرْديةْ اللّيْل
I work the night shift.	*iššíft[ə] btā3i bi-llēl.*	الشِّفْت بِتاعي بِاللّيْل.
off work, not working	*fāḍi*	فاضي
I have weekends off.	*ána fāḍi ʔāxir ilʔisbū3.*	أنا فاضي آخِر الإسْبوع.

office	*máktab (makātib)*	مكْتب (مكاتِب)
office worker	*muwáẓẓaf maktábi*	مُوَظّف مكْتبي
company representative	*mandūb šírka*	منْدوب شِرْكة
to stay late at the office	*itʔáxxar* [5s2] *fi -lmáktab*	اِتْأخّر في المكْتب
to go on a business trip	*sāfir* [3s] *f- ríḫlit šuɣl*	سافِر في رِحْلِةْ شُغْل
to have a meeting	*3ándu igtimā3*	عنْدُه اِجْتِماع
client	*3amīl (3úmala)*	عميل (عُملا)

to earn money	*gāb* [1h2] *filūs*	جاب فِلوس
wage, pay	*agr (ugūr)*	أجْر (أُجور)
salary	*muráttab*	مُرتّب
My salary is just okay.	*ilmuráttab bitā3i nuṣṣ[ə] nuṣṣ.*	المُرتّب بِتاعي نُصّ نُصّ.
to get paid	*ʔábaḍ* [1s1]	قبض
payday	*yōm ʔabḍ*	يوْم قبْض
I get paid on the first of the month.	*báʔbaḍ f- áwwal iššáhr.*	بقْبض في أوّل الشّهْر.
bonus, incentive	*ḫāfiz (ḫawāfiz)*	حافِز (حَوافِز)
pay raise	*ziyāda fi -lmuráttab*	زِيادة في المُرتّب
to get a raise	*zād* [1h2] *fi -lmuráttab*	زاد في المُرتّب

to give __ a raise	*záwwid-lu* [2s1] *-lmuráttab*	**زوِّد له المُرتّب**
promotion	*tarʔíyya*	**ترْقية**
to get promoted	*itráʔʔa* [5d]	**اِتْرقّى**
Praise be to God, I got a promotion this month.	*ilḫámdu lillāh, ána -traʔʔēt iššáhrᵊ da.*	الحمْدُ للّه أنا اتْرقّيْت الشّهْر ده.

unemployed, jobless	*3āṭil*	**عاطِل**
unemployment	*baṭāla*	**بطالة**
to resign	*istaqāl* [10h]	**اِسْتقال**
to quit one's job	*sāb* [1h2] *iššúɣl*	**ساب الشُّغْل**
to lay off, make redundant	*istáɣna* [10d1] *3an*	**اِسْتغْنى عن**
to fire	*ṭárad* [1s3]	**طرد**
to get fired	*inṭárad* [7s2] *min šúɣlu*	**اِنْطرد مِن شُغْلُه**
to retire	*ṭíli3* [1s4] *min iššúɣl* *ṭili3* [1s4] *3ála ma3āš*	**طِلِع مِن الشُّغْل** **طِلِع على معاش**
pension	*ma3āš*	**معاش**
(age of) retirement	*sinn ilma3āš*	**سِنّ المعاش**
I hope to retire when I'm sixty.	*nífsi ʔáṭla3 ma3āš 3ála sinn issittīn.*	نِفْسي أطْلع معاش على سِنّ السِّتّين.

career	*míhna (míhan)*	**مِهْنة (مِهن)**
trade, craft	*ḫírfa (ḫíraf)*	**حِرْفة (حِرف)**
What do you do?	*bitištáɣal ʔē?*	بِتِشْتغل أيْه؟
I'm a __.	*ána __.* *baštáɣal __.*	أنا __. بشْتغل.__
accountant	*muḫāsib*	**مُحاسِب**
actor	*mumássil*	**مُمثِّل**

architect	*muhándis mi3māri*	مُهنْدِس مِعْماري
artist	*fannān*	فنّان
athlete	*riyāḍi*	رِياضي
baker	*xabbāz*	خبّاز
bank teller, banker	*muwáẓẓaf fi bank*	مُوَظّف في بنْك
bank manager	*mudīr bank*	مُدير بنْك
barber	*ḫallāʔ*	حلّاق
bus driver	*sawwāʔ utubīs*	سوّاق أُتوبيس
butcher	*gazzār*	جزّار
carpenter	*naggār*	نجّار
cashier	*kašīr*	كاشير
chef	[chef]	شيف
cleaner	*3āmil (3ummāl) naḍāfa*	عامِل (عُمّال) نضافة
cook	*ṭabbāx*	طبّاخ
customer service representative	*mumássil xídmit il3úmala*	مُمثِّل خِدْمِةْ العُملا
dentist	*duktūr (dakátrit) asnān*	دُكْتور (دكاتْرِةْ) أسْنان
doctor	*duktūr (dakátra)*	دُكْتور (دكاتْرة)
editor	*muḫárrir*	مُحرِّر
electrician (repairman)	*kahrabāʔi*	كهْربائي
engineer	*muhándis*	مُهنْدِس
farmer	*fallāḫ*	فلّاح
firefighter	*rāgil (rigālit) maṭāfi*	راجِل (رِجالِةْ) مطافي
fisherman	*ṣayyād*	صيّاد
flight attendant	*muḍīf*	مُضيف
garbage collector (UK: dustman)	*zabbāl*	زبّال
gardener	*ganáyni*	جنايْني

hairdresser	*kuwafīr*	كُوافير
imam	*imām (aʔímma)*	إمام (أئِمّة)
judge	*ʔāḍi (ʔuḍāh)*	قاضي (قُضاهْ)
laborer	*3āmil (3ummāl)*	عامِل (عُمّال)
lawyer, attorney (UK: solicitor)	*muɦāmi*	مُحامي
maid	*šaɣɣāla*	شغّالة
mechanic	*mikanīki*	ميكانيكي
musician	*musiqār*	موسيقار
nurse	*mumárriḍ*	مُمرِّض
painter (of art)	*rassām*	رسّام
painter, house painter	*dahhān*	دهّان
pharmacist	*ṣaydáli (ṣayádila)*	صَيْدلي (صَيادِلة)
pilot	*ṭayyār*	طيّار
plumber	*sabbāk*	سبّاك
police officer	*ẓābiṭ (ẓubbāṭ) šúrṭa*	ظابِط (ظُبّاط) شُرْطة
politician	*siyāsi*	سِياسي
priest	*ʔissīs (ʔasāwisa)* *rāhib (ruhbān)*	قِسّيس (قساوِسة) راهِب (رُهْبان)
professor	*brufesūr* *ustāz (asátza)*	بْروفيْسور أُسْتاذ (أساتْذة)
real estate agent	*simsār (samásra)*	سِمْسار (سماسْرة)
repairman	*múṣliɦ*	مُصْلِح
sailor	*baɦɦār*	بحّار
salesperson	*mandūb mabi3āt*	منْدوب مبيعات
secretary	*sikirtēr*	سِكِرْتيرْ
servant	*šaɣɣāl*	شغّال

shop assistant	*bayyā3*	بيّاع
shopkeeper	*ba??āl*	بقّال
soldier	*3askári (3asākir)* *gúndi (gunūd)*	عسْكري (عساكِر) جُنْدي (جُنود)
taxi driver	*sawwā? táksi*	سوّاق تاكْسي
teacher	*mudárris*	مُدرِّس
technician (UK: engineer)	*fánni*	فنّي
travel agent	*wakīl (wúkala) sáfar*	وكيل (وُكلا) سفر
veterinarian	*duktūr bīṭari*	دُكْتور بيطري
waiter	*garsōn*	جرْسوْن
waitress	*garsōna*	جرْسوْنة
writer	*kātib (kuttāb)*	كاتِب (كُتّاب)

10 School and Education

education	*ta3līm*	تعْليم
educated, literate	*muta3állim*	مُتعلِّم
to learn	*it3állim* [5s1]	اِتْعلِّم
illiterate	*úmmi*	أُمّي
illiteracy	*ummíyya*	أُمّية
What is the illiteracy rate in Egypt?	*ʔē mu3áddal ilʔummíyya fi maṣr?*	أيْه مُعدّل الأُمّية في مصْر؟
school	*madrása (madāris)*	مدْرسة (مدارِس)
student	*ṭālib (ṭálaba, ṭullāb)*	طالِب (طلبة، طُلّاب)
preschool	*ḥaḍāna*	حضانة

In Egypt, children generally begin kindergarten at the age of four. Kindergarten consists of two years, called KG1 and KG2, pronounced as in English.

kindergarten	*kē žī* *kē žī* [one] *kē žī* [two]	كيْ چي(KG) كيْ چي وَن(KG1) كيْ چي توKG2))
elementary school, primary school	*(madrása) ʔibtidāʔi*	)مدْرسة) اِبْتِدائي
when I was in elementary school, ...	*lámma kunt^{ə} f- ibtidāʔi, ...*	لمّا كُنْت في اِبْتِدائي،...
first grade (year)	*sána ʔūla* *ūla ʔibtidāʔi*	سنة أولى أولى اِبْتِدائي
Her son is in first grade.	*ibnáha f- ūla ʔibtidāʔi.*	إبْنها في أولى اِبْتِدائي.
middle school	*madrása ʔi3dādi*	مدْرسة إعْدادي
high school, secondary school	*madrása sánawi*	مدْرسة ثانَوي

university, college	*gám3a*	**جامْعة**
academy	*akadimíyya* *má3had (ma3āhid)*	**أكاديمية** **معْهد (معاهِد)**
language academy	*akadimíyyit álsun* *akadimíyyit luɣāt*	**أكاديميةْ ألْسُن** **أكاديميةْ لُغات**
I'm studying Arabic at a language academy in Cairo.	*ána bádris 3árabi fi ʔakadimíyyit ilʔálsun f- ilqāhíra.*	أنا بدْرِس عربي في أكاديميةْ الألْسُن في القاهِرة.

In Egypt, elementary school consists of six years; middle school and high school are three years each.

in fifth grade	*fi xámsa -btidāʔi*	**في خامْسة ابْتِدائي**
in sixth grade	*fi sátta -btidāʔi*	**في ساتّة ابْتِدائي**
in one's second year of middle school	*fi tánya ʔi3dādi*	**قي تانْيَة إعْدادي**
in one's third year of high school	*fi tálta sánawi*	**في تالْتة ثانَوي**
in one's final year of high school	*fi ʔāxir sána f- sánawi*	**في آخِر سنة في ثانَوي**
class, period	*ḫíṣṣa (ḫíṣaṣ)*	**حِصّة (حِصص)**
I have six classes a day.	*3ándi sittᵊ ḫíṣaṣ fi -lyōm.*	عنْدي سِتّ حِصص في اليوْم.
Class starts at 8 o'clock and finishes at 9 o'clock.	*ilḫíṣṣa btíbdaʔ issā3a tamánya wi tíxlaṣ tís3a.*	الحِصّة بْتِبْدأ السّاعة تمانْيَة و تِخْلص تِسْعة.
lecture	*muḫáḍra*	**مُحاضْرة**
to attend a lecture	*ḫáḍar [1s1] muḫáḍra*	**حضر مُحاضْرة**
lesson	*dars (durūs)*	**درْس (دُروس)**
to study	*dáras [1s2]*	**درس**

studies	*dirāsa*	دِراسة
curriculum	*mánhag (manāhig)*	منْهج (مناهِج)
question	*suʔāl (asʔíla)*	سُؤال (أسْئِلة)
to ask a question in class	*sáʔal* [1s1] *suʔāl fi -lfaṣl*	سأل سُؤال في الفصْل
answer	*igāba*	إجابة
to answer	*gāwib* [3s] *3ála*	جاوِب على
to raise one's hand	*ráfa3* [1s1] *īdu*	رفع إيدُه
right, correct	*ṣaḫḫ*	صحّ
wrong, incorrect; mistake	*ɣálaṭ*	غلط
He got three questions wrong.	*gāwib ɣálaṭ 3ála tálat asʔíla.*	جاوِب غلط على تلات أسْئِلة.

classroom	*faṣl (fuṣūl)*	فصْل (فُصول)
lecture hall	*mudárrag*	مُدرّج
desk	[desk]	ديْسْك
textbook	*kitāb (kútub) madrási*	كِتاب (كُتُب) مدْرسي
notebook	*kaškūl (kašakīl)* *kurrāsa*	كشْكول (كشاكيل) كُرّاسة
to take notes	*dáwwin* [2s1] *mulaḫaẓāt*	دوِّن مُلاحْظات
to copy	*náʔal* [1s2]	نقل
Copy these sentences into your notebook.	*ínʔil ilgúmal di l-kurrástak.*	اِنْقِل الجُمل دي لِكُرّاسْتك.
backpack	*šánṭa (šúnaṭ) madrasíyya*	شنْطة (شُنط) مدْرسية
blackboard	*sabbūra*	سبّورة
chalk	*ṭabašīr* [coll.]	طباشير
whiteboard	*sabbūra bēḍa* [white board]	سبّورة بيْضا وايْت بوْرد

map	*xarīṭa (xarāyiṭ)*	خريطة (خرايِط)

library	*maktába*	مكْتبة
gymnasium	*žim*	چيم
playground, schoolyard	*ḫōš (aḫwāš)* *mál3ab (malā3ib)*	حوْش (أحْواش) ملْعب (ملاعِب)
cafeteria	*kafitírya*	كافيترْيا
laboratory	*má3mal (ma3āmil)*	معْمل (معامِل)
auditorium, theater	*másraḫ (masāriḫ)*	مسْرح (مسارِح)
school bus	*bāṣ madrása*	باص مدْرسة

summer vacation (UK: summer holidays)	*agāzit ṣēf*	أجازِةْ صيْف
winter vacation	*agāzit šíta*	أجازِةْ شِتا
break, recess	*fúsḫa (fúsaḫ)* [break]	فُسْحة (فُسح) بْريْك
We have a fifteen-minute break between classes.	*3andína fúsḫa rub3^ə sā3a bēn ilḫíṣaṣ.*	عنْدنا فُسْحة رُبْع ساعة بينْ الحِصص.
lunch break	*fúsḫit ɣáda*	فُسْحِةْ غدا

test, exam	*imtiḫān*	اِمْتِحان
to take a test	*imtáḫan* [8s1]	اِمْتحن
mid-term (exam)	*imtiḫān nuṣṣ issána*	اِمْتِحان نُصّ السّنة
final exam	*imtiḫān āxir issána*	اِمْتِحان آخِر السّنة
entrance exam	*imtiḫān qubūl*	اِمْتِحان قُبول
an oral exam	*imtiḫān šáfawi*	اِمْتِحان شفَوي
a written exam	*imtiḫān kitābi*	اِمْتِحان كِتابى
to pass a test	*nígiḫ* [1s4] *f- imtiḫān*	نِجِح في اِمْتِحان

to fail a test	*sáʔaṭ* [1s1] *f- imtiḫān*	سقط في اِمْتِحان
exam results	*natīgit imtiḫān*	نتيجةْ اِمْتِحان
grade	*dáraga* *magmū3*	درجة مجْموع
to get a good grade	*gāb* [1h2] *magmū3 kuwáyyis*	جاب مجْموع كُوَيِّس
a passing grade	*dáragit nagāḫ*	درجِةْ نجاح
a failing grade	*dáragit suʔūṭ*	درجِةْ سُقوط
report card	*sígil iddaragāt*	سِجِل الدّرجات
to study, review	*zākir* [3s]	ذاكِر
He needs to study for the test.	*lāzim yizākir li-lʔimtiḫān.*	لازِم يِذاكِر لِلاِمْتِحان.
homework	*wāgib*	واجِب
to do homework	*ḫall* [1g3] *ilwāgib* *3amal* [1s2] *ilwāgib*	حلّ الواجِب عمل الواجِب
to check, revise, review	*rāgi3* [3s] *ilwāgib*	راجِع الواجِب
essay, paper, composition	*mawḍū3 ta3bīr*	مَوْضوع تعْبير
The students have to write an essay about a historical event.	*iṭṭálaba -lmafrūḍ yiktíbu mawḍū3 ta3bīr 3an ḫádas tarīxi.*	الطّلبُه المفْروض يِكْتِبوا مَوْضوع تعْبير عن حدث تاريخي.
teacher	*mudárris*	مُدرِّس

مُدرِّس *mudárris* is a form of reference, but not a form of address. To address a teacher, أُسْتاذ *ustāz* must be used.

Good morning, teacher!	*ṣabāḫ ilxēr, ya ʔustāz!*	صباح الخيْر، يا أُسْتاذ!
lecturer	*muḫāḍir*	مُحاضِر

professor	*brufesūr* *ustāz (asátza)*	**بْروفيْسور** **أُسْتاذ (أساتْذة)**
principal	*mudīr*	**مُدير**
to teach	*dárris* [2s1]	**درِّس**
to teach a course	*dárris* [2s1] *kurs*	**درِّس كورْس**
She teaches at the university.	*híyya btidárris f- ilgám3a.*	هِيَّ بِتدِرِّس في الجامْعة.
Ahmad is teaching me Arabic.	*áɧmad biydarrísli 3árabi.*	أحْمد بِيْدرِّسْلي عربي.
to teach a lesson	*šáraɧ* [1s1] *dars*	**شرح درْس**
to correct a test	*şáɧɧaɧ* [2s2] *imtiɧān*	**صحّح اِمْتِحان**

to enroll	*ištárak* [8s1]	**اِشْترك**
enrollment	*ištirāk*	**اِشْتِراك**
I intend to enroll in an Arabic class next month.	*nāwi ʔaštírik fi faşl il3árabi -ššahr ilgáyy.*	ناوي أشْترِك في فصْل العربي الشّهْر الجايّ.
school year	*sána drasíyya* *sánit madrása*	**سنة دْراسية** **سنِة مدْرسة**
semester	[term]	**تُرْم**
tuition	*maşarīf dirāsa*	**مصاريف دِراسة**
scholarship	*mínɧa (mínaɧ)*	**مِنْحة (مِنح)**
student loan	*qarḑᵊ ţullābi (qurūḑ ţullabíyya)*	**قرْض طُلّابي (قُروض طُلّابية)**

university	*gám3a*	**جامْعة**
to get into college, start university	*xašš* [1g2] *ilgám3a* *dáxal* [1s3] *ilgám3a*	**خشّ الجامْعة** **دخل الجامْعة**
to go to college	*dáras* [1s2] *fi -lgám3a*	**درس في الجامْعة**

department, faculty	*qism (aqsām)* *kullíyya*	**قِسْم (أقْسام)** **كُلّية**
I got into the faculty of medicine, but later I changed to law.	*daxált[ə] kullíyyit iṭṭíbb, bass[ə] sibtáha wi daxált[ə] ɦuʔūʔ.*	دخلْت كُلّيةْ الطِّبّ، بسّ سِبْتها و دخلْت حُقوق.
major	*taxáṣṣuṣ*	**تخصُّص**
minor	*taxáṣṣuṣ fár3i*	**تخصُّص فرْعي**
to major in	*itxáṣṣaṣ* [5s2] *fi*	**اِتْخصّص في**
What are you majoring in?	*ínta taxaṣṣúṣak ʔē?*	إنْتَ تخصُّصك أيْه؟
I'm majoring in English literature.	*ána taxaṣṣúṣi ʔádab ingilīzi.*	أنا تخصُّصي أدب إنْجْليزي.
university campus	*ɦáram gám3i (aɦrām gam3íyya)*	**حرم جامْعي (أحْرام جامْعية)**
dormitories	*madīna gam3íyya*	**مدينة جامْعية**
Do you live on campus?	*ínta sākin fi -lmadīna -lgam3íyya?*	إنْتَ ساكِن في المدينة الجامْعية؟
to graduate from	*itxárrag* [5s2] *min*	**اِتْخرّج مِن**
When did you graduate from university?	*itxarrágt ímta min ilgám3a?*	اِتْخرّجْت إمْتى مِن الجامْعة؟
I graduated from university in 2005.	*itxarrágt[ə] min ilgám3a sánit alfēn wi xámsa.*	اِتْخرّجْت مِن الجامْعة سنِةْ ألْفين و خمْسة.

freshman (1st-year university student)	*ṭālib gidīd (ṭálaba gudād)* *ṭālib (ṭálabit) sána ʔūla*	**طالِب جِديد (طلبة جُداد)** **طالِب (طلبِةْ) سنة أولى**
sophomore (2nd year)	*ṭālib sána tánya*	**طالِب سنة تانْيَة**
junior (3rd year)	*ṭālib sána tálta*	**طالِب سنة تالْتَة**

senior (4th year)	*ṭālib sána ráb3a*	**طالِب سنة رابْعة**
All the freshmen have to attend an orientation ceremony.	*kull iṭṭullāb -lgudād ilmafrūḍ yiḥḍáru -lmuḥáḍra -tta3rifíyya.*	كُلّ الطُّلّاب الجُداد المفْروض يِحْضروا المحاضْرة التّعْريفية.

degree	*dáraga*	**درجة**
diploma	*diblōm* *diblōma*	**دِبْلوْم** **دِبْلوْمة**
certificate	*šahāda*	**شهادة**
He got a certificate for completing the course.	*ʔáxad šahāda ʔínnu xállaṣ ilkúrs.*	أخد شهادة إِنُّه خلّص الكورْس.
to get a Bachelor's degree	*ʔáxad* [i3] *dáragit ilbakaluriyūs*	**أخد درجِةْ البكالوريوس**
college student, undergraduate student	*ṭālib gám3i (ṭálaba) gam3iyyīn)*	**طالِب جامْعي (طلبة جامْعيين)**
undergraduate studies	*iddirasāt ilgam3íyya*	**الدِّراسات الجامْعية**
to do a Master's degree	*ḥáḍḍar* [2s2] *mažistēr*	**حضّر ماچِسْتيرْ**
to do a Doctorate	*ḥáḍḍar* [2s2] *dukturāh*	**حضّر دُكْتوراهْ**
thesis, dissertation	*risālit mažistēr* *risālit dukturāh*	**رِسالِةْ ماچِسْتيرْ** **رِسالِةْ دُكْتوراهْ**

subject	*mádda (mawádd)*	**مادّة (مَوادّ)**
What was your favorite subject in school?	*ʔē áktar mádda kunt*[ə] *bitḥibbáha fi -lmadrása?*	أيْه أكْتر مادّة كُنْت بِتْحِبّها في المدْرسة؟
I really enjoyed studying history, but I hated science class.	*ḥabbēt ittarīx bass*[ə] *ma-ḥabbítš il3ulūm.* *kunt*[ə] *baḥíbb ittarīx bass*[ə] *bákrah il3ulūm.*	حبّيْت التّاريخ بسّ محبّتْش العُلوم. كُنْت بحِبّ التّاريخ بسّ بكْرهْ العُلوم.

to be good at	*báʔa* [1d1] *šāṭir fi*	**بقى شاطِر في**
He's really good at math.	*húwwa šāṭir gíddan fi -rriyaḍiyāt.*	هُوَّ شاطِر جِدّاً في الرِّياضِيات.
biology	*ilʔaḥyāʔ*	**الأحْياء**
chemistry	*ilkímya*	**الكيمْيا**
dentistry	*ṭibb ilʔasnān*	**طِبّ الأسْنان**
economics	*3ilm ilʔiqtiṣād*	**عِلْم الاِقْتِصاد**
geography	*ilguɣráfya*	**الجُغْرافْيا**
geology	*ilžiyulúžya*	**الچيولوچْيا**
geometry	*ilhandása*	**الهنْدسة**
history	*ittarīx*	**التّاريخ**
law	*ilḥuʔūʔ*	**الحُقوق**
linguistics	*3ilm illuɣawiyāt*	**عِلْم اللُّغَوِيات**
literature	*ilʔádab*	**الأدب**
mathematics	*irriyaḍiyāt* *irriyāḍa*	**الرِّياضِيات** **الرِّياضة**
medicine	*iṭṭíbb*	**الطِّبّ**
philosophy	*ilfalsáfa*	**الفلْسفة**
physical education (P.E.)	*ittárbiya -rriyaḍíyya*	**التّرْبية الرِّياضية**
physics	*ilfízya*	**الفيزْيا**
political science	*il3ulūm issiyasíyya*	**العُلوم السِّياسية**
psychology	*3ilm innáfs*	**عِلْم النّفْس**
science	*il3ulūm*	**العُلوم**
social studies	*iddirasāt ilʔigtima3íyya*	**الدِّراسات الاِجْتِماعية**

Egyptians who have attended private schools tend to refer to many academic subjects by their English names: **ماث** *māt* (math), **إنْجْلِش** *īngliš* (English).

11 Health and Medicine

health	*ṣíḫḫa*	صِحّة
healthy, in good health	*bi-ṣíḫḫa kwayyísa* *salīm (sulām)* *bi-3áfya*	بِصِحّة كْوَيِّسة سليم (سُلام) بِعافْيَة
sickness, illness, disease	*máraḍ (amrāḍ)*	مرض (أمْراض)
sick, ill	*3ayyān* *marīḍ (márḍa)* *ta3bān*	عيّان مريض (مرْضى) تعْبان
to be in poor health	*ṣiḫḫítu ta3bāna*	صِحِّتُه تعْبانة
to be handicapped	*mu3āq*	مُعاق
wheelchair	*kúrsi mutaḫárrik*	كُرْسي مُتحرِّك

doctor	*duktūr (dakátra)* *ṭabīb (aṭíbba)*	دُكْتور (دكاتْرة) طبيب (أطِبّة)
I don't feel well. I think I need to go see a doctor.	*ána ta3bān. a3táqid lāzim arūḫ li-duktūr.*	أنا تعْبان .أعْتقِد لازِم أروح لِدُكْتور.
specialist	*axiṣṣāʔi*	أخِصّائي
cardiologist	*axiṣṣāʔi li-lʔálb* (lit. heart specialist)	أخِصّائي لِلقلْب
eye doctor, ophthalmologist	*duktūr 3iyūn*	دُكْتور عِيون
to make an appointment with	*ʔáxad* [i3] *mi3ād min*	أخد ميعاد مِن

hospital	*mustášfa (mustašfayāt)*	**مُسْتشْفى (مُسْتشْفَيات)**
doctor's office, clinic	*3iyāda*	**عِيادة**
nurse	*mumárriḍ*	**مُمرِّض**
patient	*marīḍ (márḍa)*	**مريض (مرْضى)**
to get a (medical) check-up	*3ámal* [1s2] *it*[check-up]	**عمل التّشيْك أپ**
to diagnose	*šáxxaṣ* [2s2]	**شخّص**
diagnosis	*tašxīṣ*	**تشْخيص**
to examine	*fáḫaṣ* [1s1] *kášaf* [1s2] *3ála*	**فحص** **كشف على**
examination	*faḫs (fuḫūṣ)*	**فحْص (فُحوص)**
The doctor examined him and diagnosed him with nasal congestion.	*idduktūr kášaf 3alē wi šáxxaṣu ʔínnu 3ándu zukām.*	الدُّكْتور كشف عليْه و شخّصُه إنُّه عنْدُه زُكام.

problem	*muškíla (mašākil, muškilāt)*	**مُشْكِلة (مشاكِل، مُشْكِلات)**
What's wrong?	*ʔē ilmuškíla?*	أيْه المُشْكِلة؟
I'm sick.	*ána 3ayyān.*	أنا عيّان.
pain	*wága3 (awgā3)*	**وَجع (أَوْجاع)**
My __ hurts.	*-i/-ya byiwgá3ni* [m.] *-i/-ya btiwgá3ni* [f.]	**ــي بيْوْجعْني.** **ــي بتْوْجعْني.**
My shoulder has been hurting for ages.	*kítfi byiwgá3ni min zamān.*	كِتْفي بيِوْجعْني مِن زمان.
It hurts here.	*ilḫítta di btiwgá3ni.*	الحِتّة دي بتِوْجعْني.

to have a backache	*3ándu wága3 fi ḍáhru*	عنْدُه وَجع في ضهْرُه
to have a headache	*3ándu şudā3*	عنْدُه صُداع
I have a really bad headache.	*3ándi şudā3 gāmid áwi.*	عنْدي صُداع جامِد أَوي.
migraine	*şudā3 níşfi*	صُداع نِصْفي
dizziness	*dōxa*	دوْخة
dizzy	*dāyix*	دايِخ
to faint	*ɣúmi 3alē*	غُمي عليْه

غُمي *ɣúmi* in the above expression is invariable.

to have a cold	*wāxid bard*	واخِد برْد
to be congested, have nasal congestion	*3ándu zukām*	عنْدُه زُكام
to have the flu	*3ándu infilwínza*	عنْدُه إنْفِلْونْزا
to have a fever	*3ándu ɧúmma*	عنْدُه حُمّى
to have a stomachache	*3ándu wága3 fi báţnu*	عنْدُه وَجع في بطْنُه
to have a sore throat	*zūru multáhib*	زورُه مُلْتهِب
to cough	*kaɧɧ* [1g2]	كحّ
to have a cough	*3ándu kúɧɧa*	عنْدُه كُحّة
to vomit, throw up	*rágga3* [2s2]	رجّع
to experience nausea, be nauseous	*3āyiz yirágga3* (lit. want to vomit)	عايِز يِرجّع
to have a rash	*3ándu ţafɧᵊ gíldi*	عنْدُه طفْح جِلْدي
to have diarrhea	*3ándu ishāl*	عنْدُه إسْهال
to be constipated	*3ándu imsāk*	عنْدُه إمْساك
to have indigestion	*3ándu 3usrᵊ haḍm*	عنْدُه عُسْر هضْم

diabetes	*issúkkar*	السُّكّر
to be diabetic	*3ándu -ssúkkar*	عنْدُه السُّكّر
to have asthma	*3ándu rabw*	عنْدُه ربْو
to have high blood pressure	*3ándu ḑayţ*	عنْدُه ضغْط
AIDS, HIV	[AIDS]	أيْدْز

Although medically there is a clear difference between HIV and AIDS, in everyday speech, this distinction is commonly ignored.

cancer	*saraţān*	سرطان

to get injured	*it3áwwar* [5s2]	اِتْعوّر
to have a bruise	*3ándu kádma*	عنْدُه كدْمة
wound, cut	*garɧ (gurūɧ)*	جرْح (جُروح)
to get stitches	*itxáyyaţ* [5s2]	اِتْخيّط
stitch	*ɣúrza (ɣúraz)*	غُرْزة (غُرز)
burn	*ɧarʔ (ɧurūʔ)*	حرْق (حُروق)
to get burned	*3ándu ɧarʔ*	عنْدُه حرْق
bandage, Band-Aid	*bilāstir*	بِلاسْتِر
to have a sprained ankle	*ríglu magzū3a*	رِجْلُه مجْزوعة
to break a bone	*kásar* [1s1] *3áḑma*	كسر عضْمة
a broken bone	*3áḑma maksūra*	عضْمة مكْسورة
cast; splint (UK: plaster)	*gabīra (gabāyir)*	جبيرة (جبايِر)

He broke his arm and has to wear a cast now.	*kásar dirā3u w lāzim yirákkib gabīra dilwáʔti.*	كسر دِراعُه و لازِم يِركِّب جبيرة دِلْوَقْتي.
x-ray	*ṣūra b-ʔaší33it iks*	صورة بِاشِعّةْ إكْس
to x-ray	*3ámal* [1s2] *aší33it iks*	عمل أشِعّةْ إكْس

medicine	*dáwa (adwíya)*	دَوا (أدْوِيَة)
prescription	*rušítta*	روشِتّة
to prescribe	*wáṣaf* [1s2]	وَصف
aspirin	*aspirīn*	أسْپيرين
pill	*ḫabbāya*	حبّايَة
antibiotics	*muḍādāt ḫayawíyya*	مُضادات حَيَوية
injection, shot	*ḫúʔna (ḫúʔan)*	حُقْنة (حُقن)
to get a shot	*ʔáxad* [i3] *ḫúʔna*	أخد حُقْنة
to draw blood	*sáḫab* [1s1] *3iyānit damm*	سحب عِيانِةْ دمّ
to run a blood test	*3ámal* [1s2] *faḫṣ^ə damm*	عمل فحْص دمّ
to cure, heal	*šáfa* [1d2]	شفى
recovery, healing	*šífa*	شِفا
to treat	*3ālig* [3s]	عالج
treatment	*3ilāg*	عِلاج
infection	*3ádwa*	عدْوى
contagious	*mú3di*	مُعْدي
Are you contagious?	*ínta máraḍak mú3di?*	إنْتَ مرضك مُعْدي؟

surgeon	*garrāɧ*	جرّاح
surgery	*girāɧa*	جِراحة
to perform surgery on, operate on	*3ámal* [1s2] *girāɧa li-* *3ámal* [1s2] *3amalíyya li-*	عمل جِراحة لِ عمل عملية لِ
to undergo surgery, have an operation	*3ámal* [1s2] *girāɧa* *3ámal* [1s2] *3amalíyya*	عمل جِراحة عمل عملية
to have an abortion	*3ámal* [1s2] *ighād*	عمل إجْهاض
plastic surgeon	*garrāɧ tagmīl*	جرّاح تجْميل
plastic surgery	*girāɧit tagmīl*	جِراحِةْ تجْميل

pregnancy	*ɧaml*	حمْل
to get pregnant by	*ɧámal* [1s2] *min*	حمل مِن
pregnant	*ɧāmil* [f.] *(ɧawāmil)*	حامِل (حَوامِل)
to give birth	*wílid* [1s5]	وِلِد
When are you due?	*hatiwlídi ʔímta?*	هتوْلِدي إمْتى؟
I'm due in early December.	*háwlid f- áwwil disímbir.*	هَوْلِد في أوِّل ديسِمْبِر.
How far along is she?	*híyya fi -ššahr ilkām?*	هِيَّ في الشّهْر الكام؟
She's six months pregnant.	*híyya fi -ššahr issādis.*	هُوَّ في الشّهْر السّادِس.
to use birth control	*istáxdim ɧubūb man3 ilɧáml*	اِسْتخْدِم حُبوب منْع الحمْل
condom	*kásbir* (lit. Casper) *wāʔi zákari* *kúndum*	كاسْبِر واقي ذكري كونْدوم

dentist	*duktūr sinān*	دُكْتور سِنان
to have a cavity	*3ándu tasáwwus*	عنْدُه تسَوُّس
to have a toothache	*sinānu btiwgá3u*	سِنانُه بْتِوْجعُه
to have a chipped tooth	*3ándu sínna maksūra*	عنْدُه سِنّة مكْسورة
to get a filling	*ḫáša* [1d2] *sínna*	حشى سِنّة
to get a tooth pulled	*xála3* [1s1] *sínna*	خلع سِنّة
to get a cleaning	*3ámal* [1s2] *tanḍīf*	عمل تنْضيف
I'm going to the dentist's to get a check-up and a cleaning.	*ána rāyiḫ li-duktūr issinān 3ašān á3mil kíšfa 3ála sināni wi ʔá3mal tanḍīf.*	أنا رايِح لِدُكْتور السِّنان عشان أعْمِل كِشْفة على سِناني و أعْمِل تنْضيف.
to get one's teeth whitened	*báyyaḍ* [2s2] *sinānu*	بيّض سِنانُه

12 Technology

technology	*tiknulúžya*	تِكْنولوچْيا
computer	[computer]	كُمْپْيوتر
to turn on the computer	*šáyɣal* [2s2] *il*[computer]	شغّل الكُمْپْيوتر
to turn off the computer	*ţáfa* [1d2] *-l*[computer]	طفى الكُمْپْيوتر
laptop	[lap top]	لاپ توْپ
monitor	[monitor]	موْنيتوْر
screen	*šāša*	شاشة
keyboard	[keyboard]	كيبوْرْد
mouse	[mouse]	ماوْس
to click on	*ḑáɣaţ* [1s1] *3ála*	ضغط على
file	*miláff* [file]	مِلفّ فايِل
folder	[folder]	فوْلْدر
I can't remember what folder the file is in.	*miš fākir ilmiláffᵊ f- ánhi* [folder].	مِش فاكِر المِلفّ في أنْهي فوْلْدر.
to open a file	*fátaɧ* [1s1] *miláff*	فتح مِلفّ
to save	*sáyyiv* [2s1] (from the English 'save') *ɧáfaẓ* [1s1]	سيِّڤ حفظ
computer program	*birnámig (barāmig)* [computer]	بِرْنامِج (برامِج) كُمْپْيوتر
to close	*ʔáfal* [1s2] *birnámig*	قفل بِرْنامِج
to delete	*másaɧ* [1s1]	مسح

Internet	[internet]	إنْترْنِت
on the Internet, online	*3ála -n*[net]	على النِّت
to get on the Internet, go online	*fátaɦ* [1s1] *in*[net]	فتح النِّت
wifi	[wireless] [wifi]	وايِرْلس وايْ فايْ
Is wifi available here?	*fī* [wireless] *hína?*	فيه وايِرْلس هِنا؟
web site	*máwqi3 (mawāqi3)* [web site]	مَوْقِع (مَواقِع) ويْبْسايْت
web page	*ṣáfɦit* [web]	صفْحِةْ ويْب
to download	*ɦámmil* [2s1]	حمِّل
to upload	*ráfa3* [1s1]	رفع
e-mail	[email]	إيميْل
to send an e-mail	*bá3at* [1s1] *risāla 3ála -lʔ*[email] *bá3at* [1s1] [email]	بعت رِسالة على الإيميْل بعت إيميْل
username	*ism* [user name]	إسْم يوزر نيْم
password	*kílmit sirr* [password]	كِلْمِةْ سِرّ پاسْوَرْد
Enter your username and password.	*íktib ísmak wi kílmit issírr.* *dáxxal il*[user name] *w il*[password].	اِكْتِب إسْمك و كِلْمِةْ السِّرّ. دخّل اليوزر نيْم و الپاسْوَرْد.

Facebook	[Facebook]	فيْسْبوك
to click "like"	*ḍáɣaṭ* [1s1] [like]	ضغط لايْك

The actual like button on Arabic Facebook says (in Modern Standard Arabic) أعْجبْني *ʔa3jabanī*.

Twitter	[Twitter]	تْويتّر

printer	*ţáb3it* [printer]	طابْعِةْ پْرِنْتر
to print	*ţába3* [1s1]	طبع
scanner	*(i)*[scanner]	سْكانِر
to scan	*másaħ* [1s1] *bi-lʔi*[scanner]	مسح بِالسْكانِر
fax, fax machine	*faks*	فاكْس
to fax	*bá3at* [1s1] *bi-lfáks*	بعت بِالفاكْس

cell phone	*mubáyl*	موبايْل
app	*taţbīq*	تطْبيق
to send a text message	*bá3at* [1s1] *risāla*	بعت رِسالة
ringtone	*ránna* *náɣama*	رنّة نغمة
vibration	*ihtizāz* [vibration]	اِهْتِزاز ڤايْبْرِيْشِن
silent mode	*şāmit* [silent]	صامِت سايْلِنْت

telephone, phone	*tilifōn*	تِليفوْن
phone number	*nímrit tilifōn*	نِمْرِةْ تِليفوْن
What's your number?	*nímrit tilifōnak kām?*	نِمْرِةْ تِليفوْنك كام ؟
to call, phone (someone)	*ittáşal* [8s1] *bi-* *ɖárab* [1s1] *tilifōn li-*	اِتّصل بِـ ضرب تِليفوْن لِـ
(phone) call	*mukálma (tilifuníyya)*	مُكالْمة (تِليفوْنية)
line	*síkka*	سِكّة
to ring	*rann* [1g3]	رنّ
The phone's ringing!	*ittilifōn biyrínn!*	التِّليفوْن بيِرِنّ!

to get a phone call	*gālu* [i1] *tilifōn*	جالُه تِليفوْن
to answer the phone	*raddᵊ* [1g2] *3ála -ttilifōn*	ردّ على التِّليفوْن
Hello?	*alō?*	آلوْ؟
on the phone	*fi -ttilifōn*	في التِّليفوْن
to talk on the phone	*itkállim* [5s1] *3ála -ttilifōn*	اِتْكلِّم على التِّليفوْن
to hang up (the phone)	*ʔáfal* [1s2] *issíkka*	قفل السِّكّة
to hang up on	*ʔáfal* [1s2] *issíkka f- wíššu*	قفل السِّكّة في وِشُّه
to call a wrong number	*ḍárab* [1s1] *nímra ɣálaṭ*	ضرب نِمْرة غلط
receiver	*sammā3it tilifōn*	سمّاعِةْ تِليفوْن

13 Getting Around

transportation	*muwáşla*	مُواصْلة
means of transportation	*wasāʔil ilmuwaşlāt* [pl.]	وَسائِل المُواصْلات
to take (a bus, taxi, etc.)	*ʔáxad* [i3]	أخد
to get on, get in, take (a bus, taxi, etc.)	*ríkib* [1s4]	رِكِب
to get off, get out of	*nízil* [1s5] *min*	نِزِل مِن

transportation, shipping	*naʔl*	نقْل
freight	*šaḫn*	شحْن
truck (UK: lorry)	*lōri*	لوْري
pick-up truck	*ʒarabíyya nuşşᵊ naʔl*	عربية نُصّ نقْل
ship	*safīna (súfun)*	سفينة (سُفُن)
boat	*márkib* [f.] *(marākib)*	مرْكِب (مراكِب)

bus	*utubīs*	أُتوبيس
I usually go to work by bus.	*ána ɣālíban barūḫ iššúɣlᵊ bi-lʔutubīs.*	أنا غالِباً بروح الشُّغْل بِالأُتوبيس.
to miss the bus	*fāt* [1h1] *ilʔutubīs*	فات الأُتوبيس
bus stop	*máwʔif (mawāʔif) utubīs*	مَوْقِف (مَواقِف) أُتوبيس
bus driver	*sawwāʔ utubīs*	سوّاق أُتوبيس

metro, subway (UK: underground)	*ilmítru*	**المِتْرو**
I take the metro every day.	*ána bárkab ilmítru kull[ə] yōm.*	أنا برْكب المِتْرو كُلّ يوْم.
metro station	*maħáttit mítru*	**محطّةْ مِتْرو**
women-only passenger car	*3arabíyyit sittāt*	**عربيةْ سِتّات**

taxi	*táksi*	**تاكْسي**
We took a taxi downtown.	*rikíbna táksi l-wist ilbálad.*	رِكِبْنا تاكْسي لِوِسْط البلد.
taxi driver	*sawwā? táksi*	**سوّاق تاكْسي**
to hail a taxi	*šāwir [3s] li-táksi*	**شاوِر لتّاكْسي**
taxi meter	*3addād táksi* *bundēra (banadīr)*	**عدّاد تاكْسي** **بُنْديْرة (بنادير)**
to negotiate the fare	*fāṣil [3s] fi -l?úgra*	**فاصِل في الأُجْرة**

left	*šimāl*	**شِمال**
Turn left!	*xušš[ə] šmāl!* *liff[ə] šmāl!*	**خُشّ شْمال.** **لِفّ شْمال.**
right	*yimīn*	**يمِين**
Turn right!	*xušš[ə] ymīn!* *liff[ə] ymīn!*	**خُشّ يمْين.** **لِفّ يمْين.**
straight	*ṭawwāli* *3ála ṭūl*	**طوّالي** **على طول**

Go straight!	*ímši ṭawwāli!*	اِمْشي طوّالي.

bicycle	*3ágala (3ágal)*	عجلة (عجل)
to ride a bicycle	*ríkib* [1s4] *3ágala*	رِكِب عجلة
cyclist	*rākib 3ágala*	راكِب عجلة
bicycle lane, bike path	*ṭarīʔ 3ágal*	طريق عجل
pedal	*baddāl*	بدّال
chain	*ganzīr (ganazīr)*	جنْزير (جنازير)
bike seat	*kúrsi 3ágala*	كُرْسي عجلة
motorcycle	*mutusíkl*	موتوسيكْل
helmet	*xōza (xíwaz)*	خوْذة (خِوَذ)

tuk-tuk, auto-rickshaw	*túktuk (takātik)*	توكْتوك (تكاتِك)

car	*3arabíyya*	عربية
to drive	*sāʔ* [1h1]	ساق
driver	*sawwāʔ*	سَوّاق
passenger	*rākib* *musāfir*	راكِب مُسافِر
driver's license	*rúxṣit (rúxaṣ) siwwāʔa*	رُخْصِة (رُخص) سِوّاقة
traffic	*murūr*	مُرور
traffic jam	*záħma*	زحْمة
to get stuck in traffic	*itzánaʔ* [7s1] *fi -zzáħma*	اِتْزنق في الزّحْمة

The traffic is horrible right now!	*iššawāri3 záɦma ʔáwi dilwáʔti!*	الشَّوارِع زحْمة أَوي دِلْوَقْتي!
rush hour	*sā3it izzúrwa*	ساعِةْ الذُّرْوَة
Forget going downtown right now. It's rush hour.	*balāš tínzal wisṭ ilbálad dilwáʔti. di sā3it izzúrwa.*	بلاش تِنْزِل وِسْط البلد دِلْوَقْتي .دي ساعِةْ الذُّرْوَة.
to pass, overtake	*3ádda* [2d] *min*	عدّى مِن
to stop	*wíʔif* [i5]	وِقِف
to yield to	*wássa3* [2s2] *li-*	وَسّع لِـ
to have the right of way	*lī -lʔawlawíyya*	ليه الأَوْلَوية
pedestrians	*mušāh* [pl.]	مُشاهْ
sidewalk (UK: pavement)	*raṣīf (arṣífa)*	رصيف (أَرْصِفة)
crosswalk, pedestrian crossing (UK: zebra crossing)	*xuṭūṭ mušāh* [pl.]	خُطوط مُشاهْ
to cross the street	*3ádda* [2d] *-ššāri3*	عدّى الشّارِع
traffic light	*išārit murūr*	إشارِةْ مُرور
green light	*išāra xáḍra*	إشارة خضْرا
red light	*išāra ɦámra*	إشارة حمْرا
yellow light	*išāra ṣáfra*	إشارة صفْرا
to run a red light	*kássar* [2s2] *ilʔišāra*	كسّر الإشارة
to park	*rákan* [1s2]	ركن
parking lot (UK: car park)	*máwʔaf (mawāʔif)*	مَوْقف (مَواقِف)
parking garage	*garāž*	جراچ

to park on the street	*rákan* [1s2] *fi -ššāri3*	ركن في الشّارِع
lane	*ħāra*	حارة
to change lanes	*ɣáyyar* [2s2] *ilħāra*	غيّر الحارة
a four-lane road	*šāri3 árba3 ħarāt*	شارِع أرْبع حارات
intersection	*taqātu3*	تقاطُع
round-about	*midān (mayadīn)*	ميدان (مَيادين)
highway, expressway (UK: motorway)	*ţarīʔ sarī3 (ţúruʔ sarī3a)*	طريق سريع (طُرُق سريعة)
bridge, overpass	*kúbri (kabāri)*	كُبْري (كباري)
speed limit	*ħudūd issúr3a* [pl.]	حُدود السُّرْعة
license plate (UK: number plate)	*lōħit arqām 3arabíyya*	لوْحِةْ أرْقام عربية
car insurance	*taʔmīn 3arabíyya*	تأْمين عربية
to pick up	*rákkib* [2s1]	ركّب
to drop off	*názzil* [2s1]	نزِّل
You can just drop me off on the corner.	*múmkin tinazzílni 3and innáşya di.*	مُمْكِن تِنزِّلْني عنْد النّاصْيَة دي.
to give a lift to, take	*wáşşal* [2s2]	وَصّل
Can you give me a ride home?	*múmkin tiwaşşálni l-ħadd ilbēt?*	مُمْكِن تِوَصّلْني لِحدّ البيْت؟
hood (UK: bonnet)	*kabbūt*	كبّوت
windshield (UK: windscreen)	*ʔizāz 3arabíyya*	قِزاز عربية

trunk (UK: boot)	*šánţit 3arabíyya*	شنْطِةْ عربية
the front seat	*ilkúrsi -lli ʔuddām*	الكُرْسي اللي قُدّام
the back seat	*ilkúrsi -lli wára*	الكُرْسي اللي وَرا
car door	*bāb 3arabíyya*	باب عربية
car door handle	*úkrit (úkar) bāb 3arabíyya*	أوكْرِةْ (أوكر) باب عربية
window	*šubbāk (šababīk)*	شُبّاك (شبابيك)
to roll the window up	*ʔáfal* [1s2] *iššubbāk*	قفل الشُّبّاك
to roll the window down	*fátaђ* [1s1] *iššubbāk*	فتح الشُّبّاك
The door is ajar.	*ilbāb miš maʔfūl kuwáyyis.*	الباب مِش مقْفول كُوَيِّس.
steering wheel	*diriksiyōn*	دِرِكْسِيوْن
to drive, steer	*sāʔ* [1h1]	ساق
turn signal	*išārit dawarān*	إشارِةْ دَوَران
He never uses his turn signal.	*húwwa miš biyistá3mil išártu.*	هُوَّ مِش بِيِسْتعْمِل إشارْتُه.
rearview mirror	*mirāya xalfíyya*	مِرايَة خلْفية
side view mirror	*mirāya ganibíyya*	مِرايَة جانِبية
glove compartment	*durgᵊ 3arabíyya*	دُرْج عربية
dashboard	*lōђit 3addadāt tablōh*	لوْحِةْ عدّادات تابْلوْه
emergency brake, hand brake	*farāmil īd* [pl.]	فرامِل إيد
tire (UK: tyre)	*3ágala (3ágal) kawítš*	عجلة (عجل) كاوِتْش

to check the tire pressure	*ʔās* [1h2] *ḍaɣṭ il3ágal*	قاس ضغْط العجل
to get a flat tire	*il3ágala fássit* [1g3]	العجلة فسِّت
spare tire	*3ágala -ḫtiyāṭi*	عجلة احْتِياطي
to change a flat tire	*ɣáyyar* [2s2] *3ágala*	غيرّ عجلة
automatic	[automatic]	أوْتوْماتيك
manual, stickshift	*manyúwal* *yádawi*	مانْيُوال يَدَوي
I can't drive a stick.	*ma-ba3ráfš asūʔ il3arabiyyāt ilmanyúwal.*	مبعْرفْش أسوق العربيات المانْيُوال.
pedal	*dawwāsa*	دوّاسة
clutch	*klitš*	كْلِتْش
brake	*farāmil* [pl.]	فرامِل
to brake	*fármil* [11s1]	فرْمِل
gas pedal (UK: accelerator)	*banzīn*	بنْزين
to accelerate, speed up	*sárra3* [2s2] *dās* [1h1] *banzīn*	سرّع داس بنْزين
to slow down	*báṭṭaʔ* [2s2]	بطّأ
stickshift	*fitīs*	فِتيس
gear	*tirs (tirūs)*	تِرْس (تِروس)
in gear	*mi3áššaʔ*	مِعشّق
1st gear	*issúr3a -lʔūla*	السُّرْعة الأولى
reverse (gear)	*maršidīr* *tirs irrugū3*	مارْشِدير تِرْس الرُّجوع

to back up	*rígi3* [1s4] *li-wára*	**رِجِع لِوَرا**
to change gears	*ɣáyyar* [2s2] *issúr3a*	**غيّر السُّرْعة**
I put the car in reverse and started backing up.	*ána gibtᵊ maršidīr wi rigí3tᵊ bi-l3arabíyya.*	أنا جِبْت مارْشِدير و رِجِعْت بِالعربية.
speedometer	*3addād issúr3a*	**عدّاد السُّرْعة**
to do the speed limit	*iltázam* [8s1] *bi-ssúr3a*	**اِلْتزم بِالسُّرْعة**
to speed, go over the speed limit	*itxáṭṭa* [5d] *-ssúr3a*	**اِتْخطّى السُّرْعة**
The police pulled me over for speeding.	*iššúrṭa waʔʔafítni 3ála gambᵊ bi-sábab issúr3a.*	الشُّرْطة وَقّفِتْني على جنْب بِسبب السُّرْعة.
gas (UK: petrol)	*banzīn*	**بنْزين**
We've run out of gas.	*ilbanzīn xíliṣ.*	البنْزين خِلِص.
The tank is full.	*ittánkᵊ malyān.*	التّنْكملْيان.
gas gauge	*3addād ilbanzīn*	**عدّاد البنْزين**
gas station (UK: petrol station)	*banzīna*	**بنْزينة**
gas pump	*miḍáxxit banzīn*	**مِضخّةْ بنْزين**
to get gas	*máwwin* [2s1] *il3arabíyya*	**موِّن العربية**
to change the oil	*ɣáyyar* [2s2] *izzēt*	**غيّر الزّيْت**
to put on one's seatbelt, wear one's seat belt	*rábaṭ* [1s3] *ḥizām ilʔamān*	**ربط حِزام الأمان**
to start a car	*dáwwar* [2s2] *il3arabíyya*	**دوّر العربية**
The car won't start.	*il3arabíyya miš bitdūr.*	العربية مِش بِتْدور.
to turn off the engine	*ṭáffa* [2d] *-lmuḥárrik*	**طفّى المُحرِّك**

bumper	*ikṣidām*	**إكْصِدام**
fender	*ráfraf (rafārif)*	**رفْرف (رفارِف)**
(car) roof	*saʔf (suʔūf)*	**سقْف (سُقوف)**
to get in a fender-bender	*3ámal* [1s2] *ḥádsa basīṭa*	**عمل حادْثة بسيطة**
dent	*xábṭa*	**خبْطة**
There's a dent in the side of the car!	*fī xábṭa fi -l3arabíyya min ilgámb.*	فيه خبْطة في العربية مِن الجنْب!
headlight	*miṣbāḥ amāmi (maṣabīḥ amamíyya)*	**مِصْباح أمامي (مصابيح أمامية)**
Turn on your headlights when it starts to get dark.	*náwwar ilmaṣabīḥ lámma -ddúnya tḍállim.*	نوّر المصابيح لمّا الدُّنْيا تْضلِّم.
to get in an accident, have an accident	*3ámal* [1s2] *ḥádsa*	**عمل حادْثة**
to crash	*xábaṭ* [1s1]	**خبط**
He crashed (his car) into a tree.	*xábaṭ 3arabītu fi šágara.*	خبط عربيتُه في شجرة.
to be totaled, destroyed	*itdášdiš* [11p1] *itdámmar* [5s2]	**اِتْدشْدِش** **اِتْدمّر**
The car was totaled in the accident.	*il3arabíyya -tdašdíšit fi -lḥádsa.*	العربية اتْدشْدِشت في الحادْثة.

14 Around Town

city	*madīna (múdun)*	مدينة (مُدُن)
town	*bálad* [f.] *(bilād)*	بلد (بِلاد)
village	*qárya (qúra)*	قرْيَة (قُرى)
downtown	*wisṭ ilbálad*	وِسْط البلد
square	*midān (mayadīn)*	ميدان (مَيادين)
park	*ginēna (ganāyin)*	جِنيْنة (جنايِن)
fountain	*nafūra*	نفورة
street	*šāri3 (šawāri3)*	شارِع (شَوارِع)
alley, narrow street	*ɦāra* *zuʔāʔ (azíʔʔa)*	حارة زُقاق (أزِقّة)
corner	*náṣya (nawāṣi)*	ناصْيَة (نَواسى)
bakery	*máxbaz (maxābiz)*	مخْبز (مخابِز)
bank	*bank (bunūk)*	بنْك (بُنوك)
butcher shop	*gazzār*	جزّار
city hall	*baladíyya*	بلدية
fire station	*núʔṭit maṭāfi (núʔaṭ maṭāfi)*	نُقْطِةْ مطافي (نُقط مطافي)
grocery store	*biʔāla*	بِقالة
museum	*mátɦaf (matāɦif)*	متْحف (متاحِف)

police station	*ʔismᵊ šúrṭa*	قِسْم شُرْطة
post office	*máktab (makātib) barīd*	مكْتب (مكاتِب) بريد
supermarket	[supermarket]	سوپرْ مارْكِت
restaurant	*máṭ3am (matā3im)*	مطْعم (مطاعِم)
café, coffee shop	*ʔáhwa* *kafēh*	قهْوَة كافيْه

قهْوَة *ʔáhwa* is a traditional coffee house, especially popular among the working class, while كافيْه *kafēh* is a Western-style café, such as Starbucks, Cilantro, and Costa Coffee, all popular chains among upper-class Egyptians.

to go to a café	*rāḥ* [1h1] *kafēh*	راح كافيْه

15 Buildings and Construction

to build	*bána* [1d2]	بنى
construction	*bināʔ* *tašyīd*	بِناء تشْييد
construction worker	*3āmil bināʔ* *fawá3li*	عامِل بِناء فَواعْلي
building, structure	*mábna*	مبْنى
skyscraper	*nāṭiḫit saḫāb*	ناطِحِةْ سحاب
apartment building (UK: block of flats)	*mábna sákani* *mábna šúʔaʔ*	مبْنى سكني مبْنى شُقق
office building	*mábna tugāri*	مبْنى تُجاري
high-rise building	*mábna šāhiq irtifā3* *mábna 3āli*	مبْنى شاهِق اِرْتِفاع مبْنى عالي
tower	*burg (abrāg)*	بُرْج (أبْراج)
to demolish	*hadd* [1g3]	هدّ
elevator (UK: lift)	*asansēr*	أسانْسيرْ
stairs, staircase	*salālim* [pl.]	سلالِم
escalator	*síllim kahrabāʔi*	سِلِّم كهْربائي
to go upstairs	*ṭíli3* [1s4] *issíllim*	طِلِع السِّلِّم
to go downstairs	*nízil* [1s5] *issíllim*	نِزِل السِّلِّم
basement	*badrōm*	بدْروْم
ground floor	*dōr árḍi*	دوْر أرْضي
top floor	*dōr axīr*	دوْر أخير

story, floor	*dōr (adwār)* *ţābiʔ (ţawābiʔ)*	دوْر (أدْوار) طابِق (طَوابِق)

concrete	*asmánt*	أسْمنْت
brick	*ţūb* [coll.]	طوب
wood	*xášab (axšāb)*	خشب (أخْشاب)
glass	*ʔizāz* [coll.]	قِزاز
metal	*má3dan*	معْدن
steel	*şulb*	صُلْب
iron	*ɧadīd*	حديد

16 Bank

bank	*bank (bunūk)*	بنْك (بُنوك)
The Central Bank of Egypt (CBE)	*ilbánk ilmarkázi ilmáṣri*	البنْك المرْكزي المصْري
to borrow money from the bank	*istálaf* [8s1] *filūs min ilbánk*	اِسْتلف فِلوس مِن البنْك
to lend money to __	*sállif* [2s1] *__ filūs*	سلِّف __ فِلوس
loan	*qarḍ (qurūḍ)*	قرْض (قُروض)
to finance	*máwwil* [2s1]	موِّل
mortgage, home loan	*rahn (ruhūn)* *tamwīl 3iqāri*	رهْن (رُهون) تمْويل عِقاري
payment, installment	*ʔisṭ (aʔsāṭ)*	قِسْط (أقْساط)
to make a payment on a loan	*dáfa3* [1s1] *ʔisṭ ilʔárḍ*	دفع قِسْط القرْض
to pay in installments	*dáfa3* [1s1] *3ála ʔaʔsāṭ*	دفع على أقْساط
to settle, pay off (a debt)	*sáddid* [2s1]	سدِّد
debt	*dēn (diyūn)*	ديْن (دِيون)
interest	*fáyda (fawāyid)*	فايْدة (فَوايِد)
This account pays 5% interest.	*ilḫisāb da biygīb fáyda xámsa fi- lmíyya.*	الحِساب ده بيِجيب فايْدة خمْسة في المية.
to earn interest	*ʔáxad* [i3] *fawāyid*	أخد فَوايِد
account	*ḫisāb*	حِساب
savings account	*ḫisāb tawfīr*	حِساب توْفير

savings	*muddaxarāt* [pl.]	مُدّخرات
to save, put aside	*ḫáwwiš* [2s1]	حوِّش
He has over 100,000 pounds in savings.	*húwwa miḫáwwiš áktar min mīt alfᵊ ginēh.*	هُوَّ مِحوِّش أكْتر مِن ميةْ ألْف جنِيْه.
I try to save a little money every month.	*baḫāwil aḫáwwiš šuwáyyit filūs kullᵊ šahr.*	بحاوِل أحوِّش شُوَيّةْ فِلوس كُلّ شهْر.
to deposit	*wáda3* [1s1]	وَدع
to withdraw	*sáḫab* [1s1]	سحب
ATM	[ATM] *mákanit iṣṣárrāf ilʔāli*	ATM مكنِةْ الصّراف الآلي
to write a check	*kátab* [1s2] *šīk*	كتب شيك
to sign	*máḍa* [1d2] *wáqqa3* [2s2]	مضى وَقّع
signature	*ímḍa* *tawqī3*	إمْضا تَوْقيع

17 Post Office

post office	*máktab (makātib) barīd*	مكْتب (مكاتِب) بريد
mail (UK: post)	*barīd*	بريد
airmail	*barīd gáwwi*	بريد جوّي
letter	*gawāb (agwíba)*	جواب (أجْوِبة)
envelope	*ẓarf (áẓruf)*	ظرْف (أظْرف)
postcard	*kart^{ə} (kurūt) pustāl*	كرْت (كُروت) پوسْتال
address	*3inwān (3anawīn)*	عِنْوان (عناوين)
stamp	*ṭābi3 (ṭawābi3)*	طابِع (طَوابِع)
to affix a stamp	*láṣaʔ* [1s1] *ṭābi3*	لصق طابِع
to stamp (with a postmark)	*xátam* [1s2]	ختم
to send, mail	*bá3at* [1s1]	بعت
package, parcel	*ṭard (ṭurūd)*	طرْد (طُرود)
mailbox (UK: letterbox)	*ṣandūʔ barīd*	صنْدوق بريد
counter, window	*šubbāk (šababīk)* *káwntar* *kašīr*	شُبّاك (شبابيك) كاوْنْتر كاشير
mail carrier (UK: postman)	*busṭági*	بوسْطجي
to deliver the mail	*wáṣṣal* [2s2] *ilbarīd*	وَصّل البريد

18 Books and Stationery

library, bookstore, stationery shop	*maktába (makātib)*	مكْتبة (مكاتِب)
book	*kitāb (kútub)*	كِتاب (كُتُب)
page	*ṣáfḥa*	صفْحة
page number	*ráqam ṣáfḥa*	رقم صفْحة
bookmark	*muʔáššir ṣafaḥāt*	مُؤشِّر صفحات
reference book	*márgi3 (marāgi3)*	مرْجِع (مراجِع)
novel	*riwāya*	رِوايَة
story	*qíṣṣa (qíṣaṣ)*	قِصّة (قِصص)
fairy tale	*qíṣṣa xayalíyya*	قِصّة خَيالية
prose	*nasr*	نثْر
writer, author	*kātib (kuttāb)* *muʔállif*	كاتِب (كُتّاب) مُؤلِّف
poetry	*ši3r*	شِعْر
poem	*qaṣīda (qaṣāyid)*	قصيدة (قصايِد)
poet	*šā3ir (šú3ara)*	شاعِر (شُعْرا)

newspaper	*gurnān (garanīn)*	جُرْنان (جرانين)
headline	*3inwān (3anawīn)*	عِنْوان (عناوين)
article	*maqāl*	مقال
column	*3amūd ṣáḥafi (3awamīd ṣaḥafíyya)*	عمود صحفي (عَواميد صحفية)

to publish	*nášar* [1s3]	نشر
to print	*ţába3* [1s1]	طبع

stationery	*adawāt maktabíyya* [pl.]	أدَوات مكْتبية
stationery store	*maђáll adawāt maktabíyya*	محلّ أدَوات مكْتبية
pen	*ʔálam (iʔlām)*	قلم (إقْلام)
ballpoint pen	*ʔálam gaff*	قلم جافّ
pencil	*ʔálam ruşāş*	قلم رُصاص
eraser (UK: rubber)	*astīka (asatīk)*	أسْتيكة (أساتيك)
to erase	*másaђ* [1s1]	مسح
(pair of) scissors	*maʔáşş*	مقصّ
ink	*ђibr (aђbār)*	حِبْر (أحْبار)

typewriter	*āla kátba*	آلة كاتْبة
paper	*wáraʔ* [coll.] *(awrāʔ)*	وَرق (أَوْراق)
a sheet of paper	*wáraʔa*	وَرقة
ruler	*masţára (masāţir)*	مسْطرة (مساطِر)
(adhesive) tape	*lázʔa*	لزْقة
pin, pushpin; paperclip; staple	*dabbūs (dababīs)*	دبّوس (دبابيس)
stapler	*dabbāsa*	دبّاسة
to staple	*dábbis* [2s1]	دبِّس
to sharpen a pencil	*bára* [1d2] *ʔálam*	برى قلم

to photocopy	*şáwwar* [2s2]	صوّر
a photocopy	*núsxa (núsax)*	نُسْخة (نُسخ)
photocopy machine	*mákanit taşwīr*	مكنِةْ تصْوير

19 Shopping

shopping	*tasáwwuq*	تسوُّق
to go shopping	*rāɧ* [1h1] *yištíri ɧagāt*	راح يِشْترِي حاجات
We went shopping downtown yesterday.	*nizílna ništíri ɧagāt min wisṭ ilbálad imbāriɧ.*	نِزِلْنا نِشْترِي حاجات مِن وِسْط البلد إمْبارِح.
to buy	*ištára* [8d]	اِشْترى
to sell	*bā3* [1h2]	باع
to pay for __	*dáfa3* [1s1] *táman __*	دفع تمن__
I've already paid for the vegetables.	*ána dafá3tᵊ táman ilxuḍār xalāṣ.*	أنا دفعْت تمن الخُضار خلاص.
How much did you pay for that?	*dafá3tᵊ kām fi da?*	دفعْت كام في ده؟
to pay in cash	*dáfa3* [1s1] *kāš*	دفع كاش
to pay by credit card	*dáfa3* [1s1] *bi-l*[credit card]	دفع بِالكْريْدِت كارْد
change (money back)	*ilbāʔi*	الباقي
You gave me too much change.	*ínta iddítni -lbāʔi zāyid.*	إنْتَ إدّيتْني الباقي زايِد.
receipt	*fatūra (fawatīr)*	فاتورة (فَواتير)

price	*si3r (as3ār)* *táman (atmān)*	سِعْر (أسْعار) تمن (أتْمان)
to cost	*itkállif* [5s1]	اِتْكلِّف
cheap	*rixīṣ (ruxāṣ)*	رِخيص (رُخاص)

expensive	*ɣāli*	**غالي**
free	*maggāni* *balāš* [invar.]	**مجّاني** **بلاش**
for free	*bi-balāš*	**بِبلاش**
fee	*rusūm* [pl.]	**رُسوم**
bill	*fatūra (fawatīr)* *ɧisāb*	**فاتورة (فَواتير)** **حِساب**
How much do I owe?	*ilɧisāb kām? (lit. How much is the bill?)*	الحِساب كام ؟

advertisement, ad	*i3lān*	**إعْلان**
discount, sale	*xaşm (xuşumāt)*	**خصْم (خُصُمات)**
40% off	*xaşm arbi3īn fi -lmíyya*	**خصْم أرْبِعين في المية**
coupon	*kubōn*	**كوبْون**
bargain	*şáfqa* *fúrşa (fúraş)*	**صفْقة** **فُرْصة (فُرص)**
Wow! That's a real bargain!	*wāw! di fúrşa háyla!* *wāw! di şáfqa gámda!*	واوْ !دي فُرْصة هايْلة! واوْ !دي صفْقة جامْدة!
to haggle over, bargain	*fāşil fi* *sāwim*	**فاصِل في** **ساوِم**
I'm not very good at haggling.	*ána miš šāţir fi -lfişāl.*	أنا مِش شاطِر في الفِصال.
fixed price	*si3r^{ə} sābit*	**سِعْر ثابِت**

shopping center	*márkaz (marākiz) ittasáwwuq*	**مرْكز (مراكِز) التّسوُّق**
(shopping) mall	*mōl*	**موْل**
market, shopping area	*sū? (aswā?)*	**سوق (أسْواق)**
Shall we go shopping this weekend?	*yálla nrūɧ issú? āxir il?isbū3?*	يَلّا نِروح السّوق آخِر الإسْبوع؟
store, shop	*maɧáll*	**محلّ**
There are a lot of nice shops on this street.	*fī maɧallāt kitīr ɧílwa fi -ššāri3 da.*	فيه محلّات كِتير حِلْوَة في الشّارِع ده.
supermarket	[supermarket]	**سوپرْ مارْكِت**
cashier	*kašīr*	**كاشير**
shop keeper	*ṣāɧib maɧáll*	**صاحِب محلّ**
shop assistant	*muwáẓẓaf fi maɧáll*	**مُوَظّف في محلّ**
customer	*zubūn (zabāyin)*	**زُبون (زبايِن)**
to serve a customer	*sā3id* [6s] *zubūn*	**ساعِد زُبون**
shopping bag	*šánṭit (šúnaṭ) tasáwwuq*	**شنْطِةْ (شُنط) تسوُّق**
plastic bag	*kīs (akyās) bilastīk*	**كيس (أكْياس) بِلاسْتيك**
Would you like a bag for that? Would you like that in a bag?	*3āyiz kīs?* *3āyiz aɧuṭṭílak da fi kīs?*	عايِز كيس؟ عايِز أحُطِّلك ده في كيس؟
to wrap	*ɣállif* [2s1]	**غلِّف**
to return (a purchased item)	*rágga3* [2s2]	**رجّع**

to exchange	*ɣáyyar* [2s2] *báddil* [2s1]	**غيّر** **بدِّل**
Can I exchange this for another color?	*múmkin aɣayyáru b-lōn tāni?*	مُمْكِن أغيرّه بِلوْن تاني؟
to get a refund	*istarádd*ᵊ [10g1] *flūsu*	**اِسْترد ّ فْلوسُه**

20 Restaurant

restaurant	*máţ3am (maţā3im)*	مطْعم (مطاعِم)
fast food restaurant	*máţ3am wagabāt sarī3a*	مطْعم وَجبات سريعة
waiter	*garsōn (garsunāt)*	جرْسوْن (جرْسوْنات)
waitress	*garsōna*	جرْسوْنة
bill	*fatūra (fawatīr)* *ɦisāb*	فاتورة (فَواتير) حِساب
to pay the bill	*dáfa3* [1s1] *ilfatūra*	دفع الفاتورة
Waiter! Can I have the bill, please?	*garsōn! múmkin ilfatūra law samáɦt?*	جرْسوْن !مُمْكِن الفاتورة لَوْ سمحْت؟
cook, chef	*ţabbāx* [chef]	طبّاخ شيْف
tip	*ba?šīš* [tips]	بقْشيش تِپْس
I never know how much to leave for a tip.	*3úmri ma-3iríft asīb* [tips] *?add^{ə} ?ē.*	عُمْري معْرِفْت أسيب تِپْس أدّ أيْه.
service	*xídma (xadamāt)*	خِدْمة (خدمات)
a table for two	*ţarabēza li-tnēn*	طرابيْزة لِاتْنيْن

21 Recreation and Relaxation

to relax	*istárxa* [10d2]	**اِسْترْخى**
relaxation	*istirxāʔ*	**اِسْترِْخاء**
to go for a walk	*itmášša* [5d]	**اِتْمشّى**
Let's go for a walk in the park.	*yálla nrūḫ nitmášša fi -lginēna.*	يَلّا نْروح نِتْمشّى في الجِنيْنة.
to fly a kite	*ţáyyar* [2s2] *ţayyāra wáraʔ*	**طيّر طيّارة وَرق**
felucca (river sailboat)	*falūka (falāyik)*	**فلوكة (فلايِك)**
day off	*yōm agāza*	**يوْم أجازة**
Today's my day off.	*innahárda yōm agázti.*	النّهارْده يوْم أجازْتي.
to rest, relax	*ráyyaḫ* [2s2]	**ريّح**
fun, enjoyable	*múmti3*	**مُمْتع**
friend	*şāḫib (aşḫāb, şuḫāb)*	**صاحِب (أصْحاب، صُحاب)**
to meet up with friends	*ʔābil* [3s] *aşḫābu*	**قابِل أصْحابُه**
to hang out (with friends)	*itfássaḫ* [5s2] *má3a şḫābu* *xárag* [1s3] *má3a şḫābu*	**اِتْفسّح معَ صُحابُه** **خرج معَ صْحابُه**
We hung out at the shopping mall yesterday evening.	*itfassáḫna fi -lmōl imbāriḫ bi-llēl.*	اِتْفسّحْنا في الموْل إمْبارِح بِاللّيْل.
to read	*ʔára* [1d1]	**قرا**
newspaper	*gurnān (garanīn)*	**جُرْنان (جرانين)**

I like to sit in a coffee shop and read the newspaper before I go to work.	*baɦíbb áʔ3ud fi -lʔáhwa wi ʔáʔra -lgurnān ʔabl^{ə} ma -rūɦ iššúɣl.*	بحِبّ أقْعُد في القهْوَة و أقْرا الجُرْنان قبْل ما أروح الشُّغْل.
magazine	*magálla*	مجلّة
book	*kitāb (kútub)*	كِتاب (كُتُب)
novel	*riwāya*	رِوايَة
comic book, graphic novel	*qíşaş mişawwára* [pl.]	قِصص مِصوّرة

television	*tilivizyōn*	تِليفِزْيوْن
Have you ever been on TV?	*ţilí3t^{ə} fi -ttilivizyōn ʔabl^{ə} kída?*	طِلِعْت في التِّليفِزْيوْن قبْل كِده؟
to watch TV	*itfárrag* [5s2] *3ála -ttilivizyōn*	اِتْفرّج على التِّليفِزْيوْن
TV show, TV program	*birnāmig (barāmig)*	بِرْنامِج (برامِج)
What's your favorite TV program?	*ʔē áktar birnāmig bitɦíbbu fi -ttilivizyōn?*	أيْه أكْتر بِرْنامِج بِتْحِبُّه في التِّليفِزْيوْن؟
What do you like to watch on TV?	*bitɦíbb^{ə} titfárrag 3ála ʔē fi -ttilivizyōn?*	بِتْحِبّ تِتْفرّج على أيْه في التِّليفِزْيوْن؟
I like watching Egyptian dramas.	*baɦíbb atfárrag 3ála -ddirāma -lmaşríy ya.*	بحِبّ أتْفرّج على الدِّراما المصْرية.
drama	*dirāma* [f.]	دِراما
comedy program	*birnāmig kōmidi*	بِرْنامِج كوْميدي
sports program	*birnāmig riyāḑi*	بِرْنامِج رِياضي
sporting event	*ɦádas riyāḑi (aɦdās riyaḑíyya)*	حدث رِياضي (أحْداث رِياضية)
soccer match	*matš^{ə} kōra*	ماتْش كوْرة
movie, film	*film (aflām)*	فيلْم (أفْلام)

documentary	*film wasāyiqi*	فيلْم وَثايِقي
children's program	*birnāmig aṭfāl*	بِرْنامِج أطْفال
cartoon	*kartūn*	كرْتون
game show	*birnāmig musabʔāt*	بِرْنامِج مُسابْقات
reality TV show	*birnāmig tilivizyōn ilwāqi3*	بِرْنامِج تِليفِزْيوْن الواقع
series	*musálsal*	مُسلْسل
sitcom	*musálsal kōmidi*	مُسلْسل كوْميدي
episode	*ḥálaʔa*	حلقة
season	*mūsim (mawāsim)* *sīzun*	موسم (مَواسِم) سيزون
I haven't seen the second season of this show yet.	*ána líssa ma-šúftiš ilmūsim ittāni min ilmusálsal da.*	أنا لِسّه مشُفْتِش الموسِم التّاني مِن المسلْسل ده.
the news	*ilʔaxbār* [pl.]	الأخْبار
weather report	*taʔrīr ṭaʔs*	تقْرير طقْس
talk show	*tōk šō* *birnāmig ḥiwāri*	توْك شوْ بِرْنامِج حِواري
channel	*qanāh (qanawāt)*	قناهْ (قنَوات)
What's on TV (now)?	*ʔē ílli šaɣɣāl 3ála -ttilivizyōn (dilwáʔti)?*	أيْه اللي شغّال على التِّليفِزْيوْن (دِلْوقْتى)؟
There's an interesting program on channel 3.	*fī birnāmig ḥilwᵊ 3ála -lqanāh ittálta.*	فيه بِرْنامِج حِلْو على القناهْ التّالْتة.
to turn the TV on	*šáɣɣal* [2s2] *ittilivizyōn*	شغّل التِّليفِزْيوْن
to turn the TV off	*ṭáfa* [1d2] *-ttilivizyōn*	طفى التِّليفِزْيوْن
volume	*ṣōt*	صوْت
to turn the volume up	*3álla* [2d] *-ṣṣōt*	علّى الصّوْت

to turn the volume down	*wáṭṭa* [2d] *-ṣṣōt*	وَطّى الصّوْت
I can't hear what they're saying. Could you turn the TV up a bit?	*ána miš sāmi3 biyʔūlu ʔē. múmkin ti3álli -ttilivizyōn šuwáyya?*	أنا مِش سامِع بيْقولوا أيْه .مُمْكِن تِعلّي التِّليفِزْيوْن شُوَيَّة؟
I'm trying to study. Could you turn the TV down a bit?	*baḫāwil azākir. múmkin tiwáṭṭi -ttilivizyōn šuwáyya?*	بحاوِل أذاكِر .مُمْكِن تِوَطّي التِّليفِزْيوْن شُوَيَّة؟
antenna	*íryal*	إرْيَل
satellite dish	*ṭábaʔ (aṭbāʔ)*	طبق (أطْباق)

radio	*rádyu*	راديْو
to listen to the radio	*sími3* [1s4] *irrádyu*	سِمِع الرّاديْو
radio station	*maḫáṭṭit rádyu*	محطّةْ راديْو

stereo (home music system)	*stéryu*	سْتيرْيو
speakers	*samma3āt*	سمّاعات
CD	[CD]	سي دى
CD player	*mišáɣɣal áqrāṣ* [CD] [CD player]	مِشغّل أقْراص سي دي سي دي پْلايِر
cassette (tape)	*kasétt*	كاسيْتّ
(vinyl) record	*isṭuwāna*	إسْطُوانة
song, track	*uɣníyya (aɣāni)*	أُغْنية (أغانى)
to play (a CD, song, etc.)	*šáɣɣal* [2s2]	شغّل
to forward, skip to the next track	*ʔáddim* [2s1]	قدِّم
to rewind, go back to (the previous track)	*rígi3 li-* [1s4]	رِجِع لِـ

to pause	*wáʔʔaf* [2s2] *3ámal* [1s2] *pōz*	وَقَّف عمل پوْز
to stop, press 'stop'	*wáʔʔaf* [2s2] *3ámal* [1s2] *(i)stōp*	وَقَّف عمل سْتوْپ
MP3	[MP3]	MP3
to download an MP3	*ɧámmil* [2s1] *miláff* [MP3]	حمِّل مِلفّMP3
MP3 player	*mišáɣɣil* [MP3] [MP3 player]	مِشغِّلMP3 MP3پْلايِر
earphones, headphones	*samma3āt*	سمّاعات

to visit	*zār* [1h1]	زار
a visit	*ziyāra*	زِيارة
to go on a visit	*rāɧ* [1h1] *fi ziyāra*	راح في زِيارة
to have guests over	*3ándu ɖuyūf*	عنْدُه ضُيوف
to entertain guests	*sálla* [2d] *ɖuyūf*	سلّى ضُيوف

to sew	*xáyyaʈ* [2s2]	خيّط
sewing machine	*mákanit xiyāʈa*	مكنِةْ خِياطة
sewing needle	*íbrit (íbar) ilxiyāʈa*	إبْرِةْ (إبر) الخِياطة
thread	*xēʈ (xuyūʈ)*	خيط (خُيوط)
a ball of wool	*kōra ʂūf*	كوْرة صوف
thimble	*kastibān*	كسْتِبان
to knit	*3ámal* [1s2] *trikō*	عمل تْريكوْ
knitting needle	*íbrit ittirikō*	إبْرِةْ التِّريكوْ
to crochet	*3ámal* [1s2] *krušēh*	عمل كْروشيْه
to embroider	*ʈárraz* [2s2]	طرّز
to patch, darn	*ráʔʔa3* [2s2]	رقّع

art	*fann (funūn)*	فنّ (فُنون)
artist	*fannān*	فنّان
to draw, sketch, paint	*rásam* [1s2]	رسم
a painting	*lōḫa*	لوْحة
a drawing	*rásma*	رسْمة

photography	*taṣwīr*	تصْوير
photo(graph)	*ṣūra (ṣúwar)*	صورة (صُوَر)
to take a photo of	*ṣáwwar* [2s2]	صوّر
Excuse me. Would you take a photo of us?	*law samáḫt, múmkin tiṣawwárna?*	لَوْ سمحْت، مُمْكِن تِصوّرْنا؟
to take a selfie	*ʔáxad* [i3] [selfie]	أخد سِلْفي
photographer	*muṣáwwir*	مُصوِّر
camera	*kámira*	كاميرا

to hunt	*iṣṭād* [8h]	اِصْطاد
hunting	*ṣēd*	صيْد
hunter	*ṣayyād*	صيّاد
hunting dog	*kalb*^{ə} *ṣēd*	كلْب صيْد
hunting rifle	*bunduʔíyyit ṣēd*	بُنْدُقيةْ صيْد
to go fishing	*iṣṭād* [8h] *sámak*	اِصْطاد سمك
fishing	*ṣēd sámak*	صيْد سمك
fishing pole	*ʔáṣabit ṣēd*	قصبِةْ صيْد
fishing tackle	*adawāt ṣēd sámak* [pl.]	أدَوات صيْد سمك
hook	*xuṭṭāf (xaṭaṭīf)*	خُطّاف (خطاطيف)
bait	*ṭu3m* [coll.]	طُعْم

cinema	*sínima* *sīma*	**سينِما** **سيما**
Let's go to the cinema this weekend.	*yálla nrūḫ issínima ʔāxir ilʔisbū3.*	يَلّا نِروح السّينِما آخِر الإسْبوع.
movie ticket	*tazkárit (tazākir) sínima*	**تذْكرِة (تذاكِر) سينِما**
How much is a (movie) ticket?	*bi-kām ittazkára?*	بِكام التّذْكرة؟
movie, film	*film (aflām)*	**فيلْم (أفْلام)**
auditorium, movie theater, screening room	*másraḫ (masāriḫ) sínima*	**مسْرح (مسارِح) سينِما**
to play, show (a movie)	*šáɣɣal* [2s2] *3áraḍ* [1s2]	**شغّل** **عرض**
What's playing?	*ʔē ílli šaɣɣāl?*	أيْه اللي شغّال؟
A new movie is coming out on Friday. Want to go?	*fī filmᵊ gdīd ha-yínzil yōm ilgúm3a. tiḫíbbᵊ nrūḫ?*	فيه فيلْم جِديد هَينْزِل يوْم الجُمْعة .تِحِبّ نِروح؟
They're showing a classic movie this evening.	*fī filmᵊ klasīki -nnahárda bi-llēl.*	فيه فيلْم كْلاسيكي النّهارْده بِاللّيْل.
seat	*kúrsi (karāsi)*	**كُرْسي (كراسى)**
What are our seat numbers?	*ilkarāsi bta3ítna raqámha kām?*	الكراسي بْتعتِنْا رقمْها كام؟
screen	*šāša*	**شاشة**
to sit close to the screen	*ʔá3ad* [1s3] *ʔuráyyib min iššāša*	**قعد قُريِّب مِن الشّاشة**
I don't like to sit too close to the screen.	*ma-baḫíbbiš áʔ3ud ʔuráyyib áwi min iššāša.*	مبحِبِّش أقْعُد قُريِّب أَوي مِن الشّاشة.
to sit in the middle	*ʔá3ad* [1s3] *fi -nnuṣṣ*	**قعد في النُّصّ**

popcorn	*fišār*	فِشار
action movie	*film* [action]	فيلْم أكْشِن
romantic comedy	*film^ə rumánsi kōmidi*	فيلْم رومانْسي كوْميدي
drama	*film^ə dirāma*	فيلْم دِراما
horror movie	*film^ə ru3b*	فيلْم رُعْب
thriller	*film isāra*	فيلْم إثارة
period piece	*film^ə tarīxi*	فيلْم تاريخي
science fiction (sci-fi)	*film^ə xayāl 3ílmi*	فيلْم خَيال عِلْمي
fantasy	*film^ə fantázya*	فيلْم فنْتازْيا
What kind of movies do you like?	*ʔē nō3 ilʔaflām ílli bitḫibbáha?*	أيْه نوْع الأفْلام اللي بِتْحِبّها؟
I love action movies, but I can't stand romantic movies.	*ána baḫíbb aflām ilʔ*[action]*, bass^ə miš baṭīʔ ilʔaflām irrumansíyya.*	أنا بحِبّ أفْلام الأكْشِن، بسّ مِش بطيق الأفْلام الرّومانْسية.
(movie) star	*nigm (nugūm)*	نِجْم (نُجوم)

theater	*másraḫ (masāriḫ)*	مسْرح (مسارِح)
on stage	*3ála -lmásraḫ*	على المسْرح
aisle	*mamárr*	ممرّ
actor	*mumássil*	مُمثِّل
to act	*mássil* [2s1]	مثِّل
to play the role of __	*lí3ib* [1s4] *dōr __* *mássil* [2s1] *dōr __*	لِعِب دوْر __ مثِّل دوْر__
intermission	*istirāḫa*	اِسْتِراحة
spectator	*mutafárrig* *mušāhid*	مُتفرِّج مُشاهِد
audience, crowd	*gumhūr (gamahīr)*	جُمْهور (جماهير)

to applaud	*sá??af* [2s2]	سقّف
applause	*tas?īf*	تسْقيف
circus	*sirk*	سيرْك
acrobat	*akrubāt*	أكْروبات
clown	*bilyátšu (bilyatšuhāt)*	بِلْياتْشو (بِلْياتْشوهات)

cigarette	*sigāra (sagāyir)*	سِجارة (سجايِر)
to smoke	*dáxxan* [2s2] *sigāra* *šírib* [1s4] *sigāra*	دخّن سِجارة شِرِب سِجارة
smoking	*tadxīn*	تدْخين
No smoking	*mamnū3 ittadxīn*	ممْنوع التّدْخين
smoker	*mudáxxin*	مُدخِّن
non-smoker	*miš mudáxxin*	مِش مُدخِّن
Do you smoke?	*ínta btíšrab sagāyir?*	إنْتَ بْتِشْرب سجايِر؟
Would you like a cigarette?	*tāxud sigāra?* *tiḫíbbᵊ tíšrab sigāra?*	تاخُد سِجارة؟ تِحِبّ تِشْرب سِجارة؟
No, thank you. I don't smoke.	*lā šúkran. ána ma-badaxxánš.*	لا شُكْراً .أنا مبدخّنْش.
to quit smoking	*báṭṭal* [2s2] *tadxīn* *báṭṭal* [2s2] *sagāyir*	بطّل تدْخين بطّل سجايِر
cigar	*sigār*	سيجار
pipe	*ɣalyūn* *bāyb*	غلْيون بايْب
tobacco	*tibɣ*	تِبْغ
matches	*kabrīt* [coll.]	كبْريت
lighter	*wallā3a*	وَلّاعة
to light a cigarette	*wálla3* [2s2] *sigāra*	وَلّع سِجارة

ashtray	*ṭaffāyit sagāyir*	طفّايةْ سجايِر
cigarette butt	*3uʔbᵊ sgāra (a3ʔāb sagāyir)*	عُقْب سِجارة (أعْقاب سجايِر)
a pack of cigarettes	*3ílbit (3ílab) sagāyir*	عِلْبةْ (عِلب) سجايِر
shisha, hookah, water-pipe	*šīša*	شيشة
to smoke a shisha	*dáxxan* [2s2] *šīša*	دخّن شيشة
mouth-piece (of shisha)	*mábsam (mabāsim)*	مبْسم (مباسِم)
glass container (of shisha)	*bannūra*	بنّورة
hose (of shisha)	*layyᵊ šīša*	ليّ شيشة
coal	*faḫm* [coll.]	فحْم

22 Music

music	*musīqa* [f.] *mazzīka* [f.]	**موسيقى** **مزّيكا**
to listen to music	*sími3* [1s4] *musīqa*	**سِمِع موسيقى**
song	*uɣníyya (aɣāni)*	**أُغْنية (أغانى)**
singer	*muɣánni*	**مُغنّي**
to sing	*ɣánna* [2d]	**غنّى**
singing	*ɣúna*	**غُنا**
I love singing, but I'm not very good at it.	*baḫíbb ilɣúna bassᵊ ṣōti miš ḫilwᵊ áwi.*	بحِبّ الغُنا بسّ صوْتي مِش حِلْو أَوي.
Who's your favorite singer?	*mīn áktar miɣánni bitḫíbbu?*	مين أكْتر مِغنّي بِتْحِبُّه؟
band, group	*fírʔa (fíraʔ)*	**فِرْقة (فِرق)**
What kind of music do you like?	*ʔē nō3 ilmusīqa -lli bitḫibbáha?*	أيْه نوْع الموسيقى اللي بِتْحِبّها؟
folk music, popular music	*ilmusīqa -ššaʒbíyya* *aɣāni šá3bi* [pl.]	**الموسيقى الشّعبية** **أغاني شعْبى**
pop music (specifically more Western-sounding music)	*musīqa -lpōp*	**موسيقى البوْپ**
rap	*ir*[rap]	**الرّاپ**
classical music	*ilmusīqa -lklasikíyya*	**الموسيقى الكْلاسيكية**
rock music	*musīqa -rrōk*	**موسيقى الرّوْك**
jazz	*ilžāz*	**الچاز**
Arabic classical music	*aɣāni 3arabíyya ʔadīma*	**أغاني عربية قديمة**

أغانى عربية قديمة *aɣāni 3arabíyya ʔadīma* refers to music from artists such as Umm Kulthum from the "Golden Age" (1940s - 1950s).

musician	*musiqār*	موسيقار
street musician, busker	*musiqār šawāri3*	موسيقار شَوارِع
musical instrument	*āla musiqíyya*	آلة موسيقية
to play (an instrument)	*3ázaf* [1s2] *3ála* *lí3ib* [1s4] *3ála*	عزف على لِعِب على
Can you play any instruments?	*bití3raf tí3zif 3ála ʔayyᵊ āla?*	بِتِعْرف تِعْزِف على إيّ آلة؟
guitar	*gitār*	جيتار
I can play the guitar.	*bá3raf á3zif 3ála -lgitār.*	بعْرف أعْزِف على الجيتار.
piano	*biyānu*	بِيانو
violin	*kamān* *kamánga*	كمان كمانْجة
trumpet	*būʔ (abwāʔ)*	بوق (أبْواق)
drum	*ṭábla (ṭúbal)*	طبْلة (طُبل)
flute	*flūt*	فْلوت
oud, lute	*3ūd (a3wād)*	عود (أعْواد)
ney (reed flute)	*nāy*	نايْ
mizmaar (wooden flute)	*muzmār (mazamīr)*	مُزْمار (مزامير)
folk mizmaar (with a flared bell like an oboe)	*muzmār báladi*	مُزْمار بلدي
guitar strings	*witrᵊ (awtār) gitār*	وِتْر (أَوْتار) جيتار
piano keys	*zarāyir biyānu* [pl.]	زرايِر بِيانو
to tune (a guitar, piano)	*ẓábaṭ* [1s3]	ظبط
in tune	*naɣámtu maẓbūṭa*	نغمْتُه مظْبوطة
out of tune	*naɣámtu miš maẓbūṭa* *našāz*	نغمْتُه مِش مظْبوطة نشاز

orchestra	*urkéstra*	أورْكِسْترا
to dance	*ráʔaṣ* [1s3]	رقص
a dance	*ráʔṣa*	رقْصة
dancer	*rāʔiṣ* *raʔʔāṣ*	راقِص رقّاص
ballet dancer	*rāʔiṣ balēh*	راقِص بليْهْ
belly dancing	*raʔṣ^ə šárʔi* *raʔṣ^ə báladi*	رقْص شرْقي رقْص بلدي

23 Games and Sports

toy, game	*lí3ba (lí3ab)*	لِعْبة (لِعب)
doll, puppet	*3arūsa (3arāyis)*	عروسة (عرايِس)
teddy bear	*dabdūb (dabadīb)*	دبْدوب (دباديب)

to play a game	*lí3ib* [1s4] *lí3ba*	لِعِب لِعْبة
to play billiards	*lí3ib* [1s4] *bilyárdu*	لِعِب بِلْيارْدو
to play cards	*lí3ib* [1s4] *bi-lwára?* *lí3ib* [1s4] *bi-lkurūt*	لِعِب بِالوَرق لِعِب بِالكُروت
turn	*dōr (adwār)*	دوْر (أدْوار)
Whose turn is it?	*dōr mīn da?*	دوْر مين ده؟
It's your turn.	*da dōrak.*	دة دوْرك.

chess	*iššaṭaráng*	الشّطْرنْج
move	*ɧáraka*	حركة
Check! (in chess)	*kišš*	كِشّ!
Checkmate!	*kiššᵊ māt*	كِشّ مات!
(chess) piece	*qíṭ3a (qíṭa3)*	قِطْعة (قِطع)
king	*málik*	ملِك
queen	*wazīr*	وَزير
bishop	*fīl*	فيل
knight	*ɧuṣān*	حُصان
rook	*ṭábya*	طابْيَة
pawn	*3askári*	عسْكري

backgammon	*ṭáwla*	طاوْلة
dice	*zahr* [coll.]	زهْر

In games such as backgammon, the numbers that appear on dice rolls have special names, numbers borrowed from Persian and Turkish.

one	*yak*	يَك
two	*dō*	دوْ
three	*sih*	سيهْ
four	*guhār*	جُهار
five	*bīš*	بيش
six	*šīš*	شيش
pair of ones, snake eyes	*hab yak*	هب يَك
pair of twos	*dubāra*	دوبارة
pair of threes	*dōsa*	دوْسة
pair of fours	*dúrgi*	دورْجي
pair of fives	*dabš*	دبْش
pair of sixes	*dušš*	دوشّ

sport	*riyāḍa*	رِياضة
Do you like sports?	*bitḫíbb irriyāḍa?*	بِتْحِبّ الرِّياضة؟
I like watching sports, but I don't play any.	*baḫíbb atfárrag 3ála -rriyāḍa, bass^ə ma-bal3abhāš.*	بحِبّ أتْفرّج على الرِّياضة، بسّ مبلْعبْهاش.
ball	*kōra*	كوْرة
soccer (UK: football)	*kōrit qádam* *kōra*	كوْرِةْ قدم كوْرة
goal	*gōn (igwān)*	جوْن (إجْوان)
to score a goal	*gāb* [1h2] *gōn*	جاب جوْن

soccer game (UK: football match)	*matšᵊ kōra* *mubarāh (mubarayāt)*	ماتْش كوْرة مُباراهْ (مُبارَيات)
soccer field (UK: football pitch)	*mál3ab (malā3ib) kōra*	ملْعب (ملاعِب) كوْرة

(American) football	*kōrit ilqádam ilʔamrikíyya* *amērikan fūtbōl*	كوْرةْ القدم الأمْريكية أميرْكان فوتْبوْل
baseball	*bēsbōl*	بيْسْبوْل
basketball	*baskitbōl*	باسْكِتْبوْل
basketball hoop	*šábakit ilbaskitbōl*	شبكِةْ الباسْكِتْبوْل
boxing	*mulákma*	مُلاكْمة
golf	*gōlf*	جوْلْف
golf ball	*kōrit gōlf*	كوْرةْ جوْلْف
golf club	*nādi gōlf*	نادي جوْلْف
golf course	*mál3ab (malā3ib) gōlf*	ملْعب (ملاعِب) جوْلْف
hockey	*hōki*	هوْكي
to ski, go skiing	*itzáɧlaʔ* [11p2] *3ála -lgalīd*	اِتْزحْلق على الجليد
tennis	*tínis*	تِنِس
tennis ball	*kōrit ittínis*	كوْرةْ التِّنِس
tennis court	*mál3ab (malā3ib) ittínis*	ملْعب (ملاعِب) التِّنِس
tennis net	*šábakit ittínis*	شبكِةْ التِّنِس
tennis racket	*máḍrab (maḍārib) ittínis*	مضْرب (مضارِب) التِّنِس
volleyball	*vōli bōl* *ilkōra -ṭṭáyra*	ڤوْلي بوْل الكوْرة الطّايْرة
volleyball net	*šábakit ilvōli bōl*	شبكِةْ الڤوْلي بوْل

to kick (a ball)	*šāṭ* [1h1]	شاط

to hit	*ḍárab* [1s1]	**ضرب**
to throw	*ráma* [1d2]	**رمى**
to catch	*mísik* [1s5]	**مِسِك**
to win (a game)	*kísib* [1s4] *fāz* [1h1] *ɣálab* [1s2]	**كِسِب** **فاز** **غلب**
to lose (a game)	*xísir* [1s4]	**خِسِر**
to beat (a team)	*fāz* [1h1] *3ála*	**فاز على**
to lose to (a team)	*xísir* [1s4] *ʔuddām*	**خِسِر قُدّام**
Who won?	*mīn kísib?*	مين كِسِب؟
player	*lā3ib*	**لاعِب**
team	*farīʔ*	**فريق**
to play against (a team, a player)	*lí3ib* [1s4] *ḍidd*	**لِعِب ضِدّ**
champion	*báṭal (ábṭal)*	**بطل (أبْطال)**
score	*natīga (natāyig)*	**نتيجة (نتايِج)**
What's the score?	*innatīga kām kām?* *ilʔiskōr kām?*	النّتيجة كام كام؟ السُّكوْر كام؟
The score is two to four.	*innatīga -tnēn arbá3a*	**النّتيجة اتْنيْن أرْبعة.**
They're tied three to three.	*ta3ādul talāta talāta.*	تعادُل تلاتة تلاتة.
The match ended in a draw (tie).	*ilmátšᵊ xíliṣ ta3ādul.*	الماتْش خِلِص تعادُل.

fitness	*liyāqa* [fitness]	**لِياقة** **فيتْنِس**
exercise	*tadrīb*	**تدْريب**
to exercise, work out	*itdárrab* [5s2] *itmárran* [5s2]	**اِتْدرّب** **اِتْمرّن**

workout	*tamrīna*	**تمْرينة**
How often do you exercise?	*bitdárrab kullᵊ ʔaddᵊ ʔē?*	بِتْدرّب كُلّ أدّ أيْه؟
I try to exercise at least twice a week.	*baḫāwil atdárrab 3ála -lʔaʔáll marritēn fi -lʔisbū3.*	بحاوِل أتْدرّب على الأقلّ مرّتيْن في الإسْبوع.
I had a really good workout at the gym this morning.	*itdarrábtᵊ kwáyyis fi -lžim iṣṣúbḫ.*	اِتْدرّبْت كُوَيِّس في الچيم الصُّبْح.
gym, health club	*žim*	**چيم**
to go to the gym	*rāḫ [1h1] ilžím*	**راح الچيم**
I go to the gym every morning.	*ána barūḫ ilžím kullᵊ yōm iṣṣúbḫ.*	أنا بروح الچيم كُلّ يوْم الصُّبْح.
to join a gym, become a member of a gym	*ištárak [8s1] fi žim*	**اِشْترك في چيم**
member	*3uḍw (a3ḍāʔ)* *muštárik*	**عُضْو (أعْضاء)** **مُشْترِك**
membership	*3uḍwíyya* *ištirāk*	**عُضْوية** **اِشْتِراك**
How much is a monthly membership at this gym?	*il3uḍwíyya fi -lžim da b-kām fi -ššahr?*	العُضْوية في الچيم ده بِكام في الشّهْر؟
Is there a contract?	*fī 3aʔd?*	فيه عقْد؟
personal trainer	*mudárrib šáxṣi* *mudárrib xuṣūṣi*	**مُدرِّب شخْصي** **مُدرِّب خُصوصي**
I'd like to hire a personal trainer.	*3āyiz mudárrib šáxṣi.*	عايِز مُدرِّب شخْصي.
training session	*ḫíṣṣit tidrīb*	**حِصّةْ تدْريب**
How much does it cost per training session?	*ḫíṣṣit ittidrīb bi-kām?*	حِصّةْ التّدْريب بِكام؟
My goal is to gain muscle.	*3āyiz arábbi 3aḍalāt.* *3āyiz azīd 3áḍal.*	عايِز أربّي عضلات. عايِز أزيد عضل.

to gain weight	*zād* [1h2]	**زاد**
I feel like I've gained a bit of weight.	*ána ɦāsis ínni zidtᵊ šwáyya.*	أنا حاسِس إنيّ زِدْت شْوَيَّة.
to lose weight	*xass* [1g3]	**خسّ**
I want to lose weight.	*3āyiz axíss.*	عايِز أخِسّ.
I need to lose five kilos.	*3āyiz axíssᵊ xámsa kīlu.*	عايِز أخِسّ خمْسة كيلو.
to go on a diet	*3ámal* [1s2] *rižīm* *míši* [1d5] *3ála ržīm*	**عمل رِجيم** **مِشي على رِجيم**
I'm on a diet.	*ána 3āmil rižīm.* *ána māši 3ála ržīm.*	أنا عامِل رِجيم. أنا ماشي على رِجيم.
locker room, changing room	*ōḍit taɣyīr ilhudūm*	**أوْضِةْ تغْيير الهُدوم**
locker	[locker]	**لوْكر**
to change one's clothes	*ɣáyyar* [2s2] *hudūmu*	**غيرّ هُدومُه**
gym clothes, workout clothes	*hudūm žim* [pl.]	**هُدوم جيم**
a barbell	*bār*	**بار**
a dumbbell	[dumbbell]	**دمْبلّ**
free weights	*awzān húrra* [pl.]	**أَوْزان حُرَّة**
to lift weights	*šāl* [1h2] *ɦadīd* *šāl* [1h2] *awzān*	**شال حديد** **شال أَوْزان**
weight machine	*gihāz (aghíza) ɦadīd*	**جِهاز (أجْهِزة) حديد**
to adjust the weight	*ẓábaṭ* [1s3] *ilwázn*	**ظبط الوَزْن**
Adjust the weight before you get on the machine.	*úẓbuṭ ilwáznᵊ ablᵊ ma tištáɣal 3ála -lgihāz.*	أُظْبُط الوَزْن قبْل ما تِشْتغل على الجِهاز.
Excuse me, how do you use this machine?	*ba3dᵊ íznak, izzāy astá3mil ilgihāz da?*	بعْد إذْنك، إزّاي أسْتعْمِل الجِهاز ده؟
to do cardio exercise	*lí3ib* [1s4] *tamarīn kardíyu*	**لِعِب تمارين كارْدِيو**

to burn calories	*ḫáraʔ* [1s1] *issu3rāt ilḫararíyya*	**حرق السُّعْرات الحرارية**
running machine, treadmill	*maššāya* *sayr (suyūr)* [treadmill]	**مشّاية** **سَيْر (سُيور)** **تْرِدْميل**
elliptical trainer	*gihāz* [elliptical]	**جِهاز إيليپْتيكال**
stationary bicycle	*3ágala sábta*	**عجلة ثابْتة**
to run	*gíri* [1d5]	**جِري**
I usually spend 20 minutes on the running machine.	*ána ɣālíban bágri tiltᵊ sā3a 3ála -lmaššāya.*	أنا غالِباً بجْري تِلْت ساعة على المشّايَة.
to jog, go jogging	*gíri* [1d5] *hárwil* [11s1]	**جِري** **هرْوِل**
exercise	*tamrīn (tamarīn)*	**تمْرين (تمارين)**
to do sit-ups, work one's abs	*lí3ib* [1s4] *baṭn*	**لِعِب بطْن**
to do pull-ups	*lí3ib* [1s4] *3úʔla*	**لِعِب عُقْلة**
to do push-ups	*lí3ib* [1s4] *ḍaɣṭ*	**لِعِب ضغْط**
How many sit-ups can you do?	*tí3raf tíl3ab kam tamrīnit baṭn?*	تِعْرف تِلْعب كام تمْرينِةْ بطْن؟
a set	*magmū3a (magamī3)*	**مجْموعة (مجاميع)**
a rep	*3ádda*	**عدّة**
Do three sets of ten reps each.	*íl3ab tálat magmu3āt fi 3ášar 3addāt.*	اِلْعب تلات مجْموعات في عشر عدّات.
Rest for one minute between sets.	*ráyyaḫ diʔīʔa bēn ilmagamī3.*	ريّح دِقيقة بينْ المجاميع.
to do aerobics	*lí3ib* [1s4] *ayrōbiks*	**لِعِب أيْروْبِكْس**
to do yoga	*lí3ib* [1s4] *yōga*	**لِعِب يوْجا**
to push	*zaʔʔ* [1g2]	**زقّ**

to pull	*šadd* [1g3]	**شدّ**
to lift	*šāl* [1h2] *ráfa3* [1s1]	**شال** **رفع**
to lower	*názzil* [2s1]	**نزِّل**
Lift the barbell over your head, then slowly lower it back down.	*írfa3 ilbār fō? rāsak wi nazzílu bi-búṭ?.*	اِرْفع البار فوْق راسك و نزِّله بِبُطْء.
to breathe in	*?áxad* [i3] *náfas*	**أخد نفس**
to breathe out	*ṭálla3* [2s2] *náfas*	**طلّع نفس**
Don't forget to breathe!	*ma-tansāš titnáffis.*	متنْساش تِتْنفِّس!
a jump rope	*ɦabl*	**حبْل**
to jump rope	*naṭṭ* [1g2] *ilɦábl*	**نطّ الحبْل**
scale	*mizān (mawazīn)*	**ميزان (مَوازين)**
to weigh oneself	*wázan* [1s2] *náfsu*	**وَزن نفْسُه**

24 Travel and Vacations

travel, traveling	*sáfar*	سفر
to travel, go on a journey	*sāfir* [3s]	سافِر
vacation (UK: holiday)	*agāza*	أجازة
to take a vacation	*ṭíli3* [1s4] *agāza*	طِلِع أجازة
a trip	*ríḫla*	رِحْلة
tourism	*siyāḫa*	سِياحة
tourist	*sāyiḫ (suyyāḫ)*	سايِح (سُيّاح)
to go on a tour	*rāḫ* [1h1] *fi gáwla*	راح في جَوْلة
tour guide	*múršid*	مُرْشِد
tourist police	*šúrṭit siyāḫa*	شُرْطِةْ سِياحة

at the seaside	*3ála -lbaḫr*	على البحْر
seaside resort	*fúnduʔ 3ála -lbaḫr*	فُنْدُق على البحْر
at the beach	*3ála -ššaṭṭ*	على الشّطّ
on the coast	*3ála -ssāḫil*	على السّاحِل
beach	*šaṭṭ (šuṭūṭ)* *bilāž*	شطّ (شُطوط) بِلاچ
I just got back from the beach.	*ána líssa rāgi3 min ilbilāž.*	أنا لِسّه راجِع مِن البِلاچ.
sand	*raml (rimāl)*	رمْل (رِمال)
to build a sandcastle	*bána* [1d2] *ʔál3a bi-rráml*	بنى قلْعة بِالرّمْل

sun umbrella, beach umbrella	*šamsíyya*	شمْسية
to sunbathe	*ʔáxad* [i3] *ɦammām šams*	أخد حمّام شمْس
to sunburn	*itɦáraʔ* [7s1] *min iššáms*	اِتْحرق مِن الشّمْس
I'm so sunburned! It hurts!	*gāli ɦarʔᵊ min iššáms! bitíwga3!*	جالي حرْق مِن الشّمْس! بِتوْجع!
to put on sunblock	*ɦaṭṭᵊ* [1g2] [sun block]	حطّ صن بْلوْك
to tan	*ismárr* [9s] *iktásab* [8s1] *sámra*	اِسْمرّ اِكْتسب سمْرة
tanned	*mismírr*	مِسْمِرّ
to go into the water	*nízil* [1s5] *ilmáyya*	نِزِل الميّة
wave	*mōg* [coll.]	موْج
to swim	*3ām* [1h1]	عام
swimming	*3ōm*	عوْم
swimming pool	*ɦammām sibāɦa* *pisīn*	حمّام سِباحة پيسين
Do you know how to swim?	*bití3raf ti3ūm?*	بِتِعْرف تِعوم؟
I can swim pretty well.	*bá3raf a3ūm kuwáyyis.*	بعْرف أعوم كُوَيِّس.
I don't know how to swim.	*ma-ba3ráfš a3ūm.*	مبعْرفْش أعوم.
to dive, go scuba diving	*ɣíṭis* [1s4]	غِطِس
to snorkel	*3ámal* [1s2] *(i)*[snorkel]	عمل سْنوْرْكِل
to go camping	*rāɦ* [1h1] *yixáyyim*	راح يِخيِّم

camp	*muxáyyam*	مُخيّم
tent	*xēma (xíyam)*	خيْمة (خِيَم)
to go hiking, trek	*míši* [1d5] *ktīr* (lit. to walk a lot)	مِشي كِتير
suitcase	*šánṭa (šúnaṭ)*	شنْطة (شُنط)
to pack one's suitcase	*wáḍḍab* [2s2] *šanṭítu* *ḫáḍḍar* [2s2] *šanṭítu*	وَضّب شنْطِتُه حضّر شنْطِتُه
to unpack one's suitcase	*fáḍḍa* [2d] *šanṭítu*	فضّى شنْطِتُه
passport	*basbōr* *gawāz sáfar*	باسْبوْر جَواز سفر
to get a passport	*ṭálla3* [2s2] *basbōr*	طلّع باسْبوْر
passport photo	*ṣūrit basbōr*	صورةْ باسْبوْر
visa	*vīza*	ڤيزا
to issue a visa	*ṭálla3* [2s2] *vīza*	طلّع ڤيزا
tourist visa	*vīza siyāḫa*	ڤيزا سِياحة
residence permit	*(taṣrīḫ) iqāma*	)تصْريح) إقامة
work permit	*taṣrīḫ 3ámal*	تصْريح عمل
valid	*ṣāliḫ*	صالح
to expire	*intáha* [8d]	اِنْتهى
abroad	*bárra*	برّه
to travel abroad	*sāfir* [3s] *bárra*	سافِر برّه
Have you ever been abroad?	*safírt^{ə} bárra ʔabl^{ə} kída?*	سافِرْت برّه قبْل كِده؟

border	*ɦudūd* [pl.]	حُدود
customs	*gamārik* [pl.]	جمارك
customs officer	*muwáẓẓaf gamārik*	مُوَظّف جمارِك
to declare	*ṣárrah* [2s2]	صرّح
to smuggle	*hárrab* [2s2]	هرّب
exchange office	*máktab (makātib) ṣirāfa*	مكْتب (مكاتِب) صِرافة
to change money	*ɣáyyar* [2s2] *filūs*	غيّر فِلوس
I'd like to change $100 to Egyptian pounds, please.	*3āyiz aɣáyyar mīt dulār li-ginēh máṣri law samáɦt.*	عايِز أغيّر ميةْ دولار لجِنيْهْ مصْري لَوْ سمحْت.
exchange rate	*si3rᵊ 3úmla*	سِعْر عُمْلة

ticket	*tazkára (tazākir)*	تذْكرة (تذاكِر)
to buy a ticket	*ištára* [8d] *tazkára* *ʔáṭa3* [1s1] *tazkára*	اِشْترى تذْكرة قطع تذْكرة

airplane	*ṭayyāra*	طيّارة
flight	*ṭayrān* *ríɦla*	طَيْران رِحْلة
to fly	*ṭār* [1h2]	طار
to book a seat	*ɦágaz* [1s2] *kúrsi*	حجز كُرْسي
I'd like to book a seat on the next available flight.	*3āyiz áɦgiz kúrsi 3ála áʔrab ríɦla.*	عايِز أحْجِز كُرْسي على أقْرب رِحْلة.
first class	*iddáraga -lʔūla*	الدّرجة الأولى

I've never flown first class before.	*3úmri ma-safártᵊ fi -ddáraga -lʔūla ʔablᵊ kída.*	عُمْري ما سافِرْت في الدّرجة الأُولى قَبْل كِده.
business class	*ilbíznis* *dáragit rigāl ilʔa3māl*	البيزْنِس درجةِ رِجال الأعْمال
economy class, coach	*iddáraga -ssiyaħíyya* *iddáraga -lʔiqtiṣadíyya*	الدّرجة السِّياحية الدّرجة الاِقْتِصادية
airfare	*táman tazkára*	تمن تذْكرة
The airfare was reasonable.	*táman ittazkára kān kuwáyyis.*	تمن التّذْكرة كان كُوَيِّس.
airport	*maṭār*	مطار
to check in	[check-in]	تْشيْك إن
aisle seat	*kúrsi gamb ilmamárr*	كُرْسي جنْب الممرّ
window seat	*kúrsi gamb iššubbāk*	كُرْسي جنْب الشُّبّاك
I prefer an aisle seat.	*baħíbb áʔ3ud gamb ilmamárr.*	بحِبّ أقْعُد جنْب الممرّ
gate	*bawwāba*	بوّابة
to board	*ṭíli3* [1s4]	طِلِع
to be delayed	*itʔáxxar* [5s2] *itʔággil* [5s1]	إتْأخَّر إتِأجِّل
Your flight has been delayed by two hours.	*riħlátak itʔaggílit sa3tēn.*	رِحْلتك اِتْأجِّلْت ساعْتيْن.
to be canceled	*itláɣa* [6d] *itkánsil* [11s1]	إتْلغى إتْكنْسِل
to take off	*ṭíli3* [1s4] *itħárrak* [5s2]	طِلِع إتْحرّك

Our flight leaves in 30 minutes from gate 5.	*riɦlítna hatíʈla3 ba3dᵊ talatīn diʔīʔa min bawwāba ráqam xámsa.*	رِحْلِتْنا هتِطْلع بعْد تلاتين دِقيقة مِن بوّابة رقم خمْسة.
to land	*hábaʈ* [1s3]	هبط
pilot	*ʈayyār*	طيّار
flight attendant	*muḍīf*	مُضيف
layover, transit	*tranzīt*	ترانْزيت
I had a 3-hour layover in Dubai.	*nizíltᵊ tránzit talāt sa3āt fi dubāy.*	نِزِلْت ترانْزيت تلات سعات في دُبىْ.

train	*ʔaʈr (ʔuʈúra)*	قطْر (قُطُرة)
to take the train	*ríkib* [1s4] *ʔaʈr*	رِكِب قطْر
first class	*iddáraga -lʔūla*	الدّرجة الأولى
second class	*iddáraga -ttánya*	الدّرجة التّانْيَة
third class	*iddáraga -ttálta*	الدّرجة التّالْتة
train station	*maɦáʈʈit ʔaʈr*	محطّةْ قطْر
one-way ticket	*tazkára -ttigāh wāɦid*	تذْكرة اتِّجاهْ واحِد
round-trip ticket (UK: return ticket)	*tazkára rāyiɦ gayy*	تذْكرة رايِح جايّ
waiting room	*ōḍit intiẓār*	أوْضِةْ اِنْتِظار
platform	*raṣīf (riṣífa)*	رصيف (رِصِفة)
track, rails	*ʔuḍbān* [pl.]	قُضْبان
railway, railroad	*síkka ɦadīd*	سِكّة حديد
to arrive	*wíṣil* [1s4]	وِصِل

arrival	*wuṣūl*	**وُصول**
to depart	*míši* [1d5] *ʔām* [1h1]	**مِشي** **قام**
departure	*qiyām*	**قِيام**
compartment	*maʔṣūra*	**مقْصورة**
(train) car	*3arabíyyit ʔaṭr*	**عربيةْ قطْر**
express	*ʔaṭrᵊ sarī3*	**قطْر سريع**
non-express train	*ʔaṭrᵊ 3ādi*	**قطْر عادي**
to change trains	*ɣáyyar* [2s2] *ilʔáṭr*	**غيّر القطْر**

bus	*utubīs*	**أُتوبيس**
to take the bus	*ʔáxad* [i3] *utubīs*	**أخد أُتوبيس**
I took a bus from Cairo to Alexandria.	*axádt utubīs min ilqāhíra li-skindiríyya.*	أخدْت أُتوبيس مِن القاهِرة لإِسْكِنْدِرية.
air-conditioned	*mukáyyaf*	**مُكيّف**
comfortable	*murīḫ*	**مُريح**
uncomfortable, tiring	*mút3ib*	**مُتْعِب**
bus station	*máwʔif (mawāʔif) utubīs*	**مَوْقِف (مَواقِف) أُتوبيس**

hitchhiking	*utustōp*	**أوتوسْتوْپ**
Hitchhiking is dangerous.	*ilʔutustōp xáṭar.*	الأوتوسْتوْپ خطر.
to hitchhike	*wáʔʔaf* [2s2] *utustōp*	**وَقّف أوتوسْتوْپ**
hitchhiker	*ílli biywáʔʔaf ilʔutustōp*	**اللي بِيْوَقّف الأوتوسْتوْپ**

hotel	*fúndu? (fanādi?)*	**فُنْدق (فنادِق)**
reservation	*ɧagz*	**حجْز**
I have a reservation.	*3ándi ɧagz.* *fī ɧagzᵊ b-?ísmi.*	عنْدي حجْز. فيه حجْز بْإِسْمي.
to reserve, book	*ɧágaz* [1s2]	**حجز**
room	*ōḍa (úwaḍ)* *ɣúrfa (ɣúraf)*	**أوْضة (أُوَض)** **غُرْفة (غُرف)**
I want to book a room.	*3āyiz áɧgiz ōḍa.*	عايِز أحْجِز أوْضة.
a single room	*ɣúrfa fardíyya*	**غُرْفة فرْدية**
a double room	*ɣúrfa li-šaxṣēn*	**غُرْفة لِشخْصينْ**
a twin room	*ɣúrfa b-sirirēn*	**غُرْفة بِسِريرينْ**
How much is it per night?	*illēla b-kām?*	اللّيلة بِكام؟
I'd like to stay for three nights.	*3āyiz á?3ud tálat layāli.*	عايِز أقْعُد تلات لَيالي.
to check in	*3ámal* [1s2] [check-in]	**عمل تْشيْك إن**
to check out	*3ámal* [1s2] [check-out]	**عمل تْشيْك أَوْت**
What time is checkout?	*it*[check-out] *issā3a kām?*	التّشيْك أوْت السّاعة كام؟
lobby	*lūbi*	**لوبي**
porter	*bawwāb*	**بوّاب**

25 Government and Politics

government	*ḩukūma*	حكومة
to govern, rule over	*ḩákam* [1s3]	حكم
cabinet	*máglis wuzarāʔ*	مجْلِس وُزراء
ministry, department	*wizāra*	وِزارة
minister, secretary	*wazīr (wuzarāʔ)*	وَزير (وُزراء)
prime minister	*raʔīs wuzarāʔ*	رئيس وُزراء
parliament	*barlamān* *máglis ša3b*	برْلمان مجْلِس شعْب
member of parliament, MP	*3uḍwᵊ fi -lbarlamān*	عُضْو في البرْلمان
president	*raʔīs (ruʔasāʔ)*	رئيس (رُؤساء)
vice president	*nāʔib raʔīs*	نائِب رئيس
republic	*gumhuríyya*	جُمْهورية
The Arab Republic of Egypt (Egypt's official name)	*gumhuríyyit maṣr il3arabíyya*	جُمْهوريةْ مصْر العربية
kingdom	*mamláka (mamālik)*	ممْلكة (ممالِك)
monarchy, royalty	*malakíyya*	ملكية
king	*málik (mulūk)*	ملِك (مُلوك)
queen	*málika*	ملِكة
prince	*amīr (umarāʔ)*	أمير (أُمراء)
princess	*amīra*	أميرة

emperor	*imbiraṭōr (abāṭíra)*	**إمْبِراطوْر (أباطِرة)**
empress	*imbiraṭōra*	**إمْبِراطوْرة**
empire	*imbiraṭuríyya*	**إمْبِراطورية**

people, nation	*ša3b (šu3ūb)*	**شعب (شُعوب)**
citizen	*muwāṭin*	**مُوَاطِن**
to vote	*ṣáwwat* [2s2]	**صوّت**
voter	*nāxib*	**ناخِب**
majority	*aɣlabíyya*	**أغْلبية**
minority	*aqallíyya*	**أقلّية**
(political) party	*ḫizb (aḫzāb)*	**حِزْب (أحْزاب)**
to nominate	*ráššaḫ* [2s2]	**رشّح**
nomination	*taršīḫ*	**ترْشيح**
elections	*intixabāt* [pl.]	**اِنْتِخابات**
to elect	*intáxab* [7s2]	**اِنْتخب**
He was elected president.	*intaxabū raʔīs.*	اِنْتخبوه رئيس.
presidential term	*fátra riʔasíyya*	**فترْة رئاسية**
In the US, a president can serve a maximum of two terms.	*fi -lwilayāt ilmuttáḫida, irraʔīs ma-yuʔ3údš áktar min fatritēn riʔasiyyitīn.*	في الوِلايات المتّحِدة، الرّئيس مَيقْعُدْش أكْتر مِن فترْتِينْ رِئاسِيّتين.

democracy	*dimuqraṭíyya*	**ديمُقْراطية**
democratic	*dimuqrāṭi*	**ديمُقْراطي**

constitution	*dustūr (dasatīr)*	دُسْتور (دساتير)
reform	*işlāɧ*	إصْلاح
dictator	*diktadōr*	دِكْتادوْر
dictatorship	*diktaduríyya*	دِكْتادورية

capital, capital city	*3āşíma (3awāşim)*	عاصِمة (عَواصِم)
Cairo is the capital of Egypt.	*ilqāhíra híyya 3āşimit maşr.*	القاهِرة هِيَّ عاصمةْ مصْر.
province	*muɧāfaẓa* *muqāţa3a*	مُحافظة مُقاطعة
state	*wilāya*	وِلايَة

politics	*siyāsa*	سِياسة
political; politician	*siyāsi*	سِياسي
summit	*qímma (qímam)*	قِمّة (قِمم)

demonstration, protest	*muẓāhara*	مُظاهرة
march	*masīra*	مسيرة
to demonstrate, protest	*itẓāhir* [3s]	اِتْظاهِر
demonstrator, protester	*mutaẓāhir*	مُتظاهِر
revolution	*sáwra*	ثَوْرة

society	*mugtáma3*	مُجْتمع
social	*igtimā3i*	اِجْتِماعي
free	*ɧurr (aɧrār)*	حُرّ (أحْرار)
freedom	*ɧurríyya*	حُرّية

26 Crime and Justice

crime	*garīma (garāyim)*	جريمة (جرايِم)
criminal	*múgrim*	مُجْرِم
to commit a crime	*irtákab* [8s1] *garīma*	اِرْتكب جريمة
to break the law	*xáraq* [1s1] *ilqanūn*	خرق القانون
theft	*sírʔa (sirʔāt)*	سِرْقة (سِرْقات)
to steal, rob	*sáraʔ* [1s1]	سرق
thief	*ɧarāmi*	حرامي
to break into a house	*iqtáɧam* [8s1] *bēt*	اِقْتحم بيْت
rape	*iɣtiṣāb*	اِغْتِصاب
to rape	*iɣtáṣab* [8s1]	اِغْتصب
murder	*ʔatl*	قتْل
to murder, kill	*ʔátal* [1s2]	قتل
murderer	*ʔātil (ʔátala)*	قاتِل (قتلة)
assault	*i3tidāʔ*	اِعْتداء
to assault, attack	*i3táda* [8d] *3ála* *hāgim* [3s]	اِعْتدى على هاجِم
vandalism	*taxrīb*	تخْريب
to vandalize	*xárrab* [2s2]	خرّب
to pickpocket	*nášal* [1s2]	نشل
a pickpocket	*náššāl*	نشّال

to arrest	*ʔábad̩* [1s1] *3ála* *i3táqal* [8s]	**قبض على** **اِعْتقل**
to be arrested	*itʔábad̩* [8s1] *3alē*	**اِتْقبض عليْه**
to interrogate	*istágwib* [10s1]	**اِسْتجْوِب**

court	*maɦkáma (maɦākim)*	**محْكمة (محاكِم)**
justice	*3adāla*	**عدالة**
judge	*ʔād̩i (ʔud̩āh)*	**قاضي (قُضاهْ)**
lawyer (UK: solicitor)	*muɦāmi*	**مُحامي**
prosecutor	*muddá3i 3āmm*	**مُدّعي عامّ**
law	*qanūn (qawanīn)*	**قانون (قَوانين)**
legal	*qanūni*	**قانوني**
illegal	*ɣēr qanūni*	**غيْر قانوني**
I think that's illegal.	*a3táqid innᵊ da miš qanūni.*	أعْتقِد إنّ ده مِش قانوني.

judgment, sentence	*ɦukm (aɦkām)*	**حُكْم (أحْكام)**
to convict	*dān* [1h2]	**دان**
punishment	*3uqūba*	**عُقوبة**
to sentence __ to	*ɦákam* [1s3] *3ála __ bi-*	**حكم على __ بِ**
The judge sentenced him to five years in prison.	*ilʔād̩i hákam 3alē bi-xámas sinīn sign.*	القاضي حكم عليْه بِخمس سِنين سِجْن.
prison	*sign (sugūn)*	**سِجْن (سُجون)**
to be sentenced	*itɦákam* [7s1] *3alē*	**اِتْحكم عليْه**

He was sentenced to life in prison.	*itḫákam 3alē bi-ssígn ilmuʔábbad.*	اِتْحكم عليْه بِالسِّجْن المُؤبّد.
in prison, imprisoned	*masgūn*	**مسْجون**
prisoner	*sagīn (suganāʔ)*	**سجين (سُجناء)**
to escape from prison	*hírib* [1s4] *min issígn*	**هِرِب مِن السِّجْن**
death sentence, capital punishment	*i3dām*	**إعْدام**
I don't believe in the death penalty.	*ána miš muqtáni3 bi-3uqūbit ilʔi3dām.*	أنا مِش مُقْتنِع بِعُقوبِةْ الإعْدام.
to accuse __ of	*ittáham* [8s1] *__ bi-*	**اِتّهم __ بِـ**
He was accused of murdering his wife.	*ittáhamū ínnu ʔátal mirātu.*	اِتّهموه إنُّه قتل مِراتُه.
accused of	*muttáhim bi-*	**مُتّهِم بِـ**
charge, accusation	*túhma (túham)*	**تُهْمة (تُهم)**
defense	*difā3*	**دِفاع**
to be hanged	*itšánaʔ* [7s1]	**اِتْشنق**

27 Money

money	*filūs* [pl.]	فِلوس
currency	*3úmla*	عُمْلة
dollar	*dulār*	دولار
euro	*yūru*	يورو
pound sterling	*ginēh isterlīni*	جِنيْهْ إسْترْليني
Egyptian pound	*ginēh máṣri*	جِنيْهْ مصْري
piastre (100 piastres = 1 pound)	*ʔirš (ʔurūš)*	قِرْش (قُروش)
25 piastres	*xámsa w 3išrīn ʔirš* *rub3ᵊ gnēh*	خمْسة و عِشْرين قِرْش رُبْع جِنيْهْ
50 piastres	*xamsīn ʔirš* *nuṣṣᵊ gnēh*	خمْسين قِرْش نُصّ جِنيْهْ
coin	*3úmla ma3daníyya*	عُمْلة معْدنية
bill	*wáraʔa (awrāʔ)* *bankinōt*	وَرقة (أَوْراق) بنْكِنوْت
a 100-pound bill	*wáraʔa b-mīt ginēh*	وَرقة بمِيةْ جِنيْهْ
change (coins)	*fákka*	فكّة
to break a bill, make change	*fakk* [1g2]	فكّ
Could you break this bill, please?	*ma3āk fákka law samáḥt?*	معاك فكّة لَوْ سمحْت؟
tax	*ḍarība (ḍarāyib)*	ضريبة (ضرايِب)

to tax	*fárad* [1s2] *ḍarība 3ála*	فرض ضريبة على
to pay taxes	*dáfa3* [1s1] *iḍḍarāyib*	دفع الضّرايِب
to evade taxes	*hírib* [1s4] *min iḍḍarāyib*	هِرِب مِن الضّرايِب
VAT (sales tax)	*ḍarībit ilmabi3āt*	ضريبِةْ المبيعات

income	*daxl*	دخْل
expenses	*maṣarīf* [pl.]	مصاريف
funds	*amwāl* [pl.]	أمْوال
financial, fiscal, monetary	*māli*	مالي
rich	*ɣáni (aɣníya)*	غني (أغْنِيا)
wealth	*sárwa*	ثَرْوَة
poor	*faʔīr (fúʔara)*	فقير (فُقرا)
poverty	*faʔr*	فقْر
upper class	*iṭṭábaʔa -lɣaníyya*	الطّبقة الغنية
middle class	*iṭṭábaʔa -lmutawassíṭa* *iṭṭábaʔa -lwúsṭa*	الطّبقة المتُوَسِّطة الطّبقة الوُسْطى
working class	*iṭṭábaʔa -l3ámla*	الطّبقة العامْلة

28 Business and Commerce

business	*a3māl* [pl.] *bíznis* *šuɣl*	أعْمال بيزْنِس شُغْل
commerce, trade; business, commercial venture	*tigāra*	تِجارة
commercial	*tugāri*	تُجاري
merchant	*tāgir (tuggār)*	تاجِر (تُجّار)
store, shop	*mátgar (matāgir)*	متْجر (متاجِر)
businessman; entrepreneur	*rāgil (rigālit) a3māl*	راجِل (رِجالِةْ) أعْمال
businesswoman	*sayyídit a3māl*	سيِّدِةْ أعْمال
to start one's own business	*báda? [1s1] iššúɣlᵊ btā3u* *báda? [1s1] šúɣlu -lxāṣṣ*	بدأ الشُّغل بِتاعُه بدأ شُغْلُه الخاصّ
company	*šírka*	شِرْكة
to go on a business trip	*sāfir [3s] fi ríḫlit šuɣl*	سافِر في رِحْلِةْ شُغْل
committee	*lágna (ligān)*	لجْنة (لِجان)
board, council	*máglis (magālis)*	مجْلِس (مجالِس)
chair, chairman	*ra?īs (ru?asā?)*	رئيس (رُؤساء)
administration	*idāra*	إدارة

to meet	*ʔābil* [3s] *igtáma3* [8s1]	قابِل اِجْتمع
meeting	*igtimā3* [meeting]	اِجْتِماع ميتينْج
appointment	*mi3ād (mawa3īd)*	ميعاد (مَواعيد)
to cancel	*láɣa* [1d2]	لغى
to postpone	*ággil* [2s1]	أجِّل
conference	*muʔtámar*	مُؤْتمر
seminar	[seminar] *nádwa (nadawāt)*	سِمينار ندْوَة (نَدَوات)
proposal	*iqtirāḫ* *3arḍ (3urūḍ)*	اِقْتِراح عرْض (عُروض)
office	*máktab (makātib)*	مكْتب (مكاتِب)
head office, headquarters	*maqárrᵊ raʔīsi (maqār raʔisíyya)* *márkaz raʔīsi (marākiz raʔisíyya)*	مقرّ رئيسي (مقار رئيسية) مرْكز رئيسي (مراكِز رئيسية)

factory	*máṣna3 (maṣāni3)*	مصْنع (مصانِع)
to manufacture	*ṣána3* [1s1]	صنع
industry	*ṣinā3a*	صِناعة

29 Agriculture

agriculture	*zirā3a*	زِراعة
farm	*mazrá3a (mazāri3)*	مزْرعة (مزارِع)
farmer	*fallāɧ*	فلّاح
barn, pen, corral, coop	*ɧaẓīra (ɧaẓāyir)*	حظيرة (حظايِر)
cattle	*báʔar* [coll.]	بقر
cow	*báʔara*	بقرة
to milk	*ɧálab* [1s2]	حلب
donkey	*ɧumār (ɧimīr)*	حُمار (حِمير)
goat	*mí3za (mi3īz)*	مِعْزة (مِعيز)
The farmer is out feeding his goats.	*ilfallāɧ bárra byiʔákkil ilma3īz bitū3u.*	الفلّاح بَرّة بِيْأكِّل المعيز بِتوعُه.
mule	*baɣl (biɣāl)*	بغْل (بِغال)
pig	*xanzīr (xanazīr)*	خنْزير (خنازير)
sheep	*xarūf (xirfān)* *ɣánam* [coll.]	خروف (خِرْفان) غنم
shepherd	*rā3i (ru3āt) ɣánam*	راعي (رُعاةْ) غنم
chicken, hen	*fárxa (firāx)*	فرْخة (فِراخ)
rooster	*dīk (diyūk)*	ديك (دِيوك)
chick	*katkūt (katakīt)*	كتْكوت (كتاكيت)

to lay an egg	*bāḍ* [1h2] *bēḍa*	باض بيْضة
duck	*baṭṭ* [coll.]	بطّ
goose	*wizz* [coll.]	وِزّ
turkey	*dīk (diyūk) rūmi*	ديك (دِيوك) رومي
camel	*gámal (gimāl)*	جمل (جِمال)
horse	*ɦuṣān (ɦiṣína)*	حُصان (حِصِنة)
stable	*iṣṭábl*	إسْطبْل
to graze	*rá3a* [1d2]	رعى
hay	*tibn*	تِبْن
field	*ɦaʔl (ɦiʔūl)* *ɣēṭ (ɣiṭān)*	حقْل (حِقول) غيْط (غِطان)
to plow	*ɦárat* [1s2]	حرت
tractor	*garrār*	جرّار
orchard	*bustān (basatīn)*	بُسْتان (بساتين)
to plant	*zára3* [1s1]	زرع
to irrigate	*ráwa* [1d2]	رَوى
harvest	*ɦaṣād*	حصاد
to harvest	*gáma3* [1s1] *ilmaɦṣūl*	جمع المحْصول
wheat	*ʔamɦ*	قمْح
corn	*dúra*	دُرة
grain, cereals	*ɦubūb* [pl.]	حُبوب

30 Military

war	*ɧarb* [f.] *(ɧurūb)*	حرْب (حُروب)
peace	*salām*	سلام
to declare war on	*á3lan* [4s] *ilɧárbᵊ 3ála*	أعْلن الحرْب على
to be at war with	*kān* [1h1] *fi ɧarbᵊ ḑidd*	كان في حرْب ضِدّ
military	*3askári*	عسْكري
army	*gēš*	جيْش
air force	*quwwāt gawwíyya* [pl.]	قُوّات جوّية
navy	*quwwāt baɧaríyya* [pl.]	قُوّات بحْرية
soldier	*gúndi (gunūdi)*	جُنْدي (جُنودى)
sailor	*baɧɧār*	بحّار
to recruit, enlist	*gánnid* [2s1]	جنِّد
battle	*ma3ráka (ma3ārik)*	معْركة (معارِك)
attack	*hugūm*	هُجوم
to attack	*hāgim* [3s]	هاجِم
to defend	*dāfi3* [3s]	دافِع
defense	*difā3*	دِفاع
bomb	*qunbíla (qanābil)*	قُنْبِلة (قنابِل)
grenade	*qunbíla yadawíyya*	قُنْبِلة يَدَوية
to explode	*infágar* [7s2]	اِنْفجر
explosion	*infigār*	اِنْفِجار
mine	*laɣm (alɣām)*	لغْم (ألْغام)

missile	*şarūx (şawarīx)*	صاروخ (صَواريخ)
tank	*dabbāba*	دبّابة
to occupy	*iђtáll* [8g]	اِحْتلّ
occupation	*iђtilāl*	اِحْتِلال
to liberate	*ђárrar* [2s2]	حرّر
liberation	*taђrīr*	تحْرير

31 The Mind

mind; intelligence	*3aʔl (3uʔūl)*	عقْل (عُقول)
consciousness	*wigdān*	وِجْدان
to think about	*fákkar* [2s2] *fi*	فكّر في
What are you thinking about?	*bitfákkar fi ʔē?*	بِتْفكّر في أيْه؟
to remember	*iftákar* [8s1]	اِفْتكر
Do you remember me?	*fakírni?*	فاكِرْني؟
to remind __ about	*fákkar* [2s2] __ *bi-*	فكّر __ بِ
Remind me to set my alarm.	*fakkárni ʔáẓbuṭ ilminábbih.*	فكّرْني أظْبُط المِنبِّه.
to plan on	*xáṭṭaṭ* [2s2] *li-*	خطّط لِ
plan	*xíṭṭa (xíṭaṭ)*	خِطّة (خِطط)
to forget	*nísi* [1d4]	نِسى
forgetful	*nassāy*	نسّايْ
memory	*zíkra (zikrayāt)*	ذِكْرى (ذِكْرَيات)
to believe	*ṣádda?* [2s2]	صدّق
I don't believe that!	*ána miš miṣádda? da!*	أنا مِش مِصدّق ده!
to understand	*fíhim* [1s4]	فِهِم
to decide	*qárrar* [2s2]	قرّر
decision	*qarār*	قرار
to know	*3írif* [1s4]	عِرِف
knowledge	*ma3rífa (ma3ārif)*	معْرِفة (معارِف)

to imagine	*itxáyyil* [5s1]	اِتْخيِّل
imagination	*xayāl*	خَيال
to guess	*xámmin* [2s1] *ɦázzar* [2s2]	خمِّن حزّر
How did you guess?	*ínta xammínt izzāy?*	إنْتَ خمِّنْت إزّايْ؟
guess	*taxmīn* *taɦzīr*	تخْمين تحْزير
to predict, expect	*itwáqqa3* [5s2]	اِتْوَقّع
crazy, insane (UK: mad)	*magnūn (maganīn)*	مجْنون (مجانين)
intelligent, clever	*záki (azkíya)*	ذكي (أذْكِيا)
intelligence	*zakāʔ*	ذكاء
stupid	*ɣábi (aɣbíya)* *3áʔlu tʔīl*	غبي (أغْبِيا) عقْلُه تْقيل
stupidity, idiocy	*ɣabāwa*	غباوَة

32 Feelings

feeling, emotion	*iħsās* *3āṭifa (3awāṭif)*	إحْساس عاطِفة (عَواطِف)
to feel	*ħass* [1g3] *bi-*	حسّ بِـ
to feel good	*ħassᵊ b-ʔiħsās kuwáyyis*	حسّ بِإحْساس كُوَيِّس
to feel bad	*ħassᵊ bi-ħsās wíħiš*	حسّ بِاحْساس وِحِش
How do you feel?	*ħāsis bi-ʔē?*	حاسِس بِأيْه؟
to laugh	*díħik* [1s4]	ضِحِك
laughter	*díħka*	ضِحْكة
to cry	*3áyyaṭ* [2s2]	عيّط
to smile	*ibtásam* [8s1]	اِبْتسم
to frown	*káššar* [2s2]	كشّر
happy	*farħān*	فرْحان
I'm really happy about the news.	*ána farħān bi-gádd 3ašān simí3t ilʔaxbār di.*	أنا فرْحان بِجدّ عشان سِمِعْت الأخْبار دي.
sad	*ħazīn (ħazāna)*	حزين (حزانى)
upset	*za3lān*	زعْلان
to annoy	*nárviz, nárfis* [11s1] *dāyiʔ* [3s]	نرْفِز ضايِق
angry with __ about, annoyed by, fed up with	*mitḍāyiʔ min __*	مِتْضايِق مِن__
I'm really annoyed at myself for that.	*ána mitdāyiʔ min náfsi 3ašān kída.*	أنا مِتْضايِق مِن نفْسي عشان كِده.

annoying	*múz3ig*	مُزْعِج
to surprise	*fāgiʔ* [3s]	فاجِئ
That really surprises me.	*ilmawdū3 da fagíʔni giddan.*	المَوْضوع ده فاجِئْني جِدّاً.
surprising	*mufāgiʔ*	مُفاجِئ
to be surprised	*itfāgiʔ* [6s]	اِتْفاجِئ
surprised	*mutafāgiʔ*	مُتفاجِئ
excited about	*mutaħámmis li-*	مُتحمِّس لِـ
exciting	*mušáwwiq*	مُشوِّق
tired	*ta3bān*	تعْبان
tiring	*mút3ib*	مُتْعِب
to fear, be afraid of	*xāf* [1h4] *min*	خاف مِن
fear	*xōf*	خوْف
proud of	*faxūr bi-*	فخور بِـ
embarrassed by	*múħrag min* *maksūf min*	مُحْرج مِن مكْسوف مِن
thankful, grateful	*šākir*	شاكِر

33 Personality

personality	*šaxṣíyya*	شخْصية
modest	*mutawāḍi3*	مُتَواضِع
shy	*xagūl*	خجول
friendly	*wadūd*	وَدود
sociable	*igtimā3i*	اِجْتِماعي
cruel, harsh	*ʔāsi*	قاسي
kind	*ṭáyyib*	طيِّب
generous	*karīm*	كريم
greedy	*ṭammā3*	طمّاع
hard-working, diligent	*mugtáhid* *biyištáɣal gāmid*	مُجْتهِد بيِشْتغل جامِد
lazy	*kaslān* *kasūl (kasāla)*	كسْلان كسول (كسالى)
serious	*gadd*	جدّ
funny, jovial, likable	*dámmu xafīf* *xafīf iddámm*	دمُّه خفيف خفيف الدّمّ
nice, pleasant, sweet	*lazīz (luzāz)*	لذيذ (لُذاذ)
jovial, merry, lively	*máriḥ*	مرِح
strange	*ɣarīb*	غريب
jealous, envious	*ɣayyūr*	غيّور

34 Likes and Dislikes

to like, love	*ħabb* [1g3]	**حبّ**
I like traveling and learning foreign languages.	*baħíbb asāfir w- at3állim luɣāt agnabíyya.*	بحِبّ أسافِر و أتْعلِّم لُغات أجْنبية.
to enjoy	*istámta3* [10s1]	**اِسْتمْتع**
to hate	*kírih* [1s4]	**كِرِهْ**
I hate getting up early.	*bákrah áṣħa bádri.*	بكْرهْ أصْحى بدْري.

interested in	*muhtímmᵊ bi-*	**مُهْتِمّ بِ**
I'm not interested in politics.	*ána miš muhtímmᵊ bi-ssiyāsa.*	أنا مِش مُهْتِمّ بِالسِّياسة.
hobby	*hiwāya*	**هِوايَة**
What are your hobbies?	*hiwáytak ʔē?*	هِوايْتك أيْه؟
to praise	*mádaħ* [1s1]	**مدح**
praise	*madħ*	**مدْح**
to criticize	*intáqad* [8s1]	**اِنْتقد**
criticism	*naqd*	**نقْد**
to complain about	*ištáka* [8d]	**اِشْتكى**
complaint	*šákwa (šakāwi)*	**شكْوى (شكاوي)**
to admire, like	*ú3gib bi-* [4sp] (lit. to be pleased by) *mú3gab bi-*	**أُعْجِب بِ** **مُعْجب بِ**
I love this color.	*ána mú3gab bi-llōn da.*	أنا مُعْجب بِاللّوْن ده.

to prefer __ to	*fáḍḍal* [2s2] *__ 3an*	**فضّل __ عن**
I prefer the train to the bus.	*bafáḍḍal ilʔáʈrᵊ 3an -lʔutubīs.*	بفضّل القطْر عن الأُتوبيس.

35 Opinions and Agreement

to get along with	*kān* [1h1] *3ála wfāq má3a* *ɧabbᵊ* [1g3] *yit3āmil má3a*	**كان على وْفاق معَ** **حبّ يِتْعامِل معَ**
They don’t get along (with each other) very well.	*húmma miš 3ála wfāq áwi má3a ba3ḍ.* *húmma miš biyɧíbbu yit3ámlu má3a ba3ḍ.*	هُمّا مِش على وْفاق أَوي معَ بعْض. هُمّا مِش بِيْحِبّوا يِتْعامْلوا معَ بعْض.
to argue about	*itnāʔiš* [6s] *fi* *gādil* [3s] *3ála*	**اِتْناقِش في** **جادِل على**
They’re always arguing about politics.	*húmma 3ála ṭūl biyitgádlu 3a -ssiyāsa.*	هُمّا على طول بِيِتْجادْلوا عَ السِّياسة.
to have a discussion	*3ándu n(i)qāš*	**عنْدُه نِقاش**
agreement	*muwáfʔa*	**مُوافْقة**
to agree with	*ittáfaʔ* [8s1] *má3a*	**اِتّفق معَ**
to disagree with	*ixtálaf* [8s1] *má3a*	**اِخْتلف معَ**
certain, sure	*mutaʔákkid*	**مُتأكِّد**
okay	*tamām* [okay]	**تمام** **أوْكيْ**

opinion	*raʔy (arāʔ)*	**رأْي (آراء)**
What do you think about __?	*ʔē ráʔyak fi __?*	أيْه رأْيَك في __؟

I think...	*a3táqid* *azúnn* *ána rá?yi*	أعْتقِد أظُنّ أنا رأْيي
in my opinion	*fi názari*	في نظري

36 Desires and Intentions

desire	*ráɣba (raɣabāt)*	**رغْبة (رغبات)**
to desire	*ráɣab* [1s1]	**رغب**
intention	*níyya (nawāya)*	**نية (نَوايا)**
to want	*3āz* [1h1] *nífsu fi*	**عاز** **نِفْسُه في**
I want to...	*ána 3āyiz* *ána 3āwiz*	**أنا عايِز** **أنا عاوِز**
I don't want to eat anything.	*miš 3āyiz ākul ḫāga.*	مِش عايِز آكل حاجة.
I want a car. I wish I had a car.	*ána nífsi f 3arabíyya.*	أنا نِفْسي في عربية.
to wish, hope	*itmánna* [5d]	**اِتْمنّى**
I hope that...	*atmánna* *in šāʔ aɫɫāh* *ya rabb*	**أتْمنّى** **إن شاء اللّه** **يا ربّ**
I hope to see you again.	*atmánna -šūfak tāni.*	أتْمنّى أشوفك تاني.
I hope nothing happened to him.	*ya rabbᵊ ma-yigralūš ḫāga.*	يا ربّ مَيجْرالوش حاجة.
to wish	*ya rēt* *ya rētu*	**يا ريْت** **يا ريْتُه**
I wish I were in Egypt.	*ya rítni kuntᵊ f maṣr.*	يا ريْتني كُنْت في مصر.
to look forward to	*nífsu*	**نِفْسُه**
I'm looking forward to meeting you.	*nífsi ʔaʔáblak.*	نِفْسي أقابْلك.

37 Religion

religion	*dīn (adyān)*	دين (أدْيان)
religious (concerning religion)	*dīni*	ديني
faith, belief	*īmān*	إيمان
secular	*3ilmāni*	عِلْماني
to believe in	*ʔāmin* [3s] *bi-*	آمِن بِـ
Do you believe in God?	*ínta múʔmin bi-llāh?*	إنْتَ مُؤْمِن بِاللّه؟
religious (person)	*mutadáyyin*	مُتديِّن
He's a very religious man.	*húwwa rāgil mutadáyyin gíddan.*	هُوَّ راجِل مُتديِّن جِدّاً.
ceremony	*ṭaʔs (ṭuʔūs)*	طقْس (طُقوس)
to pray	*dá3a* [1d2]	دعا
She prayed to God that her son would be alright.	*híyya dá3it rabbína inn ibnáha yíbʔa kwáyyis.*	هِيَّ دعِت ربِّنا إنّ إبْنها يِبْقى كْوَيِّس.
prayer	*du3āʔ*	دُعاء
soul	*rōḥ (arwāḥ)*	روْح (أرْواح)
heaven, Paradise	*ilgánna*	الجنّة
god	*ilāh (ālíha)*	إلهْ (آلِهة)
a goddess	*ilʔāha*	إلاهة
God Allah	*aɫɫāh*	اللّه
prophet	*nábi (anbíya)*	نبي (أنْبِيا)
messenger	*rasūl (rúsul)*	رسول (رُسُل)

angel	*malāk (maláyka)*	ملاك (ملايْكة)
jinn, genie	*gínni (ginn)*	جِنّي (جِنّ)
hell	*ilgaḫīm*	الجحيم
devil, demon	*šiṭān (šayaṭīn)*	شيطان (شَياطين)
the Devil, Satan	*iššiṭān*	الشّيطان
sin	*zamb (zunūb)*	ذنْب (ذُنوب)
to sin	*ʔáznab* [4s]	أذْنب
evil (noun)	*šarr (šurūr)*	شرّ (شُرور)
evil (adjective)	*širrīr (ašrār)*	شِرّير (أشْرار)

superstition	*xurāfa*	خُرافة
superstitious (person)	*múʔmin bi-lxurāfa*	مُؤْمِن بِالخُرافة
good luck	*ḫazẓᵊ ḫilw*	حظّ حِلْو
bad luck	*ḫazzᵊ wíḫiš*	حظّ وِحِش
pagan	*wásani*	وَثني
paganism	*ilwasaníyya*	الوَثنية

Islam	*islām*	إسْلام
Muslim	*múslim*	مُسْلِم
Islamic	*islāmi*	إسْلامي
The Prophet Muhammad	*innábi muḫámmad*	النّبي مُحمّد
Christianity	*ilmasiḫíyya*	المسيحية
Christian	*masīḫi*	مسيحي

Christ	*ilmasīḫ*	المسيح
Jesus	*3īsa* *yasū3*	عيسى يَسوع

Jesus is called عيسى *3īsa* by Muslims, and يَسوع *yasū3* by Christians.

Judaism	*ilyahudíyya*	اليَهودية
Jew, Jewish	*yahūdi*	يَهودي
Buddhism	*ilbuzíyya*	البوذية
Buddhist	*būzi*	بوذي
Buddha	*būza*	بوذا
Hinduism	*ilhindusíyya*	الهِنْدوسية
Hindu	*hindūsi*	هِنْدوسي
atheism	*ilḫād*	إلْحاد
atheist	*múlḫid*	مُلْحِد

mosque	*gāmi3 (gawāmi3)*	جامِع (جَوامِع)
masjid	*másgid (masāgid)*	مَسْجِد (مساجِد)
Friday prayer	*ṣalāt ilgúm3a*	صلاةْ الجُمْعة
imam	*imām (aʔímma)*	إمام (أئِمّة)
Friday sermon	*xúṭbit ilgúm3a*	خُطْبِةْ الجُمْعة
to preach	*wá3aẓ* [1s2]	وَعظ
call to prayer	*adān*	أدان
to call to prayer	*áddin* [2s1]	أدِّن
ablution (ceremonial washing before praying)	*wuḍūw*	وُضوء

to perform ritual ablutions	*itwáḍḍa* [5d]	اِتْوَضّى
to perform prayer	*ṣálla* [2d]	صلّى
prayer	*ṣalā (ṣalawāt)*	صلاة (صلَوات)
dawn prayer	*ṣalāt ilfágr* *ṣalāt iṣṣubḥ*	صلاةْ الفجْر صلاةْ الصُّبْح
Duha prayer (voluntary morning prayer)	*ṣalāt iḍḍúḥa*	صلاةْ الضُّحى
noon prayer	*ṣalāt iḍḍúhr*	صلاةْ الضُّهْر
afternoon prayer	*ṣalāt il3áṣr*	صلاةْ العصْر
sunset prayer	*ṣalāt ilmáɣrib*	صلاةْ المغْرِب
evening prayer	*ṣalāt il3išāʔ*	صلاةْ العِشاء
Eid prayers	*ṣalāt il3īd*	صلاةْ العيد
Quran	*ilqurʔān*	القُرْآن
to recite the Quran	*tála* [1d3] *-lqurʔān*	تلا القُرْآن
sura (chapter of Quran)	*sūra (síwar)*	سورة (سِوَر)
verse	*āya*	آيَة
Hadith	*ḥadīs (aḥdās)*	حديث (أحْداث)
Sunnah	*issúnna*	السُّنّة

church	*kinīsa (kanāyis)*	كِنيسة (كنايِس)
church service	*xídmit (xadamāt) kinīsa*	خِدْمِةْ (خدمات) كِنيسة
minister, pastor	*kāhin (káhana)*	كاهِن (كهنة)

priest (Catholic, Orthodox)	*ʔissīs (ʔasāwisa)* *rāhib (ruhbān)*	قِسّيس (قساوِسة) راهِب (رُهْبان)
nun	*rahíba*	راهِبة
pope	*bāba*	بابا
to preach about	*báššar* [2s2] *bi-*	بشّر بِـ
sermon	*maw3íẓa (mawā3iẓ)*	مَوْعِظة (مَواعِظ)
pulpit	*mínbar (manābir)*	مِنْبر (منابِر)
altar	*mázbaḫ (mazābiḫ)*	مذْبح (مذابِح)
choir	*gōqa*	جوْقة
Bible	*ilkitāb ilmuqáddis*	الكِتاب المُقدِّس
The New Testament	*ilʔingīl*	الإنْجيل
evangelical	*ingīli*	إنْجيلي
to baptize	*3ámmid* [2s1]	عمِّد
baptism	*ta3mīd*	تعْميد

38 Language

language	*lúɣa*	لُغة
foreign language	*lúɣa ʔagnabíyya*	لُغة أجْنبية
(foreign) accent	*lákna*	لكْنة
native language	*lúɣa ʔumm*	لُغة أُمّ
Chinese	*ṣīni*	صيني
Dutch	*hulándi*	هولنْدي
English	*ingilīzi* [English]	إنْجِليزي إنْجْليش
Farsi	*fársi*	فارْسي
French	*faransāwi*	فرنْساوي
German	*almāni*	ألْماني
Greek	*yunāni*	يوناني
Hebrew	*3íbri*	عِبْري
Hindi	*híndi*	هِنْدي
Italian	*iṭāli*	إيطالي
Japanese	*yabāni*	ياباني
Korean	*kūri*	كوري
Portuguese	*burtuɣāli*	بُرْتُغالي
Russian	*rūsi*	روسي
Spanish	*asbāni*	أسْباني
Turkish	*túrki*	تُرْكي

Arabic	*3árabi*	عربي
Classical Arabic	*3árabi -lqurʔān* (lit. Arabic of the Quran)	عربي القُرْآن
Modern Standard Arabic	*ilfúṣḫa*	الفُصْحى
dialect	*láhga*	لهْجة
colloquial language	*3ammíyya*	عامية
Egyptian Arabic	*il3ammíyya (-lmaṣríyya)* *il3árabi -lmáṣri* *máṣri* *illáhga -lmaṣríyya*	العامية (المصْرية) العربي المصْري مصْري اللّهْجة المصْرية
Moroccan Arabic	*il3árabi -lmaɣrábi*	العربي المغْربي
Levantine Arabic	*il3árabi -ššāmi*	العربي الشّامي
Gulf Arabic	*il3árabi -lxalīgi*	العربي الخليجي

to learn	*it3állim* [5s1]	اِتْعلِّم
practice, exercise	*tadrīb* *tamrīn (tamarīn)*	تدْريب تمْرين (تمارين)
to practice	*itdárrab* [5s2] *3ála* *itmárran* [5s2] *3ála*	اِتْدرّب على اِتْمرّن على
level	*mustáwa (mustawayāt)*	مُسْتَوى (مُسْتَوَيات)
beginner's	*mubtádi*	مُبْتدي
intermediate	*mutawássiṭ*	مُتَوَسِّط
advanced	*3āli*	عالي

writing	*kitāba*	كِتابة
to write	*kátab* [1s2]	كتب
reading	*ʔirāya*	قِرايَة
to read	*ʔára* [1d1]	قرا
alphabet	*ilḫurūf ilʔabgadíyya*	الحُروف الأبْجدية
letter	*ḫarf (ḫurūf)*	حرف (حُروف)
Chinese characters	*ilḫurūf iṣṣiníyya*	الحُروف الصِّينية
to spell	*istahágga* [10.d2]	اِسْتهجّى
spelling	*higāʔ*	حِجاء
How do you spell that?	*ilkílma di titkítib izzāy?* (lit. How is that word written?)	الكِلْمة دي تِتْكِتِب إزّايْ؟
handwriting, penmanship	*xaṭṭ*	خطّ
I have such bad penmanship.	*ána xáṭṭi wíḫiš.*	أنا خطّي وِحِش.
legible	*biyitʔíri*	بِيِتْقِري
illegible	*ma-byitʔirīš*	مبْيِتْقِريش
His handwriting is completely illegible.	*xáṭṭu ma-yitʔirīš xāliṣ.*	خطُّه مَيِتْقِريش خالِص.
calligraphy	*fann irrásmᵊ bi-lxáṭṭ*	فنّ الرّسْم بِالخطّ

speaking, speech	*muḫádsa* *kalām*	مُحادْثة كلام

I need to practice speaking more.	*ána miђtāg atdárrab 3ála -lmuђádsa ʔáktar min kída.*	أنا مِحْتاج أتْدرّب على المُحادْثة أكْتر مِن كِده.
You can't understand anything he says.	*kalāmu ma-byitfihímš.*	كلامُه مبْيِتْفِهِمْش.
to speak	*itkállim* [5s1]	**اِتْكلِّم**
Can you speak Arabic?	*bití3raf titkállim 3árabi?*	بِتِعْرف تِتْكلِّم عربي؟
I know a few words.	*ána 3ārif šuwáyyit kalamāt.*	أنا عارِف شُوَيِّةْ كلمات.
I know some basic Arabic.	*á3raf ђagāt basīṭa fi -l3árabi.*	**أعْرف حاجات بسيطة في العربي.**
I can speak a little Arabic.	*bá3raf atkállim šuwáyya 3árabi.*	بعْرف أتْكلِّم شُوَيَّة عربي.
I can get by in Arabic.	*ána māši fi -l3árabi.*	أنا ماشي في العربي.
I speak Arabic pretty well.	*batkállim 3árabi kuwáyyis.*	بتْكلِّم عربي كُوَيِّس.
broken Arabic	*3árabi mikássar*	**عربي مِكسّر**
fluently	*líblib* *zayy illíblib* *bi-ṭalāqa*	**لِبْلِب** **زيّ اللِّبْلِب** **بِطلاقة**
I speak Arabic fluently.	*ána líblib fi -l3árabi.*	أنا لِبْلِب في العربي.
pronunciation	*nuṭʔ*	**نُطْق**
How do you pronounce this word?	*ilkílma di nuṭʔáha izzāy?*	الكِلْمة دي نُطْقها إزّايْ؟
to pronounce	*náṭaʔ* [1s1]	**نطق**

Your Arabic pronunciation is quite good.	*bitínṭaʔ 3árabi kuwáyyis áwi.*	بِتِنْطق عربي كْوَيِّس أَوي.

listening	*samā3*	**سماع**
I need to work on my listening skills in Arabic.	*lāzim aštáɣal 3ála tamarīn issamā3 bi-l3árabi.*	لازِم أشْتغل على تمارين السّماع بِالعربي.
to listen to	*sími3* [1s4]	**سِمِع**

vocabulary	*mufradāt* [pl.]	**مُفْردات**
word	*kílma (kalamāt)*	**كِلْمة (كلمات)**
dictionary	*qamūs (qawamīs)*	**قاموس (قَواميس)**
to look up a word in the dictionary	*dáwwar* [2s2] *3ála kílma min ilqamūs*	**دوّر على كِلْمة مِن القاموس**
flashcard	*biṭāʔit istizkār*	**بِطاقِةْ اِسْتِذْكار**
to repeat	*kárrar* [2s2]	**كرّر**
repetition	*tikrār*	**تِكْرار**

grammar	*naħw*	**نحْو**
grammatical	*náħawi*	**نحَوي**
grammatical rule	*qá3da (qawā3id) naħawíyya*	**قاعْدة (قَواعِد) نحَوية**
to inflect, conjugate, decline	*ṣárraf* [2s2]	**صرّف**

inflection, conjugation, declension	*taşrīf*	تصْريف
suffix	*ɧarfᵊ f- āxir ilkílma*	حرْف في آخِر الكِلْمة
prefix	*ɧarfᵊ f- áwwil ilkílma*	حرْف في أوِّل الكِلْمة
case	*ɧāla*	حالة
tense	*záman (azmān)*	زمن (أزْمان)
gender	*gins (agnās)*	جِنْس (أجْناس)
singular	*múfrad*	مُفْرد
dual	*musánna*	مُثنّى
plural	*gam3*	جمْع
masculine	*muzákkar*	مُذكّر
feminine	*muʔánnas*	مُؤنّث
neuter	*muɧāyid*	مُحايِد
the present tense	*záman ilmuḑāri3*	زمن المُضارِع
the past tense	*záman ilmāḑi*	زمن الماضي
the future tense	*záman ilmustáʔbal*	زمن المُسْتقْبل
article	*adāt ta3rīf* [pl.]	أداةْ تعْريف
preposition	*ɧarfᵊ garr*	حرْف جرّ
noun	*ism (asmāʔ)*	إسْم (أسْماء)
verb	*fi3l (af3āl)*	فِعْل (أفْعال)
adjective	*şífa*	صِفة
adverb	*ẓarf (ẓurūf)*	ظرْف (ظُروف)
subject	*fā3il*	فاعِل

object	*maf3ūl bíhi*	مفْعول بِهِ
definite	*muħáddad*	مُحدّد
indefinite	*ɣēr muħáddad*	غيْر مُحدّد
word order	*tartīb ilkalamāt*	ترْتيب الكلمات
sentence	*gúmla (gúmal)*	جُمْلة (جُمل)
paragraph	*fáqra (faqarāt)*	فقْرة (فقرات)
vowel	*ħarfᵉ mutaħárrik*	حرْف مُتحرِّك
consonant	*ħarfᵉ sākin*	حرْف ساكِن
syllable	*máqṭa3*	مقْطع

punctuation	*tarqīm*	ترْقيم
punctuation mark	*3alāmit tarqīm*	علامِةْ ترْقيم
period (UK: full stop)	*núʔṭa (núʔaṭ)*	نُقْطة (نُقط)
comma	*fáṣla*	فاصْلة
exclamation mark	*3alāmit ta3ággub*	علامِةْ تعجُّب
question mark	*3alāmit istifhām*	علامِةْ اِسْتِفْهام
quotation mark	*faṣlitēn* [dual]	فصْلِتيْن

Quotation marks are not consistently used in Arabic. Quotes are often introduced with a colon.

colon	*nuʔṭitēn* [dual]	نُقْطِتيْن
parenthesis, bracket	*qōs (aqwās)*	قوْس (أقْواس)
(a pair of) parentheses	*qusēn* [dual]	قوسيْن

39 Countries and Nationalities

country, nation	*bálad* [f.] *(bilād)*	**بلد (بِلاد)**
What countries have you been to?	*ʔē ilbilād ílli zurtáha?*	أيْه البِلاد اللي زُرْتها؟
international	*dáwli*	**دَوْلي**
worldwide	*3ālami*	**عالمي**
culture	*saqāfa*	**ثقافة**
foreign; foreigner	*agnábi (agānib)*	**أجْنبي (أجانِب)**

nationality, citizenship	*ginsíyya*	**جِنْسية**
Where are you from?	*ínta mnēn?*	إنْتَ مِنيْن؟
I'm from Egypt.	*ána min maşr.*	أنا مِن مصْر.
I'm Egyptian.	*ána máşri.*	أنا مصْري.

Arab	*3árabi (3árab)*	**عربي (عرب)**

Although Egyptians consider themselves part of the Arab world, when they speak of 'an Arab' they are usually referring to someone from the Arabian Peninsula.

The Arab World	*il3ālam il3árabi*	**العالم العربي**

Countries are feminine in Arabic. The only exceptions are five Arab countries, noted as masculine below.

Egypt **Egyptian**	*maşr* *máşri*	**مصْر** **مصْري**
Sudan **Sudanese**	*issudān* [m.] *sudāni*	**السّودان** **سوداني**

Libya **Libyan**	*líbya* *lībi*	ليبْيا ليبي
Tunisia **Tunisian**	*tūnis* *túnsi*	تونِس تونْسي
Algeria **Algerian**	*ilgazāyir* *gazáyri*	الجزايِر جزايْري
Morocco **Moroccan**	*ilmáɣrib* [m.] *maɣríbi*	المغْرِب مغْرِبي
Palestine **Palestinian**	*filisṭīn* *filisṭīni*	فِلِسْطين فِلِسْطيني
Jordan **Jordanian**	*ilʔúrdun* [m.] *urdúni*	الأُرْدُن أُرْدُني
Lebanon **Lebanese**	*libnān* [m.] *libnāni*	لِبْنان لِبْناني
Syria **Syrian**	*súrya* *sūri*	سورْيا سوري
Iraq **Iraqi**	*il3irāʔ* [m.] *3irāʔi*	العِراق عِراقي
Kuwait **Kuwaiti**	*ilkuwēt* *kuwēti*	الكُويْت كُويْتي
Qatar **Qatari**	*qáṭar* *qáṭari*	قطر قطري
Bahrain **Bahraini**	*ilbaḥrēn* *baḥrēni*	البحْريْن بحْريْني

The Emirates	*ilʔimarāt*	الإمارات
Emirati	*imarāti*	إماراتي
Saudi Arabia	*issu3udíyya*	السُّعودية
Saudi	*su3ūdi*	سُعودي
Oman	*3umān*	عُمان
Omani	*3umāni*	عُماني
Yemen	*ilyáman*	اليَمن
Yemeni	*yámani*	يَمني
Somalia	*iṣṣumāl*	الصّومال
Somali	*ṣumāli*	صومالي

Nationalities, adjectives, and languages are regularly formed from the names of countries by adding the suffix ـي *-i,* as seen in the section above. This requires first removing any definite articles and ـا *-a* or ـيا *-ya* endings. These forms are only listed for countries in the following section if there is a notable variation or irregular plural.

Ethiopia	*asyōbiya*	أثْيوْبِيا
Nigeria	*nayžírya*	نَيْچيرْيا
South Africa	*ganūb afríqya*	جنوب أفْريقْيا

Norway	*innurwīg*	النّرْويج
Sweden	*issiwīd*	السِّويد
Swedish	*siwīdi*	سِويدي
Finland	*finlánda*	فِنْلنْدا
Denmark	*iddanimárk*	الدّانمِارْك

Germany **German**	*almánya* *almāni (almān)*	أَلْمانْيا أَلْماني (أَلْمان)
The Netherlands, Holland	*hulánda*	هولانْدا
Belgium	*balžīka*	بلْچيكا
Ireland	*ayirlánda*	أَيِرْلنْدا
Great Britain	*biriṭánya*	بِريطانْيا
England **English**	*ingiltíra* *ingilīzi (ingilīz)*	إنْجِلْترِا إنْجِليزي (إنْجِليز)
Scotland	*iskutlánda*	إسْكُتْلنْدا
Wales	*welz*	ويْلز
France **French**	*faránsa* *faransāwi*	فرنْسا فرنْساوي
Spain	*asbánya*	أَسْبانْيا
Portugal	*burtuɣāl*	بُرْتُغال
Switzerland	*suwísra*	سُويسْرا
Italy	*iṭálya*	إيطالْيا
Austria **Austrian**	*innímsa* *nimsāwi*	النِّمْسا نِمْساوي
The Czech Republic **Czech**	*tšīkiya* *tšīki*	تْشيكِيا تْشيكي
Slovakia	*siluvákya*	سِلوڤاكْيا
Poland	*bulánda*	بولنْدا
Hungary	*ilmágar*	المجر
Romania	*rumánya*	رومانْيا

Bulgaria	*bulɣárya*	بُلْغارْيا
Turkey **Turkish**	*turkíya* *túrki (atrāk)*	تُرْكِيا تُرْكي (أتْراك)
Ukraine	*ukránya*	أوكْرانْيا
Russia	*rúsya*	روسْيا

Iran	*irān*	إيران
Afghanistan **Afghan**	*afɣanistān* *afɣāni*	أفْغانِسْتان أفْغاني
Pakistan	*bakistān*	باكِسْتان
India	*ilhínd*	الهِنْد
China	*iṣṣīn*	الصّين
South Korea	*kúrya -lganubíyya*	كورْيا الجنوبية
Japan	*ilyabān*	اليابان
Taiwan	*taywān*	تايْوان
Thailand	*taylánda*	تايْلانْدا
Vietnam	*vitnām*	ڤيتْنام
Malaysia	*malēziya*	ماليْزِيا
Indonesia	*indunīsiya*	إنْدونيسِيا
The Philippines	*ilfilibīn*	الفِلِبين

Australia	*usturálya*	أُسْتُرالْيا
New Zealand	*nyuzilánda*	نْيوزيلنْدا

Canada	*kánada*	كندا
The United States **American**	*ilwilayāt ilmuttáɦida* *amrikāni (amrikān)*	الوِلايات المتّحِدة أمْريكاني (أمْريكان)
Mexico	*ilmiksīk*	المِكْسيك
Colombia	*kulumbíya*	كولومْبِيا
Venezuela	*vinziwēla*	ڤِنْزِويْلا
Brazil	*ilbarazīl*	البرازيل
Argentina	*ilʔaržantīn*	الأرْچِنْتين
Chile	*tšīli*	شيلي

40 Egypt

In Arabic, all cities are feminine.

The Mediterranean Sea	*ilbáħr ilmutawássiṭ*	البحْر المُتَوَسِّط
The North Coast	*issāħil iššamāli*	السّاحِل الشّمالي
Mersa Matruh	*mársa maṭrūħ*	مرْسى مطْروح
The Delta (region)	*iddílta*	الدِّلْتا
Alexandria	*iskindiríyya*	إسْكِنْدِرية
Cairo-Alexandria Desert Road (highway)	*ṭarīʔ maṣr - iskindiríyya -ṣṣaħrāwi*	طريق مصْر - إسْكِنْدِرية الصّحْراوي
Agami	*il3ágami*	العجمي
Damanhur	*damanhūr*	دمنْهور
Tanta	*ṭánṭa*	طنْطا
Port Said	*bur sa3īd*	بور سعيد
Al-Mahalla Al-Kubra	*ilmaħálla -lkúbra*	المحلّة الكُبْرى
Mansoura	*ilmanṣūra*	المنْصورة
Zagazig	*izzaʔazīʔ*	الزّقازيق
Benha	*bánha*	بنْها
Damietta	*dumyāṭ*	دُمْياط
Suez	*issuwēs*	السُّويْس
Ismaïlia	*ilʔisma3ilíyya*	الإسْماعيلية

The Gulf of Suez	*xalīg issuwēs*	خليج السُّويْس
The Suez Canal	*qanāt issuwēs* *ilqanāl*	قناةْ السُّويْس القنال

Sinai (region and peninsula)	*sīna*	سينا
Sharm el-Sheikh	*šarm iššēx*	شرْم الشّيْخ
The Gulf of Aqaba	*xalīg il3áqaba*	خليج العقبة

Cairo	*ilqāhíra* *maṣr*	القاهِرة مصْر
Giza	*ilgīza*	الجيزة
Saqqara	*saʔʔāra*	سقّاره

Upper Egypt	*iṣṣi3īd* *ṣi3īd maṣr*	الصّعيد صِعيد مصْر
Faiyum	*ilfayyūm*	الفيّوم
Beni Suef	*baniswēf*	بني سْويْف
Minya	*ilmínya*	المِنْيا
Asyut	*asyūṭ*	أسْيوط
Sohag	*suhāg*	سوهاج
Qena	*ʔína*	قِنا
Luxor	*ilʔúʔṣur*	الأُقْصُر
The Valley of the Kings	*wádi -lmulūk*	وادي المُلوك

Aswan	*aswān*	أسْوان
The Aswan Dam	*issádd il3āli* (lit. the High Dam)	السّد العالي
Abu Simbel	*abū símbil*	أبو سِمْبِل

The Eastern Desert (desert region to the east of the Nile)	*iṣṣáɦara -ššarʔíyya*	الصّحْرا الشّرْقية
The Red Sea	*ilbáɦr ilʔáɦmar*	البحْر الأحْمر
Hurghada	*ilɣardáʔa*	الغرْدقة

The Western Desert (desert region to the west of the Nile)	*iṣṣáɦara -lɣarbíyya*	الصّحْرا الغرْبية
Siwa (oasis and village)	*sīwa*	سيوَة
The White Desert	*iṣṣáɦara -lbēḍa*	الصّحْرا البيْضا
Farafra (oasis and village)	*ilfaráfra*	الفرافْرة
Bahariya Oasis	*ilwaɦāt ilbaɦríyya*	الواحات البحْرية

41 Greater Cairo

Greater Cairo	*ilqāhíra -lkúbra*	القاهِرة الكُبْرى

Greater Cairo is made up Cairo itself, as well as the cities of Giza, Shubra El-Kheima, Helwan, 6th of October City, and Obour City.

Cairo (on the east bank of the Nile)	*ilqāhíra* *maşr*	القاهِرة مصْر

Egyptians, especially those in rural areas, habitually refer to Cairo as مصْر *maşr* 'Egypt.' Context, of course, makes it clear whether the country of Egypt or the city of Cairo is being referred to.

I'm going into Cairo to sell my tomatoes.	*ána nāzil maşr abī3 maђşūl ilʔūţa.*	أنا نازِل مصْر أبيع محْصول القوطة.
Shubra El-Kheima	*šúbra -lxēma*	شُبْرا الخيْمة
Helwan	*ђilwān*	حِلْوان
6th of October City	*assādis min uktōbar* *sítta -ktōbar*	السّادِس مِن أُكْتوْبر سِتّة أُكْتوبر
Obour City	*madīnit il3ubūr*	مدينِةْ العُبور

Tahrir Square	*midān ittaђrīr*	ميدان التّحْرير
The Egyptian Museum	*ilmátђaf ilmáşri*	المتْحف المصْري
Mogamma (government building including immigration office)	*ilmugámma3*	المُجمّع
Qasr al-Ainy Street	*šāri3 ilʔáşr il3ēni*	شارِع القصْر العيْني
The American University in Cairo (AUC)	*ilgám3a -lʔamrikíyya fi -lqāhíra*	الجامْعة الأمْريكية في القاهِرة

Garden City (district)	[Garden City]	جارْدِن سيتى
The Nile Corniche	*kurnīš innīl* *ilkurnīš*	كورْنيش النّيل الكورْنيش
The Ring Road	*iṭṭarīʔ iddáyri*	الطّريق الدّايْري

Talaat Harb Square	*midān ṭál3at ɦarb*	ميدان طلْعت حرْب
Groppi Café	*grúppi kafēh*	جْروبّي كافيْهْ
Café Riche	*kafēh rīš*	كافيْهْ ريش

The Nile	*innīl*	النّيل
Gazira Island	*ilgizīra*	الجِزيرة
Cairo Tower	*burg ilqāhíra*	بُرْج القاهِرة
Cairo Opera House	*dār ilʔúbra -lmaṣríyya* *dār ilʔúbra -lgidīda*	دار الأوبْرا المصْرية دار الأوبْرا الجِديدة
Zamalek (district)	*izzamālik*	الزّمالِك
Gezira Sporting Club	*nādi -lgizīra -rriyāḍi*	نادي الجِزيرة الرِّياضي
El Sawy Culture Wheel	*sáʔyit iṣṣāwi*	ساقْيِةْ الصّاوي
The Qasr Al-Nil Bridge	*kúbri ʔaṣr innīl*	كوبْري قصْر النّيل
The 6th of October Bridge	*kúbri sítta -ktōbar*	كوبْري ٦ أُكْتوْبر

Islamic Cairo	*ilqāhíra -lfaṭimíyya*	القاهِرة الفاطِمية
Al-Azhar Park	*ɦadīqit ilʔázhar*	حديقِةْ الأزْهر
The Citadel	*ilʔál3a*	القلْعة

City of the Dead (cemetary and slum)	*ilʔarāfa*	القرافة
Khan el-Khalili (souk in Islamic Cairo)	*xān ilxalīli*	خان الخليلي
The Mosque of Muhammad Ali	*gāmi3 muђámmad 3áli*	جامع مُحمّد علي
Al-Azhar Mosque	*ilgāmi3 ilʔázhar*	الجامع الأزْهر
Al-Azhar University	*gám3it ilʔázhar*	جامْعِةْ الأزْهر

Old Cairo	*maṣr ilʔadīma*	مصْر القديمة
Coptic Cairo	*ilqāhíra -lʔibṭíyya*	القاهرة القِبْطية
The Hanging Church (Saint Virgin Mary's Coptic Orthodox Church)	*ilkanīsa -lmi3alláʔa*	الكنيسة المِعلّقة
The Coptic Museum	*ilmátђaf ilʔíbṭi*	المتْحف القِبْطي

Heliopolis (district)	*maṣr ilgidīda*	مصْر الجِديده
Nasr City (district)	*madīnit naṣr*	مدينِةْ نصْر
Maadi (district)	*ilma3ādi*	المعادي

Giza (on the west bank of the Nile)	*iggīza*	الجّيزة
Cairo University	*gám3it ilqāhíra*	جامعِةْ القاهِرة
Doqqi (district)	*iddúʔʔi*	الدُّقّي
Agouza (district)	*il3agūza*	العجوزة
Mohandessin (district)	*ilmuhandisīn*	المُهنْدِسين

Gameat Al Dewal Al Arabeya Street	*šāri3 gám3it iddúwal il3arabíyya*	شارِع جامْعِةْ الدُّوَل العربية
Sphinx Square	*midān sifínkis*	ميدان سِفِنْكْس
Ahmed Orabi Street	*šāri3 áḥmad 3urābi*	شارِع أحْمد عُرابي
Pyramids Street	*šāri3 ilʔahrām*	شارِع الأهْرام
The Pyramids of Giza	*ilʔahramāt*	الأهْرامات
The Sphinx	*abū -lhōl*	أبو الهوْل

42 Earth and Space

land; ground, soil; earth	*arḍ* [f.] *(arāḍi)*	أرْض (أراضي)
island	*gizīra (gúzur)*	جِزيرة (جُزُر)
peninsula	*šibh^{ə} gzīra*	شِبْهْ جِزيرة
mountain	*gábal (gibāl)*	جبل (جِبال)
tunnel	*náfaʔ (anfāʔ)*	نفق (أنْفاق)
mountain range	*silsílit gibāl*	سِلْسِلِةْ جِبال
mountainous, hilly	*gábali*	جبلي
hill	*tall (tilāl)*	تلّ (تِلال)
flat	*musáṭṭaḥ*	مُسطّح
plateau	*háḍaba (hiḍāb)*	هضبة (هِضاب)
valley	*wādi (widyān)*	وادي (وِدْيان)
ravine, gorge	*wādi 3amīq*	وادي عميق
cliff	*gáraf (gurūf)*	جرف (جُروف)

continent	*qárra*	قارّة
North America	*amrīka -ššamalíyya* [f.]	أمْريكا الشّمالية
South America	*amrīka -lganubíyya* [f.]	أمْريكا الجنوبية
Europe	*urúbba* [f.]	أوروبّا
Africa	*afríqya* [f.]	أفْريقْيا
Asia	*ásya* [f.]	آسْيا
Australia	*usturálya* [f.]	أُسْتُرالْيا

water	*máyya*	ميّة
to freeze	*itgámmid* [5s1]	اِتْجمّد
to melt	*sāɧ* [1h2]	ساح
sea	*baɧr (biɧār, buɧūr)*	بحْر (بِحار، بُحور)
bay, gulf	*xalīg (xilgān)*	خليج (خِلْجان)
canal	*qanāh (qanawāt)* *tír3a (tíra3)*	قناهْ (قَنوات) تِرْعة (تِرع)
river	*nahr (anhār)*	نهْر (أنْهار)
stream	*gádwal (gadāwil)*	جدْوَل (جداوِل)
lake	*buɧēra*	بُحيْرة
waterfall, cataract	*šallāl*	شلّال
swamp	*mustánqa3*	مُسْتنْقع
ocean	*muɧīṭ*	مُحيط
Pacific Ocean	*ilmuɧīṭ ilhādi*	المُحيط الهادي
Atlantic Ocean	*ilmuɧīṭ ilʔaṭlánṭi*	المُحيط الأطْلنْطي
Indian Ocean	*ilmuɧīṭ ilhíndi*	المُحيط الهِنْدي
equator	*xaṭṭ ilʔistiwāʔ*	خطّ الاِسْتِواء
the tropics	*ilmanāṭiq ilmadaríyya*	المناطِق المدارية
the arctic	*ilqúṭb iššamāli*	القُطْب الشّمالي
desert	*ṣáɧara (ṣaɧāri)*	صحرا (صحارى)
forest, jungle	*ɣāba*	غابة

plains, grasslands	*suhūl* [pl.]	سُهول
sand dunes	*kusbān ramlíyya* [pl.]	كُثْبان رملية
oasis	*wāɦa*	واحة

volcano	*burkān (barakīn)*	بُرْكان (براكين)
lava	*ɦímam*	حِمم
to erupt	*infágar* [7s2] *sār* [1h1]	اِنْفجر ثار
eruption	*infigār*	اِنْفِجار
dormant, extinct	*xāmid*	خامِد
This volcano hasn't erupted in millions of years.	*ilburkān da xāmid min malayīn issinīn.*	البرُكان ده خامِد مِن ملايين السِّنين.
earthquake	*zilzāl (zalāzil)*	زِلْزال (زلازِل)
an earthquake struck	*zilzāl ḍárab*	زِلْزال ضرب
Did you feel the earthquake this morning?	*ɦassēt bi- zzilzāl innahárda -ṣṣubɦ?*	حسّيْت بِالزِّلْزال النّهارْده الصُّبْح؟

air	*háwa*	هَوا
sky	*sáma (samawāt)*	سما (سمَوات)
moon	*ʔámar (iʔmār)*	قمر (إقْمار)
planet	*káwkab (kawākib)*	كَوْكب (كَواكِب)
sun	*šams* [f.] *(šumūs)*	شمْس (شُموس)
star	*nígma*	نِجْمة
universe, cosmos	*kōn (akwān)*	كوْن (أكْوان)

space, outer space	*ilfaḍāʔ*	**الفضاء**
comet	*muzánnab*	**مُذنّب**
meteorite, falling star	*šihāb (šúhub)*	**شِهاب (شُهُب)**
sunlight	*nūr iššáms*	**نور الشّمْس**
sunrise	*šurūʔ (iššáms)*	**شُروق (ألشّمْس)**
The sun rises in the east.	*iššámsᵊ btúšruʔ min iššárʔ.*	الشّمْس بْتُشْرُق مِن الشّرْق.
sunset	*ɣurūb (iššáms)*	**غُروب (الشّمْس)**
The sun sets in the west.	*iššámsᵊ btúɣrub min ilɣárb.*	الشّمْس بْتُغْرُب مِن الغرْب.
dusk, twilight	*ɣásaʔ*	**غسق**

compass	*búṣla*	**بوصْلة**
map	*xarīṭa (xarāyiṭ)*	**خريطة (خرايِط)**
north	*šamāl*	**شمال**
south	*ganūb*	**جنوب**
west	*ɣarb*	**غرْب**
east	*šarʔ*	**شرْق**
northwest	*šamāl ɣarb*	**شمال غرْب**
southwest	*ganūb ɣarb*	**جنوب غرْب**
northeast	*šamāl šarʔ*	**شمال شرْق**
southeast	*ganūb šarʔ*	**جنوب شرْق**
Alexandria is in the north of Egypt.	*iskindiríyya f- šamāl maṣr.*	إسْكِنْدِرية في شمال مصْر.

Sudan is to the south of Egypt.	*issudān ganūb maʂr.*	السّودان جنوب مصْر.
northern	*šamāli*	**شمالي**
southern	*ganūbi*	**جنوبي**
western	*ɣárbi*	**غرْبي**
eastern	*šárʔi*	**شرْقي**
the north pole	*ilqúʈb iššamāli*	**القُطْب الشّمالي**
the south pole	*ilqúʈb ilganūbi*	**القُطْب الجنوبي**

43 Weather

weather	*gaww* *ţaʔs*	**جوّ** **طقْس**
What's the weather like today?	*ilgáwwᵊ 3āmil ʔē innahárda?*	الجوّ عامِل أيْه النّهارْده؟
The weather is __.	*ilgáww(ᵊ) __.*	الجوّ.__
good, nice, fair	*ɧilw* *gamīl*	**حِلْو** **جميل**
bad, miserable	*wíɧiš* *bíši3*	**وِحِش** **بِشِع**
What a nice day!	*innahárda yōm ɧilw!*	**النّهارْده يوْم حِلْو!**

temperature	*dáragit ɧarāra*	**درجِةْ حرارة**
What's the temperature?	*dáragit ilɧarāra kām?*	درجِةْ الحرارة كام؟
Keep in mind that Egyptians use Celsius, and not Fahrenheit.		
(It's) 25 degrees.	*xámsa wi 3išrīn dáraga.*	خمْسة و عِشْرين درجة.
It's in the low twenties.	*dáragit ilɧarāra f- bidayāt il3išrīn.*	درجِةْ الحرارة في بِدايات العِشْرين.
in the mid-twenties	*fi wisţ il3išrīn*	**في وِسْط العِشْرين**
in the high twenties	*fi ʔawāxir il3išrīn*	**في أَواخِر العِشْرين**
It's around 30 degrees.	*ɧawāli talatīn dáraga.*	حَوالي تلاتين درجة.
It's over 30 degrees.	*áktar min talatīn dáraga.*	أكْتر مِن تلاتين درجة.

It's below zero. It's below freezing.	*dáragit ilħarāra taħt iṣṣífr.*	درجِةْ الحرارة تحْت الصِّفْر.
the maximum temperature, the high	*dáragit ilħarāra -lkúbra*	**درجِةْ الحرارة الكُبْرى**
the minimum temperature, the low	*dáragit ilħarāra -ṣṣúɣra*	**درجِةْ الحرارة الصُّغْرى**

الجوّ *ilgáww* or الدُّنْيا *iddúnya* serve as subjects when talking about the weather, where in English the subject would be "it," as in "It's hot," "It's sunny." The predicate can be a true adjective, or a noun used adjectivally. Keep in mind that nouns, unlike true adjectives, are invariable and do not have a feminine form.

It's __.	*ilgáww(e)__.* *iddúnya __.*	الجوّ __. الدُّنْيا.__
heat	*ħarr*	**حرّ**
It's very hot.	*ilgáwwᵊ ħarrᵊ áwi.* *iddúnya ħarrᵊ áwi.*	الجوّ حرّ أَوي. الدُّنْيا حرّ أَوي.
warmth	*dáfa*	**دفا**
coolness, coldness	*bard*	**برْد**
It's really cold.	*iddúnya bardᵊ áwi.*	الدُّنْيا برْد أَوي.
It's freezing outside.	*ilgáwwᵊ talgᵊ bárra.*	الجوّ تلْج برّه.
heatwave	*mōga ħárra* *mōgit ħarr*	**موْجة حارّة** **موْجِةْ حرّ**
How hot does it get where you're from?	*ilgáwwᵊ ħarrᵊ ʔaddᵊ ʔē fi baládkum?*	الجوّ حرّ أدّ أيْه في بلدْكُم؟

Where I'm from, it doesn't usually get over 30 degrees in the summer.	*ɣālíban dáragit ilḫarāra ma-bit3addīš talatīn fi -ṣṣēf fi báladi.*	غالِباً درجِةْ الحرارة مبِتْعدّيش تلاتين في الصّيْف في بلدي.
It's hotter than it was yesterday.	*ilgáwwᵊ ḫarr áktar min imbāriḫ.*	الجوّ حرّ أكْتر مِن إمْبارِح.
I don't like hot weather.	*ma-baḫíbbiš ilḫárr.*	مبحِبِّش الحرّ.

sky	*sáma (samawāt)*	**سما (سمَوات)**
The sky is clear.	*issáma ṣáfya.*	السّما صافْيَة.
It's sunny.	*ilgáwwᵊ múšmis.*	الجوّ مُشْمِس.
sun	*šams* [f.] *(šumūs)*	**شمْس (شُموس)**
The sun has come out.	*iššámsᵊ ẓáharit.*	الشّمْس ظهرِت.
The sun is shining.	*iššámsᵊ mušríʔa.*	الشّمْس مُشْرِقة.
darkness	*ḍálma*	**ضلْمة**
It's dark.	*iddúnya ḍálma.*	الدُّنْيا ضلْمة.
cloud	*saḫāba (súḫub)*	**سحابة (سُحُب)**
It's cloudy. It's overcast.	*ilgáwwᵊ mɣáyyim.*	الجوّ مُغيِّم.

rain	*máṭar* *máṭara*	**مطر** **مطرة**
It is raining. It's rainy.	*iddúnya bitmáṭṭar.*	الدُّنْيا بِتْمطّر.
It's started to rain.	*iddúnya bádaʔit timáṭṭar.*	الدُّنْيا بدأِت تِمطّر.

It's stopped raining.	*ilmáṭara wíʔfit.*	المطْرة وِقْفِت.
It is pouring.	*iddúnya bitrúxx.*	الدُّنْيا بِترُخّ.
It is drizzling.	*iddúnya bitnádda3.*	الدُّنْيا بِتْندّع.
rainbow	*qōs (aqwās) qázaḫ*	**قوْس (أقْواس) قزح**

wind	*rīḫ (riyāḫ)*	ريح (رِياح)
It's windy.	*ilḫáwa gāmid. (lit. The air is strong.)*	الهَوا جامِد.
to blow	*habb* [1g3]	**هبّ**
khamsin (hot, dusty southerly wind in the spring)	*ilxamasīn*	**الخماسين**

snow	*talg*	**تلْج**
It's snowing.	*iddúnya bitmáṭṭar talg.*	الدُّنْيا بِتْمطّر تلْج.
Does it snow where you're from?	*iddúnya bitmáṭṭar talgᵊ 3andúkum?*	الدُّنْيا بِتْمطّر تلْج عنْدُكُم؟
Where I'm from, it snows a lot in the winter.	*iddúnya bitmáṭṭar talgᵊ ktīr fi -ššíta fi báladi.*	الدُّنْيا بِتْمطّر تلْج كِتير في الشِّتا في بلدي.
hail	*bard*	**برْد**
It's hailing.	*iddúnya bitmáṭṭar bard.*	الدُّنْيا بِتْمطّر برْد.
fog	*ḍabāb*	**ضباب**
It's foggy.	*fī ḍabāb.*	فيه ضباب.

storm	*3āṣífa (3awāṣif)*	**عاصِفة (عَواصِف)**

There's a windstorm. It's stormy.	*ilgáwwᵊ 3āşif.*	الجوّ عاصِف.
There's a rainstorm.	*fī 3āşífa mumṭira.*	فيه عاصِفة مُمْطِرة.
sandstorm, dust storm	*3āşífa turabíyya*	**عاصِفة تُرابية**
hurricane, typhoon, cyclone	*i3şār (a3aşīr)*	**إعْصار (أعاصير)**
tornado	*i3şār qáma3i*	**إعْصار قمعي**
dust devil	*zawbá3a (zawābi3)*	**زَوْبعة (زَوابِع)**
the eye of the storm	*márkaz ilʔi3şār*	**مرْكز الإعْصار**
lightning	*barʔ*	**برْق**
There was a flash of lightning.	*kān fī barʔ.*	كان فيه برْق.
Lightning struck the tree.	*ilbárʔᵊ ḍárab iššágara.*	البرْق ضرب الشّجرة.
thunder	*ra3d*	**رعْد**
The thunder woke me up last night.	*şōt irrá3dᵊ şaħħāni -mbāriħ bi-llēl.*	صوْت الرّعْد صحّاني إمْبارِح بِاللّيْل.

weather forecast	*tawaqqa3āt ilgáww*	**تَوَقّعات الجوّ**
What's the forecast for tomorrow?	*búkra tawaqqa3āt ilgáwwᵊ ʔē?* *axbār ilgáwwᵊ ʔē búkra?*	بُكْره تَوَقّعات الجوّ أيْه؟ أخْبار الجوّ أيْه بُكْره؟
Do you think it's going to rain?	*tiftíkir iddúnya hatmáṭṭar?*	تِفْتِكِر الدُّنْيا هتْمطّر؟
It looks like (it's going to) rain.	*iddúnya šakláha hatmáṭṭar.*	الدُّنْيا شكْلها هتْمطّر
We're expecting a storm.	*íħna mutawaqqa3īn 3āşífa.*	إحْنا مُتوقّعين عاصِفة.

climate	*munāx*	**مُناخ**
arid, dry	*gaff*	**جافّ**
Cairo has a very arid climate.	*gaww ilqāhíra gaffᵊ giddan.*	جوّ القاهرة جافّ جِدّاً.
humid	*ráṭib*	**رطِب**
tropical	*istiwāʔi*	**اِسْتِوائي**
The weather is quite changeable.	*ilgáwwᵊ byitɣáyyar áwi.*	الجوّ بْيِتْغيرّ أَوي.
drought	*qaħṭ* *gafāf*	**قحْط** **جفاف**
flood	*fayaḍān*	**فَيَضان**

44 Animals

animal	*ḫayawān*	**حَيَوان**
pet	*ḫayawān alīf*	**حَيَوان أليف**
Do you have any pets?	*3ándak ḫayawanāt alīfa?*	عنْدك حَيَوانات أليفة؟
dog	*kalb (kilāb)*	**كلْب (كِلاب)**
cat	*ʔúṭṭa (ʔúṭaṭ)*	**قُطّة (قُطط)**
I like cats, but I don't like dogs so much.	*ána baḫíbb ilʔúṭaṭ bassᵊ ma-baḫíbbiš ilkilāb áwi.*	أنا بحِبّ القُطط بسّ مبحِبِّش الكِلاب أَوي.
cage	*ʔáfaṣ (iʔfāṣ)*	**قفص (إقْفاص)**
kennel	*bēt (biyūt) ḫayawanāt*	**بيْت (بِيوت) حَيَوانات**
leash	*ḫablᵊ (ḫibāl) kalb*	**حبْل (حِبال) كلْب**
dog collar	*ṭōʔ (aṭwāʔ) kalb*	**طوْق (أطْواق) كلْب**
to train	*dárrab* [2s2]	**درّب**
(pet) food, feed	*akl*	**أكْل**
to feed	*ʔákkil* [2s1]	**أكِّل**

Both masculine and feminine noun forms exist for most animals. These are, of course, used when referring to animals of a specific gender. Otherwise, it is usually the masculine form that is used to refer to an animal. However, certain animals are more commonly referred to by their feminine forms. The more common form is listed below.

bear	*dibb (díbab)*	**دِبّ (دِبب)**
beaver	*qúndus (qanādis)*	**قُنْدُس (قنادِس)**
buffalo	*gamūsa (gawamīs)*	**جاموسة (جَواميس)**

cheetah	*fahd (fuhūd)*	فهْد (فُهود)
deer, gazelle	*ɣazāla (ɣizlān)*	غزالة (غِزْلان)
elephant	*fīl (afyāl)*	فيل (أفْيال)
fox	*tá3lab (ta3ālib)*	تعْلب (تعالِب)
giraffe	*zarāf* [coll.]	زراف
hippopotamus	*sáyyid ʔíšta (ɧayawanāt sáyyid ʔíšta)*	سيِّد قِشْطة (حَيَوانات سيِّد قِشْطة)
kangaroo	*kangáru*	كنْجارو
koala	*kawāla*	كَوالا
leopard	*fahd*	فهْد
lion	*ásad (usūd)*	أسد (أُسود)
mouse; rat	*fār (firān)*	فار (فِران)
polar bear	*dibbᵊ qúʈbi*	دِب قُطْبي
rabbit	*árnab (arānib)*	أرْنب (أرانِب)
rhinoceros	*waɧīd ilʔárn (ɧayawanāt waɧīd ilʔárn)*	وَحيد القرْن (حَيَوانات وَحيد القرْن)
skunk	*ʐarbān*	ظرْبان
squirrel	*singāb (sanagīb)*	سِنْجاب (سناجيب)
tiger	*nimr (numūr)*	نمِر (نُمور)
wolf	*dīb (diyāba)*	ديب (دِيابة)

seal	*kalb (kilāb) baɧr*	كلْب (كِلاب) بحْر
sealion	*ásad (usūd) baɧr*	أسد (أُسود) بحْر

dolphin	*dúlfin*	دولْفين
whale	*ḫūt (ḫitān)*	حوت (حِتان)

bird	*ţēr (ţuyūr)*	طيْر (طُيور)
canary	*kanárya*	كنارْيا
crow, raven	*ɣurāb (ɣirbān)*	غُراب (غِرْبان)
dove	*yamāma*	يَمامة
eagle, condor, vulture	*nisr (nusūr)*	نِسْر (نُسور)
hawk, falcon	*şaʔr (şuʔūr)*	صقْر (صُقور)
ostrich	*na3āma*	نعامة
parrot	*baɣbaɣān*	بغْبغان
peacock	*ţawūs (ţawawīs)*	طاووس (طَواويس)
penguin	*baţrīq (batāriq)*	بطْريق (بطارِق)
pigeon	*ḫamāma*	حمامة
seagull	*nōras (nawāris)*	نوْرس (نَوارِس)
small bird (sparrow, finch, etc.)	*3aşfūr (3aşafīr)*	عصْفور (عصافير)
stork	*luʔlāʔ (laʔāliʔ)*	لُقْلاق (لقالِق)
swallow	*sunūnu (sununuwāt)*	سُنونو (سُنونُوات)
swan	*bág3a*	بجْعة

reptiles	*zawāḫif* [pl.]	زَواحِف
cobra	*kúbra*	كوبْرا
crocodile	*timsāḫ (tamasīḫ)*	تِمْساح (تماسيح)

lizard	*siɦlíyya (saɦāli)*	سِحْلية (سحالى)
snake	*ti3bān (ta3abīn)*	تِعْبان (تعابين)
turtle, tortoise	*sulɦífa (salāɦif)*	سُلْحِفة (سلاحِف)

frog	*ḍufdá3a*	ضُفْضعة

fish	*sámak* [coll.]	سمك
shark	*(sámak) ʔirš*	(سمك) قِرْش
jellyfish	*ʔandīl baɦr*	قنْديل بحْر

insect, bug	*ɦášara*	حشرة
ant	*naml* [coll.]	نمْل
bee	*naɦl* [coll.]	نحْل
A bee stung me.	*fī náɦla ʔaraṣítni.*	فيه نحْلة قرصِتْني.
bee-sting	*ʔárṣit náɦla*	قرْصِةْ نحْلة
beehive	*xalíyyit naɦl*	خليةْ نحْل
beetle	*xunfísa (xanāfis)*	خُنْفِسة (خنافِس)
butterfly	*farāša*	فراشة
cockroach	*ṣurṣār (ṣaraṣīr)*	صُرْصار (صراصير)
cricket	*ṣurṣār (ṣaraṣīr) ɣēṭ*	صُرْصار (صراصير) غيْط
dragon-fly	*dibbān tinīn* [coll.]	دِبّان تِنين
flea	*barɣūt (baraɣīt)*	برْغوت (براغيت)
fly	*dibbān* [coll.]	دِبّان

grasshopper, locust	*garād* [coll.]	جراد
louse (lice)	*ʔaml* [coll.]	قمْل
The child has head lice.	*il3áyyil 3ándu ʔamlᵊ f rāsu.*	العيِّل عنْدُه قمْل في راسُه.
mosquito	*namūs* [coll.]	نموس
mosquito bite	*ʔárṣit namūsa*	قرْصِةْ نموسة
A mosquito bit me.	*fī namūsa ʔaraṣítni.*	فيه نموسة قرصِتْني.
moth	*3ítta*	عِتّة
scorpion	*3áʔrab* [coll.] *(3aʔārib)*	عقْرب (عقارِب)
snail	*ḩalazōn* [coll.]	حلزوْن
spider	*3ankabūt (3anākib)*	عنْكبوت (عناكِب)
spider web	*šábakit 3ankabūt*	شبكِةْ عنْكبوت
I'm afraid of spiders.	*ána baxāf min il3anākib.*	أنا بخاف مِن العناكِب.
wasp	*dabbūr (dababīr)*	دبّور (دبابير)
worm	*dūd* [coll.]	دود

beak, bill	*munʔār (manaʔīr)*	مُنْقار) مناقير)
claw, talon	*máxlab (maxālib)*	مخْلب (مخالِب)
feathers	*rīš* [coll.]	ريش
feeler, antenna	*málmas (malāmis)*	ملْمس (ملامِس)
fur	*farw* [coll.]	فرْو
horn, antler	*ʔarn (ʔurūn)*	قرْن (قُرون)
paw, leg	*rigl (riglēn)*	رِجْل (رِجْليْن)

tail	*dēl (diyūl)*	دِيْل (دِيول)
udder, teats	*ḍurū3* [pl.]	ضُروع
wing	*ginā<u>h</u> (agní<u>h</u>a)*	جِناح (أجْنِحة)

45 Plant Life

plant	*nabāt* [coll.] *nábta*	نبات نبْتة
tree	*šágar* [coll.]	شجر
bush, shrub	*šugáyra*	شُجَيْرة
leaf	*wáraʔ (awrāʔ) šágar* [coll.]	وَرق (أَوْراق) شجر
branch	*far3 (furū3)*	فرْع (فُروع)
trunk	*giz3 (guzū3)*	جِذْع (جُذوع)
bark	*liḫāʔ*	لِحاء
bamboo	*bámbu* [coll.]	بامْبو
date palm	*dōm* [coll.]	دوْم
oak tree	*ballūṭ* [coll.]	بلّوط
palm tree	*naxl* [coll.]	نخْل
pine tree	*ṣinōbar* [coll.]	صِنوْبر
Royal Poinciana tree	*bunsiyāna* [coll.]	بونْسِيانا
sycamore tree	*gimmēz* [coll.]	جِمّيْز
willow tree	*ṣafṣāf* [coll.]	صفْصاف

flower	*ward* [coll.]	وَرْد
petal	*bátla*	بتْلة
stem, stalk	*sāq (siqān)*	ساق (سِقان)
carnation	*ʔurúnful* [coll.]	قُرُنْفُل

daisy, mum, chrysanthemum	*uqɧuwān* [coll.]	أُقْحُوان
poppy	*xišxāš* [coll.]	خِشْخاش
rose	*zahr* [coll.] *(zuhūr)*	زهْر (زُهور)
sunflower	*3abbād iššáms*	عبّاد الشّمْس
tulip	*tūlib* [coll.]	توليب
violet	*banáfsig* [coll.]	بنفْسِج

cactus	*ṣabbār* [coll.]	صبّار
moss	*ṭáɧlab (ṭaɧālib)*	طحْلب (طحالِب)
vine	*nabāt mutasálliʔ*	نبات مُتسلِّق

seed	*bízra (buzūr)*	بِذْرة (بُذور)
to plant (a seed)**, grow** (a plant)	*zára3* [1s1]	زرع
(a plant) **to grow**	*kíbir* [1s4]	كِبِر
This plant is really growing fast!	*innábta di btíkbar bi-súr3a!*	النّبْتة دي بْتِكْبر بِسُرْعة!
to water (a plant)	*sáʔa* [1d2]	سقى
to fertilize	*ɧaṭṭ*ᵊ [1g2] *simād*	حطّ سِماد
to weed a garden	*náḍḍaf* [2s2] *ilginēna*	نضّف الجِنيْنة
plant pot	*ʔaṣríyyit zar3*	قصْريةْ زرْع

46 Colors

color	*lōn (alwān)*	لوْن (ألْوان)
black	*íswid* [m.], *sōda* [f.] *(sūd)*	إسْوِد،سوْدا (سود)
white	*ábyaḍ* [m.], *bēḍa* [f.] *(bēḍ)*	أبْيَض، بيْضا (بيْض)
blue	*ázraʔ* [m.], *zárʔa* [f.] *(zurʔ)*	أزْرق، زرْقا (زُرْق)
red	*áḫmar* [m.], *ḫámra* [f.] *(ḫumr)*	أحْمر، حمْرا (حُمْر)
yellow	*áṣfar* [m.], *ṣáfra* [f.] *(ṣufr)*	أصْفر، صفْرا (صُفْر)
green	*áxḍar* [m.], *xáḍra* [f.] *(xuḍr)*	أخْضر، خضْرا (خُضْر)

Colors ending in ـي *-i* and those borrowed from other languages are invariable (that is, they do have feminine or plural forms). Egyptians will often simply use English words for specific shades of color.

beige	*bēž* [invar.]	بيْج
brown	*búnni* [invar.]	بُنّى
fuchsia	*fūšíya* [invar.]	فوشِيا
gray	*ruṣāṣi* [invar.] *ramādi* [invar.]	رُصاصي رمادي
lemon-yellow	*lamūni* [invar.]	لمونى
light blue	*lábani* [invar.]	لبنى
navy blue	*kúḫli* [invar.]	كُحْلى

olive	*zitūni* [invar.]	زيتوني
orange	*burtuʔāni* [invar.]	بُرْتُقاني
pink	*bámbi* [invar.] *pīnk* [invar.]	بمْبي پينْك
purple, violet	*banafsígi* [invar.]	بنفْسِجي
turquoise	*turkwāz* [invar.]	تُرْكْواز

shade	*dáraga*	درجة
light __	*__ fātiḫ*	فاتِح
light green	*áxḍar fātiḫ*	أخْضر فاتِح
dark __	*__ ɣāmiʔ*	غامِق
dark red	*áḫmar ɣāmiʔ*	أحْمر غامِق
colorful, multi-colored	*miláwwin*	مِلوِّن

47 Shapes, Sizes, and Measurements

shape	*šakl (aškāl)*	شكْل (أشْكال)
circle	*dáyra (dawāyir)*	دايْرة (دَوايِر)
circular	*dáyri*	دايْري
oval	*šakl^ə bayḍāwi*	شكْل بَيْضاوي
oval(-shaped)	*bayḍāwi*	بَيْضاوي
square; square(-shaped)	*murábba3*	مُربّع
rectangle; rectangular	*mustaṭīl*	مُسْتطيل
triangle; triangular	*musállas*	مُثلّث

big, large	*kibīr (kubār)*	كِبير (كُبار)
small, little	*ṣuɣáyyar (ṣuɣār)*	صُغيرّ (صُغار)
length **height** (person)	*ṭūl (aṭwāl)*	طول (أطْوال)
long **tall** (person)	*ṭawīl (ṭuwāl)*	طَويل (طُوال)
short	*ʔuṣáyyar (ʔuṣār)*	قُصيرّ (قُصار)
width	*3arḍ (a3rāḍ)*	عرْض (أعْراض)

measurement	*miqyās (maqayīs)*	مِقْياس (مقاييس)
to measure	*ʔās* [1h2]	قاس
size, volume	*ɧagm (aɧgām)*	حجْم (أحْجام)
surface area	*misāɧa*	مِساحة

distance	*masāfa*	مسافة
millimeter	*millimítr*	مِلّيمِتْر
centimeter	*santimítr* *sánti*	سنْتِمِتْر سنْتي
meter	*mitr (amtār)*	مِتْر (أمْتار)
kilometer	*kīlumítr* *kīlu*	كيلومِتْر كيلو
inch	*būşa*	بوصة
foot	*ʔádam (aʔdām)*	قدم (أقْدام)
mile	*mīl (amyāl)*	ميل (أمْيال)
square meter	*mitr^{ə} murábba3*	مِتْر مُربّع
cubic meter	*mitr^{ə} muká33ab*	مِتْر مُكعّب
weight	*wazn (awzān)*	وَزْن (أَوْزان)
to weigh	*wázan* [1s2]	وَزن
gram	*girām*	جِرام
kilogram	*kīlugrām* *kīlu*	كيلوجْرام كيلو
ton (metric)	*ţinn (aţnān)*	طِنّ (أطْنان)
ounce	*únşa*	أونْصة
pound	[pound] *raţl (artţāl)*	پاوْنْد رطْل (أرْطال)

48 Quantity

every; all	*kull*	**كُلّ**
every child	*kullᵊ ṭifl*	كُلّ طِفْل
all of the children	*kull ilʔaṭfāl*	كُلّ الأطْفال
most	*mú3ẓam*	**مُعْظم**
most people	*mú3ẓam innās*	مُعْظم النّاس
some	*ba3ḍ*	**بعْض**
some people	*ba3ḍ innās*	بعْض النّاس
no, none of	*wála wāḥid min* *wála ḥaddᵊ min*	**وَلا واحِد مِن** **وَلا حدّ مِن**
no students, none of the students	*wála wāḥid min iṭṭálaba*	وَلا واحِد مِن الطّلبة
a lot of	*kitīr [often invar.]*	**كِتير**
a lot of money	*filūs kitīr*	فِلوس كِتير
a lot of people	*nās kitīr*	ناس كِتير
a little	*ʔuláyyil*	**قُليِّل**
a little time	*waʔtᵊ ʔuláyyil*	وَقْت قُليِّل
a little money	*filūs ʔulayyíla*	فِلوس قُليِّلة
a few	*šuwáyyit* *kām*	**شُوَيّة** **كام**
a few people	*šuwáyyit nās* *nās ʔulayyilīn*	شُوَيّة ناس ناس قُليِّلين
a few days	*kam yōm*	كام يوْم

a couple of __	__-*ēn* [dual]	**ـــين**
a couple of months	*šahrēn* [dual]	شهْريْن
several	*káza*	**كذا**
several kinds	*káza nō3*	كذا نوْع

49 Numbers

number, numeral	*ráqam (arqām)*	رقم (أرْقام)
number (quantity)	*3ádad (a3dād)*	عدد (أعْداد)
to count	*3add* [1g3]	عدّ
odd	*fárdi*	فرْدي
even	*záwgi*	زَوْجي
zero	*şifr*	صِفْر
cardinal number	*3ádad áşli*	عدد أصْلي
one	__ *wāħid* [m.] __ *wáħda* [f.]	__واحِد واحْدة __

واحِد *wāħid* and واحْدة *wáħda* follow the noun they modify and agree with it in gender.

two	*itnēn*	اِتْنينْ

اِتْنينْ *itnēn* is generally not needed to modify a noun. Instead, the suffix *-ēn* is used, as in the example below.

two tables and two chairs	*ţarabiztēn wi kursiyēn*	طرابيزْتينْ و كُرْسِيينْ

The numbers 3-10 have two forms. The full form, ending in ـة *-a,* is used when not followed by a noun, most notably when counting: واحِد *wāħid,* اِتْنينْ *itnēn,* تلاتة *talāta,* أرْبعة *arbá3a* 'one, two, three, four...'. The shortened form precedes the noun it modifies.

three	*talāta* *tálat* __	تلاتة تلات__
four	*arbá3a* *árba3* __	أرْبعة أرْبع__

five	*xámsa* *xámas* __	خمْسة خمس__
six	*sítta* *sitt* __	سِتّة سِتّ__
seven	*sáb3a* *sába3* __	سبْعة سبع__
eight	*tamánya* *táman* __	تمانْيَة تمان__
nine	*tís3a* *tísa3* __	تِسْعة تِسع__
ten	*3ášara* *3ášar* __	عشرة عشر__
eleven	*ḩidāšar*	حِداشر
twelve	*itnāšar*	اِتْناشر
thirteen	*talattāšar*	تلاتّاشر
fourteen	*arba3tāšar*	أرْبعْتاشر
fifteen	*xamastāšar*	خمسْتاشر
sixteen	*sittāšar*	سِتّاشر
seventeen	*saba3tāšar*	سبعْتاشر
eighteen	*tamantāšar*	تمانْتاشر
nineteen	*tisa3tāšar*	تِسعْتاشر
twenty	*3išrīn*	عِشْرين

Compound numbers with 20, 30, etc., are literally phrased 'one and twenty', 'two and twenty', etc.

twenty-one	*wāḩid wi 3išrīn*	واحِد و عِشْرين

twenty-two	*itnēn wi 3išrīn*	اِتْنين و عِشْرين

In compound numbers the numbers 3-9 appear in their full forms.

twenty-three	*talāta w 3išrīn*	تلاتة و عِشْرين
thirty	*talatīn*	تلاتين
forty	*arbi3īn*	أرْبِعين
fifty	*xamsīn*	خمْسين
sixty	*sittīn*	سِتّين
seventy	*sab3īn*	سبْعين
eighty	*tamanīn*	تمانين
ninety	*tis3īn*	تِسْعين
one hundred	*míyya* *mīt* __	مية ميةْ__
two hundred	*mitēn*	ميتيْن
three hundred	*tultumíyya* *tultumīt* __	تُلْتُمية تُلْتُميةْ__
four hundred	*rub3umíyya* *rub3umīt* __	رُبْعُمية رُبْعُميةْ__
five hundred	*xumsumíyya* *xumsumīt* __	خُمْسُمية خُمْسُميةْ__
six hundred	*suttumíyya* *suttumīt* __	سُتُّمية سُتُّميةْ__
seven hundred	*sub3umíyya* *sub3umīt* __	سُبْعُمية سُبْعُميةْ__
eight hundred	*tumnumíyya* *tumnumīt* __	تُمْنُمية تُمْنُميةْ__

nine hundred	*tus3umíyya* *tus3umīt* __	تُسْعُمية تُسْعُميةْ__
one thousand	*alf*	ألْف
two thousand	*alfēn*	ألْفينْ
three thousand	*tálat-talāf*	تلاتّلاف
four thousand	*árba3-talāf*	أرْبعْتلاف
five thousand	*xámas-talāf*	خمسْتلاف
six thousand	*sit-talāf*	سِتّلاف
seven thousand	*sába3-talāf*	سبعْتلاف
eight thousand	*táman-talāf*	تمنْتلاف
nine thousand	*tísa3-talāf*	تِسعْتلاف
ten thousand	*3ášar-talāf*	عشرْتلاف
eleven thousand	*ɧidāšar alf*	حِداشر ألْف
twenty thousand	*3išrīn alf*	عِشْرين ألْف
one hundred thousand	*mīt alf*	ميةْ ألْف
million	*milyōn*	ميلْيوْن
billion	*bilyōn*	بيلْيوْن

arithmetic, calculation	*ɧisāb*	حِساب
to calculate, to work out	*ɧásab* [1s2]	حسب
calculator	*āla ɧásba* [calculator]	آلة حاسْبة كلْكوليْتر

How did you work that out in your head? I need a calculator!	*ínta ɧasábtᵊ da b-dimāɣak izzāy? ána miɧtāg āla ɧásba!*	إنْتَ حسبْت ده بِدِماغك إزّايْ؟ أنا مِحْتاج آلة حاسْبة!
to add, add up	*gáma3* [1s1]	**جمع**
Add up the price of all the items to get the total.	*ígma3 si3rᵊ kull ilɧagāt 3ašān tí3raf igmāli -ssi3r.*	اِجْمع سِعْر كُلّ الحاجات عشان تِعْرف إجْمالي السِّعْر.
to subtract	*ţáraɧ* [1s1]	**طرح**
Subtract the smaller amount from the larger one to find the difference.	*íţraɧ irráqam işşuɣáyyar min ilkibīr 3ašān tí3raf ilfár?.*	اِطْرح الرّقم الصُّغيرّ مِن الكِبير عشان تِعْرف الفرْق.
to multiply by	*ɖárab* [1s1] *fi*	**ضرب في**
Multiply the length and width to find the area of the rectangle.	*íɖrab iţţūl fi -l3arɖ 3ašān tíɧsib misáɧt ilmustaţīl.*	اِضْرب الطّول في العرْض عشان تِحْسِب مِساحْةْ المُسْتطيل.
to divide by	*?ásam* [1s2] *3ála*	**قسم على**
Divide the total by the number of people to find the average.	*í?sim irráqam 3ála 3ádad innās 3ašān tí3raf ilmutawássiţ.*	اِقْسِم الرّقم على عدد النّاس عشان تِعْرف المُتَوَسِّط.
to equal, be equal to	*sāwa* [3d]	**ساوى**
equals, is	*yisāwi* *yíb?a* *bi*	**يِساوي** **يِبْقى** **بِـ**
plus, and	*zā?id* *wi*	**زائِد** **و**

Three plus two equals five.	*talāta zāʔid itnēn yisāwi xámsa.*	تلاتة زائِد اِتْنين يِساوي خمْسة.
minus	*nāʔiṣ* *min*	**ناقِص** **مِن**
Ten minus nine equals one.	*3ášara nāʔiṣ tís3a ysāwi wāɧid.* *tís3a min 3ášara ysāwi wāɧid.* (lit. nine from ten equals one)	عشرة ناقِص تِسْعة يِساوي واحِد. تِسْعة مِن عشرة يِساوي واحِد.
times	*fi*	**في**
Three times four equals twelve.	*talāta f- arbá3a bi-tnāšar.*	تلاتة في أرْبعة بِاتْناشر.
divided by	*3ála*	**على**
Twenty divided by four equals five.	*3išrīn 3ála ʔarbá3a b-xámsa.*	عِشْرين على أرْبعة بِخمْسة.

ordinal number	*3ádad tartībi*	**عدد ترْتيبي**
first	*áwwal* [m.] *ūla* [f.]	**أوّل** **أولى**
second	*tāni* [m.] *tánya* [f.]	**تاني** **تانْية**
third	*tālit* [m.] *tálta* [f.]	**تالِت** **تالْتة**
fourth	*rābi3* [m.] *ráb3a* [f.]	**رابِع** **رابْعة**
fifth	*xāmis* [m.] *xámsa* [f.]	**خامِس** **خامْسة**

sixth	*sādis* [m.] *sádsa* [f.]	سادِس سادْسة
seventh	*sābi3* [m.] *sáb3a* [f.]	سابِع سابْعة
eighth	*tāmin* [m.] *támna* [f.]	تامِن تامْنة
ninth	*tāsi3* [m.] *tás3a* [f.]	تاسِع تاسْعة
tenth	*3āšir* [m.] *3ášra* [f.]	عاشِر عاشْرة

There are no unique ordinal forms for numbers over 10. The cardinal number is used. An ordinal number can be distinguished from a cardinal number because it follows the noun it modifies and usually takes the definite article. Compare the following:

There are **twenty books**, and **the twentieth book** is mine.	*fī 3išrīn kitāb w ilkitāb il3išrīn bitā3i.*	فيه عِشْرين كِتاب و الكِتاب العِشْرين بِتاعي.
the last __	*āxir __*	آخِر__

fraction	*guz? (agzā?)*	جُزْء (أجْزاء)
whole	*kull*	كُلّ
half	*nuşş (anşāş)*	نُصّ (أنْصاص)
Two halves make a whole.	*innuşşēn yi3mílu guz?ᵊ kāmil.*	النُّصّينْ يِعْمِلوا جُزْء كامِل.
a third	*tilt (atlāt)*	تِلْت (أتْلات)
a fourth, a quarter	*rub3 (arbā3)*	رُبْع (أرْباع)

a fifth	*xums (axmās)*	**خُمْس (أخْماس)**
three fifths	*tálat axmās*	**تلات أخْماس**

Fractions above 10 are formed with ordinal numbers separated by على *3ála*.

one twelfth (1/12)	*wāɧid 3ála -tnāšar*	**واحِد على اتْناشر**
three twentieths (3/20)	*talāta 3ála 3išrīn*	**تلاتة على عِشْرين**

percentage	*nísba (nísab) miʔawíyya*	**نِسْبة (نِسب) مِئَوية**
a large percentage	*nísba kbīra*	نِسْبة كْبيرة
what percentage of __	*kām fi -lmíyya min __*	**كام في المية مِن__**
percent	*fi -lmíyya*	**في المية**
fifty percent of people	*xamsīn fi -lmíyya min iššá3b*	خمْسين في المية مِن الشّعْب

50 Time

time	*waʔt (awʔāt)*	وَقْت (أَوْقات)
day	*yōm (ayyām)*	يوْم (أيّام)
in the morning	*iṣṣúbḥ*	الصُّبْح
at noon	*iḍḍúhr*	الضُّهْر
in the afternoon	*ba3d iḍḍúhr*	بعْد الضُّهْر
in the evening, at night	*bi-llēl*	بِاللّيْل
at midnight	*fi nuṣṣ illēl*	في نُصّ اللّيْل
three days ago	*min tálat tiyyām*	مِن تلات تِيّام
the day before yesterday	*áwwil imbāriḥ*	أوِّل إمْبارِح
yesterday	*imbāriḥ*	إمْبارِح
yesterday morning	*imbāriḥ iṣṣúbḥ*	إمْبارِح الصُّبْح
last night	*imbāriḥ bi-llēl*	إمْبارِح بِاللّيْل
today	*innahárda*	النّهارْده
this morning	*innahárda -ṣṣubḥ*	النّهارْده الصُّبْح
this afternoon	*innahárda ba3d iḍḍúhr*	النّهارْده بعْد الضُّهْر
this evening, tonight	*innahárda bi-llēl*	النّهارْده بِاللّيْل
tomorrow	*búkra*	بُكْره
tomorrow morning	*búkra -ṣṣubḥ*	بُكْره الصُّبْح

tomorrow evening	*búkra bi-llēl*	بُكْره بِاللّيْل
the day after tomorrow	*ba3d^{ə} búkra*	بعْد بُكْره
in three days	*ba3d^{ə} tálat tiyyām*	بعْد تلات تِيّام

every day	*kull^{ə} yōm*	كُلّ يوْم
every other day	*márra kull^{ə} yumēn*	مرّة كُلّ يومينْ
all day	*ṭūl ilyōm*	طول اليوْم

week	*isbū3 (asabī3)*	إسْبوع (أسابيع)
weekday, workday	*yōm iššúɣl*	يوْم الشُّغْل
(on) the weekend	*āxir ilʔisbū3* *nihāyit ilʔisbū3*	آخِر الإسْبوع نِهايِةْ الإسْبوع
Sunday	*ilḩádd*	الحدّ
Monday	*ilʔitnēn*	الاِتْنينْ
Tuesday	*ittalāt*	التّلات
Wednesday	*ilʔárba3*	الأرْبع
Thursday	*ilxamīs*	الخميس
Friday	*ilgúm3a*	الجُمْعة
Saturday	*issábt*	السّبْت
See you on Saturday!	*ašūfak yōm issábt!*	أشوفك يوْم السّبْت!

last week	*ilʔisbū3 ílli fāt*	الإسْبوع اللي فات
this week	*ilʔisbū3 da*	الإسْبوع ده

next week	*il?isbū3 ilgáyy* *il?isbū3 ílli gayy*	**الإسْبوع الجايّ** **الإسْبوع اللي جايّ**
I'll tell you next week or the week after.	*a?úllak il?isbū3 ilgáyy aw ílli bá3du.*	أقولّك الإسْبوع الجايّ أوْ اللي بعْدُه.

month	*šahr (ášhur)*	**شهْر (أشْهر)**
January	*yanāyir*	**يَنايِر**
February	*fibrāyir*	**فِبْرايِر**
March	*māris*	**مارِس**
April	*ibrīl*	**إبْريل**
May	*māyu*	**مايو**
June	*yúnyu* *yúnya*	**يونْيو** **يونْيَة**
July	*yúlyu* *yúlya*	**يولْيو** **يولْيَة**
August	*aɣústṭus*	**أغُسْطُس**
September	*sibtímbir*	**سِبْتِمْبِر**
October	*uktōbir*	**أُكْتوْبِر**
November	*nufímbir, nuvímbir*	**نوفِمْبِر**
December	*disímbir*	**ديسِمْبِر**
I was born in December.	*ána -twaládtᵊ f šahrᵊ disímbir.*	أنا اتْوَلَدْت في شهْر ديسِمْبِر.
calendar	*taqwīm (taqawīm)*	**تقْويم (تقاويم)**

last month	*iššáhr ílli fāt*	الشّهْر اللي فات
this month	*iššáhr*^{ə} *da*	الشّهْر ده
next month	*iššáhr ilgáyy* *iššáhr ílli gayy*	الشّهْر الجايّ الشّهْر اللي جايّ
season	*faşl (fuşūl)*	فصْل (فُصول)
spring	*irrabī3*	الرّبيع
summer	*işşēf*	الصّيْف
fall, autumn	*ilxarīf*	الخريف
winter	*iššíta*	الشِّتا
I like to go to Alexandria in the winter.	*baḫíbb arūḫ iskindiríyya fi -ššíta.*	بحِبّ أروح إسْكِنْدِرية في الشِّتا.
holiday	*3īd (a3yād)*	عيد (أعْياد)
New Year's Eve	*lēlit rās issána*	ليلِةْ راس السّنة
New Year's Day	*rās issána*	راس السّنة
Valentine's Day	*3īd il*[Valentine] *3īd ilḫúbb*	عيد الفالانْتايْن عيد الحُبّ
Independence Day	*3īd ilʔistiqlāl*	عيد الاِسْتِقْلال
Halloween	*il*[Halloween]	الهالُوين
Thanksgiving	*yōm iššúkr*	يوْم الشُّكْر
Dates for holidays celebrated in Egypt are specified in parentheses.		
National Police Day (January 25)	*3īd iššúrţa*	عيد الشُّرْطة

2011 Revolution Day (January 25)	*3īd sáwrit xámsa wi 3išrīn yanāyir*	عيد ثَوْرِة ٢٥ يَنايِر
Mother's Day (March 21)	*yōm il?úmm*	يوْم الأُمّ
Sham el-Nessim (day after Coptic Orthodox Easter)	*šamm innisīm*	شمّ النّسيم

Sham el-Nessim is a spring festival celebrated by all Egyptians, regardless of religion. Families typically spend the day outdoors, picnicking and going on outings.

Sinai Liberation Day (April 25)	*3īd taħrīr sīna*	عيد تحْرير سينا
Labor Day (May 1)	*3īd il3ummāl*	عيد العُمّال
Revolution Day (July 23)	*sáwrit talāta wi 3išrīn yúlyu*	ثَوْرِة ٢٣ يولْيو
Wafaa el-Nil (Flooding of the Nile) (August 15)	*3īd wafā? innīl*	عيد وَفاء النّيل
Armed Forces Day (October 6)	*3īd ilquwwāt ilmusalláħa*	عيد القُوّات المُسلّحة

Muslim holidays follow the Islamic lunar calendar, and thus may fall at various times of the year.

Ramadan	*ramaḍān*	رمضان
Eid Al-Fitr, the Lesser Eid (3 days)	*3īd ilfiṭr* *il3īd iṣṣuɣáyyar*	عيد الفِطْر العيد الصُّغيرّ
Eid Al-Adha, the Feast of the Sacrifice, the Greater Eid (4 days)	*3īd il?áḍħa* *il3īd ilkibīr*	عيد الأضْحى العيد الكِبير
Mawlid (Birth of the Prophet Mohammad)	*ilmáwlid (innábawi)* *máwlid innábi*	المَوْلِد (ألنَّبَوي) مَوْلِد النّبي

Christmas (in Egypt, Coptic Christians celebrate Christmas on January 7.)	*3īd ilmilād* *il*[Christmas]	عيد الميلاد الكْريسْماس
Epiphany (celebrated in January)	*ilɣuṭās*	الغُطاس
Easter (Coptic Easter may follow Western Christianity's Easter by a week or two.)	*3īd ilʔiyāma*	عيد القِيامة

year	*sána (sinīn)*	سنة (سِنين)
twenty years ago	*min 3išrīn sána*	مِن عِشْرين سنة
last year	*issána -lli fātit*	السّنة اللي فاتِت
this year	*issanā-di*	السّنة دي
next year	*issána -lgáyya*	السّنة الجايّة
in five years	*ba3dᵊ xámas sinīn*	بعْد خمس سِنين

period, era, age	*3aṣr (3uṣūr)*	عصْر (عُصور)
decade	*3aʔd (3uʔūd)*	عقْد (عُقود)
in the 1980s	*fi -ttamaninát*	في التّمانينات
century	*qarn (qurūn)*	قرْن (قُرون)
in the 19th century, in the 1800s	*fi -lqarn ittisa3tāšar*	في القرْن التِّسعْتاشر
millennium	*alfíyya*	ألْفية

in the present	*fi -lħāḍir*	**في الحاضِر**
now	*dilwáʔti*	**دِلْوَقْتي**
in the past	*ʔablᵊ kída* *fi -lmāḍi*	**قبْل كِده** **في الماضي**
just, just now	*líssa*	**لِسّه**
I just went to the bank.	*ána kuntᵊ líssa fi -lbank.*	أنا كُنْت لِسّه في البنْك.
a long time ago, in the past	*zamān*	**زمان**
in the future	*fi -lmustáʔbal*	**في المُسْتقْبل**
right now, right away	*dilwáʔti ħālan*	**دِلْوَقْتي حالاً**
Okay, I'll do it right away!	*tamām, ána há3mil kída dilwáʔti ħālan!*	تمام، أنا هعْمِل كِده دِلْوَقْتي حالاً!
soon, in a bit	*ba3dᵊ šwáyya ṣuɣayyarīn* *kamān šuwáyya*	**بعْد شْوَيَّة صُغيرّين** **كمان شُوَيَّة**
I'll go to bed soon.	*ána dāxil issirīr ba3dᵊ šwáyya ṣuɣayyarīn.* *ána hanām kamān šuwáyya.*	أنا داخِل السِّرير بعْد شْوَيَّة صُغيرّين. أنا هنام كمان شُوَيَّة.
later	*ba3dēn*	**بعْديْن**
one day, someday	*fi yōm min ilʔayyām*	**في يوْم مِن الأيّام**

hour	*sā3a*	**ساعة**
minute	*diʔīʔa (daʔāyiʔ)*	**دِقيقة (دقايِق)**
second	*sánya (sawāni)*	**ثانْيَة (ثَواني)**
What time is it?	*issā3a kām?*	السّاعة كام؟

It's one o'clock. (1:00)	*issā3a wáɦda.*	السّاعة واحْدة.
It's two o'clock. (2:00)	*issā3a -tnēn.*	السّاعة اتْنينْ.
It's three o'clock. (3:00)	*issā3a talāta.*	السّاعة تلاتة.
It's five past three. (3:05)	*issā3a talāta wi xámsa.*	السّاعة تلاتة و خمْسة.
It's ten past three. (3:10)	*issā3a talāta wi 3ášara.*	السّاعة تلاتة و عشرة.
It's a quarter past three. (3:15)	*issā3a talāta wi rub3.*	السّاعة تلاتة و رُبْع.
It's twenty past three. (3:20)	*issā3a talāta wi tilt.* (lit. ... and a third.)	السّاعة تلاتة و تِلْت.
It's twenty-five past three. (3:25)	*issā3a talāta wi nuṣṣ ílla xámsa.* (lit. ... and half except five)	السّاعة تلاتة و نُصّ إلّا خمْسة.
It's three thirty. (3:30)	*issā3a talāta wi nuṣṣ.* (lit. ... and half)	السّاعة تلاتة و نُصّ.
It's twenty-five to four. (3:35)	*issā3a talāta wi nuṣṣ^{ə} w xámsa.* (lit. and half and five)	السّاعة تلاتة و نُصّ و خمْسة.
It's twenty to four. (3:40)	*issā3a ʔarbá3a ʔílla tilt.* (lit. except a third)	السّاعة ارْبعة إلّا تِلْت.
It's a quarter to four. (3:45)	*issā3a ʔarbá3a ʔílla rub3.* (lit. except a quarter)	السّاعة ارْبعة إلّا رُبْع.
It's ten to four. (3:50)	*issā3a ʔarbá3a ʔílla 3ášara.*	السّاعة ارْبعة إلّا عشرة.
It's five to four. (3:55)	*issā3a ʔarbá3a ʔílla xámsa.*	السّاعة ارْبعة إلّا خمْسة.
It's almost four o'clock.	*issā3a dáxla 3ála ʔarbá3a.* *issā3a ʔarbá3a taʔrīban.*	السّاعة داخْلة على أرْبعة. السّاعة أرْبعة تقْريباً.

The following expressions are the Arabic equivalents of 'a.m.' and 'p.m.' The hours for which each expression is commonly used is listed. There is some overlap, allowing more than one expression for certain times of the day.

in the morning (4-11 a.m.)	*iṣṣúbḥ*	الصُّبْح
9 a.m.	*issā3a tís3a -ṣṣubḥ*	السّاعة تِسْعة الصُّبْح
in the afternoon (12-3 p.m.)	*iḍḍúhr*	الضُّهْر
3 p.m.	*issā3a talāta -ḍḍuhr*	السّاعة تلاتة الضُّهْر
in the afternoon (3-6 p.m.)	*il3áṣr*	العصْر
in the evening (5-7 p.m.)	*ilmáɣrib*	المغْرِب
at night (7 p.m. - 3 a.m.)	*bi-llēl*	بِاللّيْل
in the morning (3-6 a.m.)	*ilfágr*	الفجْر

what time, when	*issā3a kām*	السّاعة كام
What time do you get up?	*bitíṣḥa -ssā3a kām?*	بتِصْحى السّاعة كام؟
at __ o'clock	*issā3a __* *il__*	السّاعة __ الـ__
around __ o'clock	*ḥawāli -ssā3a __* *3a-ssā3a __* *kída -ssā3a __*	حَوالي السّاعة __ عَ السّاعة __ كِده السّاعة__
I usually get up around seven.	*ána fi -l3āda báṣḥa 3a-ssáb3a.*	أنا في العادة بصْحى عَ السّبْعة.
at __ o'clock sharp	*issā3a __ bi-ẓẓábṭ*	السّاعة __ بِالظّبْط

early	*bádri*	**بدْري**
I went home early from school today.	*rawwáɧt ilbēt bádri min ilmadrása -nnahárda.*	روّحْت البيْت بدْري مِن المدْرسة النّهارْده.
late	*mitʔáxxar* *wáxri*	**متْأخّر** **وَخْري**
He got home late at night.	*rígi3 ilbēt bi-llēl mitʔáxxar.*	رِجِع البيْت بِاللّيْل متْأخّر.

since	*min*	**مِن**
I've been living in Cairo since 2010.	*ána 3āyiš fi -lqāhíra min alfēn wi 3ášara.*	أنا عايِش في القاهِرة مِن ألْفيْن و عشرة.
for	*baʔālu*	**بقالُه**
I've been learning Arabic for two years.	*bat3állim 3árabi baʔāli sanatēn.*	بتْعلِّم عربي بقالي سنتيْن.
until	*li-ɧádd*	**لِحدّ**
I watched TV until eleven o'clock.	*itfarrágtᵊ 3ála -ttilivizyōn li-ɧádd issā3a ɧidāšar.*	اِتْفرّجْت على التِّليفِزْيوْن لِحدّ السّاعة حِداشر.

51 Pronouns

I	*ána*	**أنا**
we	*íħna*	**إحْنا**
you	*ínta* [m. sing.]	**إنْتَ**
you	*ínti* [f. sing.]	**إنْتي**
you, you guys	*íntu* [pl.]	**إنْتو**
he, it	*húwwa*	**هُوَّ**
she, it	*híyya*	**هِيَّ**
they	*húmma*	**هُمّا**

this, that	*da*	**دة**
this, that, these, those	*di*	**دي**
these, those	*dōl*	**دوْل**

everyone	*kull innās*	**كُلّ النّاس**
Everyone needs friends.	*kull innās miħtagīn aṣħāb.*	كُلّ النّاس مِحْتاجين أصْحاب.
someone	*ħadd*	**حدّ**
Someone is at the door.	*fī ħaddᵊ 3ála -lbāb.*	فيه حدّ على الباب.
anyone	*ayyᵊ ħadd*	**أيّ حدّ**
Anyone can do it.	*ayyᵊ ħaddᵊ múmkin yí3mil kída.*	أيّ حدّ مُمْكِن يِعْمِل كِده.

no one	*ma-ɦáddiš* *ma-fīš ɦadd*	**محدِّش** **مفيش حدّ**
No one lives forever.	*ma-ɦáddiš biy3īš li-l?ábad.*	محدِّش بِيْعيش لِلابد.
everything	*kullᵊ ɦāga* *kúllu*	**كُلّ حاجة** **كُلُّه**
Everything is ready.	*kullᵊ ɦāga gáhza.*	كُلّ حاجة جاهْزة.
something	*ɦāga*	**حاجة**
I want to eat something sweet.	*3āyiz ākul ɦāga msakkíra.*	عايِز آكل حاجة مْسكِّرة.
anything	*ayyᵊ ɦāga*	**أيّ حاجة**
What do you want to eat? - Anything is fine.	*3āyiz tākul ?ē? - ayyᵊ ɦāga.*	عايِز تاكُل أيْه؟ - أيّ حاجة.
nothing	*wála ɦāga*	**وَلا حاجة**
What did you buy? - Nothing!	*ištarēt ?ē? - wála ɦāga.*	اِشْتريْت أيْه؟ - وَلا حاجة.

52 Question Words

what	*ʔē*	**أيْه**
What is that?	*ʔē da?*	أيْه ده؟
What do you want?	*ínta 3āyiz ʔē?*	إنْتَ عايِز أيْه؟
who	*mīn*	**مين**
Who told you that?	*mīn ʔállak kída?*	مين قالّك كِده؟
Who did you tell?	*ínta ʔultᵊ l-mīn?*	إنْتَ قُلْت لِمين؟
which __	*ánhi __*	**أنْهي__**
Which movie do you want to see?	*3āyiz tišūf ánhi film?*	عايِز تِشوف أنْهي فيلْم؟
where	*fēn*	**فيْن**
Where do you live?	*ínta 3āyiš fēn?*	إنْتَ عايِش فيْن؟
when	*ímta*	**إمْتى**
When are you going on vacation?	*hatíṭla3 agāza ʔímta?*	هتِطْلع أجازة إمْتى؟
what time	*issā3a kām*	**السّاعة كام**
What time did you get here?	*ínta gīt hína -ssā3a kām?*	إنْتَ جيت هِنا السّاعة كام؟
how	*izzāy*	**إزّايْ**
How do you usually get to work?	*bitrūḥ iššúɣl izzāy fi-l3ādi?*	بِتْروح الشُّغْل إزّايْ في العادي؟
why	*lē*	**ليْه**
Why are you late?	*itʔaxxártᵊ lē?*	اِتْأخّرْت ليْه؟

how many, how much	*kām*	**كام**

When كام *kām* precedes a noun, it is pronounced *kam*.

How many people are there in your family?	*fī kam fardᵊ f 3íltak?*	فيه كام فرْد في عيلْتك؟
How much does this cost?	*bi-kām da?*	بِكام ده؟
how much, how many; how long, how much time	*ʔaddᵊ ʔē*	**أدّ أيْه، قدّ أيْه**
How much water is there in the bottle?	*fī máyya ʔaddᵊ ʔē gúwwa -lʔizāza?*	فيه ميّة أدّ أيْه جُوّه الإزازة؟
How many people died in the revolution?	*nās ʔaddᵊ ʔē mātit fi -ssáwra?*	ناس أدّ أيْه ماتِت في الثَوْرة؟
How long does it take you to get to work?	*ínta btāxud ʔaddᵊ ʔē 3ašān tíwṣal iššúɣl?*	إنْتَ بِتاخُد أدّ أيْه عشان توْصل الشُّغْل؟
How long have you been married?	*ínta mitgáwwiz baʔālak ʔaddᵊ ʔē?*	إنْتَ مِتْجوِّز بقالك أدّ أيْه؟
How long is this carpet?	*ṭūl issiggāda di ʔaddᵊ ʔē?*	طول السِّجادة دي أدّ أيْه؟
how old	*kam sána*	**كام سنة**
How old are you?	*ínta 3ándak kam sána?*	إنْتَ عنْدك كام سنة؟
how big	*misáḥtu ʔaddᵊ ʔē*	**مِساحْتُه أدّ أيْه**
How big is your house?	*bētak misáḥtu ʔaddᵊ ʔē?*	بيْتك مِساحْتُه أدّ أيْه؟
how far	*ilmasāfa ʔaddᵊ ʔē*	**المسافة أدّ أيْه**
How far is it from here to downtown?	*ilmasāfa ʔaddᵊ ʔē min hína l-wisṭ ilbálad?*	المسافة أدّ أيْه مِن هِنا لِوِسْط البلد؟

how often	*kullᵊ ʔaddᵊ ʔē*	**كُلّ أدّ أيْه**
How often do you exercise?	*bititmárran kullᵊ ʔaddᵊ ʔē?*	بِتِتْمرّن كُلّ أدّ أيْه؟

53 Adverbs

slowly	*bi-rrāḫa*	**بِالرّاحة**
fast, quickly	*bi-súr3a*	**بِسُرْعة**
especially	*xuşūşan*	**خُصوصاً**
at least	*3ála -lʔaʔáll*	**على الأقلّ**
almost, nearly, around, about	*taʔrīban*	**تقْريباً**
again	*tāni*	**تاني**
alone	*li-wáḫdu*	**لِوَحْدُه**
also, too, as well	*bárḍu*	**برْضُه**

here	*hína*	**هِنا**
there	*hināk*	**هِناك**
everywhere	*fī kullᵊ makān*	**في كُلّ مكان**
I see him everywhere.	*ána bašūfu fi kullᵊ makān.*	أنا بشوفُه في كُلّ مكان.
somewhere	*ḫitta* *makān*	**حِتّة** **مكان**
I want to go somewhere fun.	*3āyiz arūḫ ḫitta mumtí3a.*	عايِز أروح حِتّة مُمْتِعة.
anywhere	*ayyᵊ makān*	**أيّ مكان**
You can buy it anywhere.	*múmkin tištirī min ayyᵊ makān.*	مُمْكِن تِشْترِية مِن أيّ مكان.
nowhere	*ma-fīš makān*	**مفيش مكان**

Nowhere is safe.	*ma-fīš makān amān.*	مفيش مكان أمان.
always	*dáyman* *3ála ṭūl*	**دايْماً** **على طول**
She always does her homework.	*híyya 3ála ṭūl biti3mil ilwāgib.*	هِيَّ على طول بِتِعْمِل الواجِب.
sometime	*fi márra*	**في مرّة**
Let's have coffee sometime.	*ma tīgi nísrab ʔáhwa f- márra.*	ما تيجي نِشْرب قهْوَة في مرّة.
sometimes	*aḫyānan* *sa3āt*	**أحْياناً** **ساعات**
I sometimes get up late.	*ána sa3āt báṣḫa mitʔáxxar.*	أنا سعات بصْحى مِتْأخّر.
anytime	*ayyᵊ waʔt*	**أيّ وَقْت**
You can call me anytime.	*múmkin tikallímni fi ʔayyᵊ waʔt.*	مُمْكِن تِكلِّمْني في أيّ وَقْت.
never	*3úmru ma-*	**عُمْرُه ما**
I never eat breakfast.	*3úmri ma báfṭar.*	عُمْري ما بفْطر.
They've never been out of Egypt.	*3umrúhum ma sáfru bárra maṣr.*	عُمْرُهُم ما سافْروا برّه مصْر.
usually	*3ādatan* *fi -l3ādi* *3umūman*	**عادةً** **في العادي** **عُموماً**
I usually go to work by car, but I sometimes walk.	*ána 3ādatan barūḫ iššúɣlᵊ bi-l3arabíyya, bass aḫyānan bámši.*	أنا عادةً بروح الشُّغْل بِالعربية، بسّ أحْياناً بمْشي.

often	*kitīr* *ɣālíban*	**كِتير** **غالِبًا**
I often see him at the café.	*ána bašūfu ktīr fi -lʔáhwa.*	أنا بشوفُه كِتير في القهْوه.

somehow	*ma-3ráfš izzāy* (lit. I don’t know how)	**معْرفْش إزّايْ**
The cat somehow got in the house.	*ma-3ráfš izzāy ilʔúṭṭa dáxalit ilbēt.*	معْرفْش إزّايْ القُطّة دخلِت البيْت.
very	*ʔáwi* *gíddan* *xāliṣ*	**أَوي** **جِدّاً** **خالِص**
very good	*kuwáyyis gíddan*	كُوَيِّس جِدّاً

__ enough	*kifāya*	**كِفايَة**
big enough	*kibīr kifāya*	كِبير كِفايَة
too __	*__ áwi*	**__أَوي**
too big	*kibīr áwi*	كِبير أَوي
too much, too many	*kitīr áwi*	**كِتير أَوي**
too much money	*filūs kitīr áwi*	فِلوس كِتير أَوي
too many people	*nās kitīr áwi*	ناس كِتير أَوي

well	*kuwáyyis*	**كُوَيِّس**
She speaks Arabic well.	*híyya btitkállim 3árabi kwáyyis.*	هِيَّ بِتِتْكلِّم عربي كْوَيِّس.

still	*líssa*	**لِسّه**
I'm still hungry.	*ána líssa ga3ān.*	أنا لِسّه جعان.

not... yet	*li-ɧádd^{ə} dilwáʔti* *líssa*	**لِحدّ دِلْوَقْتي** **لِسّه**
Isn't he here yet?	*húwwa líssa ma-gāš li-ɧádd^{ə} dilwáʔti?*	هُوَّ لِسّه مجاش لِحدّ دِلْوَقْتي؟
I haven't finished my coffee yet.	*ma-xallástiš ʔahwíti li-ɧádd^{ə} dilwáʔti.* *ána líssa ma-xallástiš ʔahwíti.*	مخلّصْتِش قَهْوِتي لِحدّ دِلْوَقْتي. أنا لِسّه مخلّصْتِش قَهْوِتي.

already	*xalāş*	**خلاص**
I already told you!	*ána ʔultílak xalāş!*	أنا قُلْتِلك خلاص!
I've already eaten lunch.	*ána -tɣaddēt xalāş!*	أنا اتْغدّيْت خلاص.

just	*líssa* *yadōb*	**لِسّه** **يادوْب**
I just ate.	*ána líssa wākil.*	أنا لِسّه واكِل.
I just told you!	*ána líssa yadōb ʔáylak.*	أنا لِسّه يادوْب قايْلك!

inside	*gúwwa*	**جُوّه**
It's hot today. Let's stay inside.	*iddúnya ɧarr innahárda. xallīna gúwwa ʔáɧsan.*	الدُّنْيا حرّ النّهارْده .خلّينا جُوّه أحْسن.

outside	*bárra*	**برّه**
Let's sit outside.	*yálla nú?3ud bárra.*	يَلّا نُقْعُد برّه.
abroad, overseas	*bárra (-lbálad)*	**برّه (البلد)**
Does he live abroad?	*húwwa 3āyiš bárra -lbálad?*	هُوَّ عايِش برّه البلد؟
I'm going abroad next week.	*ána msāfir bárra -l?isbū3 ilgáyy.*	أنا مْسافِر برّه الإِسْبوع الجايّ.

upstairs	*fō?*	**فوْق**
Come upstairs!	*íṭla3 fō?!*	اِطْلع فوْق!
downstairs	*taḥt*	**تحْت**

54 Conjunctions

and	*wi*	**و**
or	*aw*	**أَوْ**
but	*bass*	**بسّ**
whether, if	*law*	**لَوْ**
that	*inn*	**إنّ**
because	*3ašān* *3alašān*	**عشان** **علشان**
I'm tired today because I went to bed late last night.	*ána ta3bān innahárda 3ašān nimtᵊ mitʔáxxar imbāriḫ.*	أنا تعْبان النّهارْده عشان نمِْت مِتْأخّر إمْبارِح.
I feel good because I exercise every day.	*ána kwáyyis 3ašān batmárran kullᵊ yōm.*	أنا كْوَيِّس عشان بتْمرّن كُلّ يوْم.
so	*3ašān kída*	**عشان كِده**
I went to bed late last night, so I'm tired today.	*ána nimtᵊ mitʔáxxar imbāriḫ, 3ašān kída, ána ta3bān innahárda.*	أنا نمِْت مِتْأخّر إمْبارِح، عشان كِده أنا تعْبان النّهارْده.
so that, in order to	*3ašān* *3alašān*	**عشان** **علشان**
You have to study hard in order to learn Arabic well.	*lāzim tizākir kuwáyyis 3ašān tit3állim il3árabi kwáyyis.*	لازِم تِذاكِر كُوَيِّس عشان تِتْعلِّم العربي كْوَيِّس.

We had to leave home early in order to get there on time.	*lāzim nímši min ilbēt bádri 3ašān níwṣal fi mi3ádna.*	لازِم نِمْشي مِن البيْت بدْري عشان نِوْصل في ميعادْنا.
after	*ba3dᵊ ma*	**بعْد ما**
I had dinner after I got home last night.	*it3aššēt ba3dᵊ ma rawwáḫt ilbēt imbāriḫ bi-llēl.*	اِتْعشّيْت بعْد ما روّحْت البيْت إمْبارِح بِاللّيْل.
I always have dinner after I get home.	*ána dáyman bit3ášša ba3dᵊ ma -ráwwaḫ ilbēt.*	أنا دايْماً بِتْعشّى بعْد ما أروح البيْت.
I'll have dinner after I get home this evening.	*hat3ášša ba3dᵊ ma -ráwwaḫ ilbēt innahárda bi-llēl.*	هتْعشّى بعْد ما أروح البيْت النّهارْده بِاللّيْل.
before	*ʔablᵊ ma*	**قبْل ما**
He opened the window before he went to bed last night.	*húwwa fátaḫ iššubbāk ʔablᵊ ma ynām imbāriḫ.*	هُوَّ فتح الشُّبّاك قبْل ما يْنام إمْبارِح.
He always opens the window before he goes to bed.	*húwwa dáyman biyíftaḫ iššubbāk ʔablᵊ ma ynām.*	هُوَّ دايْماً بِيِفْتح الشُّبّاك قبْل ما يِنام.
He'll open the window before he goes to bed tonight.	*húwwa hayíftaḫ iššubbāk ʔablᵊ ma ynām innahárda.*	هُوَّ هَيِفْتح الشُّبّاك قبْل ما يِنام النّهارْده.
until, by the time	*li-ḫáddᵊ ma*	**لِحدّ ما**
I lived in Alexandria until I graduated from university.	*ána 3ištᵊ f- iskindiríyya l-ḫaddᵊ ma -txarrágtᵊ min ilgám3a.*	أنا عِشْت في إسْكِنْدِرية لِحدّ ما اتْخرّجْت مِن الجامْعة.
I'll stay in a hotel until I find an apartment.	*ána hánzil fi fúnduʔ li-ḫáddᵊ ma -lāʔi šáʔʔa.*	أنا هنْزِل في فُنْدق لِحدّ ما ألاقي شقّة.

It was nine o'clock by the time he got up.	*li-ḫádd[ə] ma ṣíḫi min innōm kānit issā3a báʔit tís3a.*	لِحدّ ما صِحي مِن النّوم كانِت السّاعة بقِت تِسْعة.

while	*wi*	**و**
I did my homework while I was watching TV.	*ána 3amált ilwāgib w-ána batfárrag 3ála -ttilivizyōn.*	أنا عملْت الواجِب و أنا بتْفرّج على التِّليفِزْيوْن.
if	*law*	**لَوْ**
If I have enough money, I'll buy it.	*law kān ma3āya flūs kifāya, haštirīha.*	لَوْ كان معايا فِلوس كِفايَة هشْترِيها.
If I had enough money, I'd buy it.	*law kān ma3āya flūs kifāya, kunt[ə] haštirīha.*	لَوْ كان معايا فِلوس كِفايَة كُنْت هشْترِيها.
If I had had enough money, I would have bought it.	*law kān ma3āya flūs kifāya, kunt ištarítha.*	لَوْ كان معايا فِلوس كِفايَة كُنْت اِشْتريتْها.
when	*lámma* *ímta*	**لمّا** **إمْتى**
When we got home from work, we went straight to bed.	*lámma rawwáḫna -lbēt min iššúgl, nímna 3ála ṭūl.*	لمّا روّحْنا البيْت مِن الشُّغْل نِمْنا على طول.
I don't know when they're coming.	*ána ma-3ráfš húmma gayyīn ímta.*	أنا معْرفْش هُمّا جايّين إمْتى.
where	*fēn*	**فيْن**
I can't remember where I put my keys.	*ána miš fākir ḫaṭṭēt ilmafatīḫ fēn.*	أنا مِش فاكِر حطّيْت المفاتيح فيْن.

why	*lē*	**لِيْه**
Do you know why he said that?	*tí3raf húwwa ʔāl kída lē?*	تِعْرف هُوَّ قال كِده لِيْه؟
who	*mīn*	**مين**
I want to know who did it.	*3āyiz á3raf mīn ílli 3ámal kída.*	عايِز أعْرف مين اللي عمل كِده.
what	*ílli* *ʔē*	**اللي** **أيْه**
I want to know what you did.	*ána 3āyiz á3raf ínta 3amáltᵊ ʔē.*	أنا عايِز أعْرف إنْتَ عملْت أيْه؟
I know what you did.	*ána 3ārif ílli -nta 3amáltu.*	أنا عارِف اللي إنْتَ عملْتُه.

55 Prepositions

at, in, on	*fi*	**في**
in, inside; into	*gúwwa*	**جُوّه**
in the box	*gúwwa -ṣṣandūʔ*	**جُوّه الصّنْدوق**
outside of; out of	*bárra*	**برّه**
on; onto	*3ála*	**على**
on the table	*3ála -ṭṭarabēza*	**على الطّرابيْزة**
He fell onto the hood of the car.	*húwwa wíʔi3 3ála kabbūt il3arabíyya.*	هُوَّ وِقع على كبّوت العربية.
to	*li-*	**لِـ**
from	*min*	**مِن**
from my house to school	*min bēti li-lmadrása*	**مِن بيْتي لِلمدْرسة**
above, over	*fōʔ* *min fōʔ*	**فوْق** **مِن فوْق**
The painting is hanging over the sofa.	*illōḥa mit3állaʔa fōʔ ilkánaba.*	اللّوْحة مِتْعلّقة فوْق الكنبة.
The airplane flew over the mountains.	*iṭṭayyāra ṭārit fōʔ ilgibāl.*	الطّيّارة طارِت فوْق الجِبال.
He jumped over the fence.	*húwwa naṭṭᵊ min fōʔ issūr.*	هُوَّ نطّ مِن فوْق السّور.

under, beneath	*taḫt*	**تحْت**
under the table	*taḫt iṭṭarabēza*	**تحْت الطّرابيْزة**
between	*bēn*	**بيْن**
The post office is between the bank and the supermarket.	*máktab ilbarīd bēn ilbánk w is*[supermarket].	مكْتب البريد بيْن البنْك و السّوپر مارْكِت.
near, close to	*ʔuráyyib min*	**قُريِّب مِن**
The Sphinx is near the Pyramids.	*abū -lhōl ʔuráyyib min ilʔahramāt.*	أبو الهوْل قُريِّب مِن الأهْرامات.
far from	*bi3īd (bu3ād) 3an*	**بِعيد (بُعاد) عن**
Aswan is far from Alexandria.	*aswān bi3īda 3an iskindiríyya.*	أسْوان بِعيدة عن إسْكِنْدِرية.
next to; along	*gamb*	**جنْب**
There's a coffee shop next to my office.	*fī ʔáhwa gambᵊ maktábi.*	فيه قهْوَة جنْب مكْتبي.
We walked along the river.	*mišēna gamb innáhr.*	مِشيْنا جنْب النّهْر.
in front of; across from, opposite	*ʔuddām*	**قُدّام**
I sat down in front of the TV.	*ána ʔa3ádtᵊ ʔuddām ittilivizyōn.*	أنا قعدْت قُدّام التِّليفِزْيوْن.
He sat across from the interviewer.	*húwwa ʔá3ad ʔuddām iššáxṣ ílli byi3mílu muʔábla.*	هُوَّ قعد قُدّام الشّخْص اللي بِيِعْمِلُه مُقابْلة.
behind	*wára*	**وَرا**
I parked behind the house.	*ána rakánt il3arabíyya wára -lbēt.*	أنا ركنْت العربية وَرا البيْت.
around, surrounding	*ḫawalēn*	**حَواليْن**

There's a fence surrounding the house.	*fī sūr ɧawalēn ilbēt.*	فيه سور حَوالينْ البيْت.
through	*min gúwwa*	**مِن جُوّه**
The train went through the tunnel.	*il?áţr^ə 3ádda min gúwwa -náfa?.*	القطْر عدّى مِن جُوّه النّفق.

Often a verb followed by a preposition in English will translate as a verb without a preposition in Arabic.

He swam across the river.	*3ádda -nnahr^ə 3ōm.* (lit. He crossed the river swimming.)	عدّى النّهْر عوْم.
Don't go down the ladder.	*ma-tinzílš issíllim da.*	متِنْزِلْش السِّلِّم ده.
The cat climbed up the tree.	*il?úţţa ţíl3it iššágara.* (lit. The cat ascended the tree.)	القُطّة طِلْعِت الشّجرة.
down from; off	*min 3ála*	**مِن على**
The cat climbed down the tree.	*il?úţţa nízlit min 3ála -ššágara.*	القُطّة نزِلْت مِن على الشّجرة.
The book fell off the table.	*ilkitāb wí?i3 min 3ála -ţţarabēza.*	الكِتاب وِقع مِن على الطّرابيْزة.
past	*min ?uddām* *min gamb*	**مِن قُدّام** **مِن جنْب**
I walked past the restaurant.	*ána mšīt min ?uddām ilmáţ3am.*	أنا مْشيت مِن قُدّام المطْعم.

Prepositions are highly idiomatic, making them notoriously tricky to translate. Notice how 'against' is translated in the following English sentences literally as 'on' and 'in front of' in Arabic.

He leaned against the car.	*húwwa sánad 3ála -l3arabíyya.*	هُوَّ سند على العربية.

The table is against the wall.	*iṭṭarabēza ʔuddām ilḫēṭa.*	الطّرابيْزة قُدّام الحيْطة.
toward	*náḫyit*	**ناحْيِةْ**
He ran toward the door.	*húwwa gíri náḫyit ilbāb.*	هُوَّ جِري ناحْيِةْ الباب.
The train is heading toward Cairo.	*ilʔáṭr rāyiḫ náḫyit ilqāhíra.*	القطْر رايِح ناحْيِةْ القاهِرة.
with	*má3a*	**معَ**
I had dinner with my friends.	*it3aššēt má3a -ṣḫābi.*	اِتْعشّيْت معَ أصْحابي.
by, with	*bi-*	**بِـ**
I came to work by bus.	*ána gīt iššúɣlᵊ bi-lbāṣ.*	أنا جيت الشُّغْل بِالباص.
She wrote the letter by hand.	*híyya kátabit ilgawāb bi-ídha.*	هِيَّ كتبْت الجَواب بإيدْها.
She wrote the letter with a pencil.	*híyya kátabit ilgawāb bi-ʔálam ruṣāṣ.*	هِيَّ كتبِت الجَواب بِقلم رُصاص.
without	*min ɣēr*	**مِن غيْر**
I can't live without you.	*ma-ʔdárš a3īš min ɣērak.*	مقْدرْش أعيش مِن غيْرك.

56 Verbs

The following common verbs did not fit neatly into other categories. If you cannot find a verb here, try the index in the back of the book to see if it is listed under another category. Also, you can find over 1,000 verbs listed in the indexes of Lingualism's *Colloquial Arabic Verbs: Conjugation Tables and Grammar.*

to abandon, desert	*hágar* [1s3]	هجر
to accept	*wāfiʔ* [3s]	وافِق
to accompany	*rāɧ* [1h1] *má3a* *míši* [1d5] *má3a*	راح معَ مِشي معَ
to adjust	*ẓábbaṭ* [2s2]	ظبّط
to admit	*i3táraf* [8s1]	اِعْترف
to advise, recommend	*náṣaɧ* [1s1]	نصح
to affect	*ʔássar* [2s2] *3ála*	أثّر على
to allow	*sámaɧ* [1s1]	سمح
to answer, respond, reply	*raddᵊ* [1g2] *3ála* *gāwib* [3s] *3ála*	ردّ على جاوِب على
to apologize for	*i3tázar* [8s1] *3an*	اِعْتذر عن
to appear	*ẓáhar* [1s1]	ظهر
to appreciate	*qáddar* [2s2]	قدّر
to approve of	*ríḍi* [1d4] *bi-*	رِضي بِـ
to arrange, organize	*náẓẓam* [2s2]	نظّم
to ascend, go up	*ṭíli3* [1s4]	طِلع
to ask	*sáʔal* [1s1]	سأل

to attend	*ḩáḑar* [1s1]	**حضر**
to be	*kān* [1h1]	**كان**
to be able to, can	*ʔídir* [1s4] *3írif* [1s4]	**قِدِر** **عِرِف**
Can you swim?	*tí3raf ti3ūm?*	تِعْرف تِعوم؟
I can't understand a word you're saying.	*ma-ʔdárš áfham ḩāga min kalāmak.*	مقْدرْش أفْهم حاجة مِن كلامك.
to become, be	*báʔa* [1d1]	**بقى**
to beg, plead	*itwássil* [5s1]	**اِتْوَسِّل**
to begin, start	*bádaʔ* [1s1]	**بدأ**
to behave	*iḩtáram* [8s1]	**اِحْترم**
to bet	*rāhin* [3s]	**راهِن**
to blame __ for	*lām* [1h1] *__ 3ála*	**لام __ على**
to break	*kásar* [1s1]	**كسر**
to bring, get	*gāb* [1h2]	**جاب**
to burn	*ḩáraʔ* [1s1]	**حرق**
to care	*ihtámm* [8g]	**اِهْتمّ**
to carry, lift, pick up	*šāl* [1h2]	**شال**
Did she carry the box to the kitchen?	*híyya šālit iṣṣandūʔ li-lmáţbax?*	هِيَّ شالِت الصّنْدوق للمطْبخ؟
He lifted the child up.	*šāl iţţífl.*	شال الطِّفْل.
He picked the book up from the table.	*húwwa šāl ilkitāb min 3ála -ţţarabēza.*	هُوَّ شال الكِتاب مِن على الطّرابيْزة.
to change	*ɣáyyar* [2s2]	**غيّر**

to change, be changed	*ityáyyar* [5s2]	اِتْغيّر
to chase, pursue	*ţārid* [3s]	طارِد
to cheat, deceive	*ɣašš* [1g3]	غشّ
to cheer, encourage	*šágga3* [2s2]	شجّع
to choose	*ixtār* [8h]	اِخْتار
to climb, ascend	*ţíli3* [1s4]	طِلِع
to close, lock	*ʔáfal* [1s2]	قفل
to come	*gih* [i1]	جِهْ
to compare	*qārin* [3s]	قارِن
to contact	*ittáşal* [8s1] *bi-*	اِتّصل بِـ
to continue	*kámmil* [2s1]	كمِّل
to decline	*ráfaḍ* [1s3]	رفض
to decrease, reduce	*ʔall* [1g3]	قلّ
to demand	*ţálab* [1s3]	طلب
to deny	*nákar* [1s2]	نكر
to descend, go down	*nízil* [1s5]	نِزِل
to describe	*wáşaf* [1s2]	وَصف
to design	*şámmim* [2s1]	صمِّم
to differ	*ixtálaf* [8s1]	اِخْتلف
to disappear	*ixtáfa* [8d]	اِخْتفى
to do, make	*3ámal* [1s2]	عمل
to drop	*wáʔʔa3* [2s2]	وَقّع
He dropped his book.	*wáʔʔa3 kitābu.*	وَقّع كِتابُه.

to edit, correct	*ḥárrar* [2s2] *3áddil* [2s1]	حرّر عدِّل
to express	*3ábbar* [2s2] *3an*	عبرّ عن
I can't express myself in Arabic very well.	*ma-baʔdárš a3ábbar 3an náfsi bi-l3árabi kwáyyis.*	مبقْدرْش أعبرّ عن نفْسي بِالعربي كْوَيِّس.
to fall	*wíʔi3* [i5]	وِقِع
to find	*lāʔa* [3d] *láʔa* [i4]	لاقى لقى
to finish, come to an end	*intáha* [8d]	اِنْتهى
to finish, end, complete, accomplish	*xállaṣ* [2s2] *náha* [1d2]	خلّص نهى
to fix	*ṣállaḥ* [2s2]	صلّح
to float	*ṭáfa* [1d2]	طفا
The ball is floating in the water.	*ilkōra btíṭfu fōʔ ilmáyya.*	الكوْرة بْتِطْفو فوْق الميّة.
to get, take, receive, obtain	*ḥáṣal* [1s1] *3ála*	حصل على
to give	*ídda* [i2]	إدّى
to go	*rāḥ* [1h1]	راح
to happen	*gára* [1d1] *ḥáṣal* [1s1]	جرى حصل
to have	*kān* [1h1] *3ándu*	كان عنْدُه
to help	*sā3id* [3s]	ساعِد
to hit	*ḍárab* [1s1] *xábaṭ* [1s1]	ضرب خبط

to imagine	*itxáyyil* [5s1]	اِتْخيِّل
to intend to	*náwa* [1d2]	نَوى
I intend to succeed at my job.	*ána nāwi ʔángaħ fi šúɣli.*	أنا ناوي أنْجح في شُغْلي.
to jump	*naṭṭ* [1g2]	نطّ
to keep, continue (doing)	*istamárrᵊ* [10g1] *fi-* *fíḍil* [1s4]	اِسْتمرّ في فِضِل
to leave; quit	*sāb* [1h2]	ساب
to lie	*kídib* [1s5]	كِدِب
to live	*3āš* [1h2]	عاش
to look	*baṣṣᵊ* [1g2] *li-*	بصّ لِـ
to lose	*xísir* [1s4]	خِسِر
to mean	*ʔáṣad* [1s3]	قصد
to move	*itħárrak* [5s2]	اِتْحرّك
He hasn't moved in ten minutes.	*húwwa ma-tħarrákšᵊ baʔālu 3ášar daʔāyiʔ.*	هُوَّ متْحرّكْش بقالُه عشر دقايِق.
to move (something)	*ħárrak* [2s2]	حرّك
I can't move my leg!	*miš ʔādir aħárrak rígli!*	مِش قادِر أحرّك رِجْلي!
to open	*fátaħ* [1s1]	فتح
to order, command	*ʔámar* [1s3]	أمر
to order, request	*ṭálab* [1s3]	طلب
to pass, go past	*3ádda* [2d]	عدّى
to prepare	*gáhhiz* [2s1]	جهِّز
to prohibit	*mána3* [1s1]	منع

to punish	*3āqib* [3s]	عاقِب
to put, set (down)	*ɧaṭṭ* [1h1]	حطّ
He set down the book on the table.	*húwwa ɧaṭṭ ilkitāb 3ála -ṭṭarabēza.*	هُوَّ حطّ الكِتاب على الطّربيْزة.
to say, tell	*ʔāl* [1h1]	قال
to show	*wárra* [2d]	وَرى
to sink	*ɣíriʔ* [1s4]	غِرِق
The Titanic sank over a hundred years ago.	*it*[Titanic] *ɣírʔit min áktar min mīt sána.*	التّايْتانيك غِرْقِت مِن أكْتر مِن ميةْ سنة.
to stay	*istánna* [10.2i] *ʔá3ad* [1s3]	اِسْتنّى قعد
to succeed	*nígiɧ* [1s4]	نِجِح
to suggest, propose	*iqtáraɧ* [8s1]	اِقْترح
to take	*ʔáxad* [i3] *xad* [i3]	أخد خد
to tear	*mázzaʔ* [2s2]	مزّق
to thank	*šákar* [1s3]	شكر
to tie	*rábaṭ* [1s3]	ربط
to touch	*lámas* [1s2]	لمس
to try, attempt	*ɧāwil* [3s]	حاوِل
to try, try out	*gárrab* [2s2]	جرّب
to use	*istá3mil* [10s1] *istáxdim* [10s1]	اِسْتعْمِل اِسْتخْدِم
to wait	*istánna* [10.2i]	اِسْتنّى

to walk, go, leave	*míši* [1d5]	مِشى
to welcome, greet	*ráђђab* [2s2]	رحّب

57 Adjectives

The following common adjectives did not fit neatly into other categories. If you cannot find a verb here, try the index in the back of the book to see if it is listed under another category.

good	*kuwáyyis*	كُوَيِّس
bad	*wíħiš*	وِحِش
hard	*şulb*	صُلْب
soft	*ţári*	طري
difficult, hard	*şa3b*	صعْب
easy	*sahl*	سهْل
important	*muhímm*	مُهِمّ
necessary	*ḑarūri*	ضروري
strong	*ʔáwi (aʔwíya)*	قَوي (أقْوِيا)
weak	*ḑa3īf (ḑú3afa)*	ضعيف (ضُعفا)
deep	*3amīq*	عميق
shallow	*ḑaħl*	ضحْل
long; tall (person)	*ţawīl (ţuwāl)*	طَويل (طُوال)
He's very tall.	*húwwa ţawīl áwi.*	هُوَّ طَويل أَوي.
short	*ʔuşáyyar (ʔuşār)*	قُصيرّ (قُصار)
She's quite short.	*híyya ʔuşayyára ʔáwi.*	هِيَّ قُصيرّة أَوي.
old, ancient	*ʔadīm (ʔudām)*	قديم (قُدام)
new	*gidīd (gudād)*	جِديد (جُداد)
clear, obvious	*wāḑiħ*	واضِح

His answer was very clear.	*igábtu kānit wáḍḫa giddan.*	إجابْته كانِت واضْحة جِدّاً.
unclear	*miš wāḍiḫ*	مِش واضِح
clean	*niḍīf (nuḍāf)*	نِضيف (نُضاف)
dirty	*wísix*	وِسِخ
heavy	*tiʔīl*	تِقيل
light	*xafīf (xufāf)*	خفيف (خُفاف)
ready	*gāhiz*	جاهِز
Are you ready yet?	*ínta gāhiz?*	إنْتَ جاهِز؟
I'm ready!	*ána gāhiz!*	أنا جاهِز!
right (person)	*ṣaḫḫ* [invar.] *3ándu ḫaʔʔ*	صحّ عنْدُه حقّ
Yes, you're right!	*áywa, ínta ṣaḫḫ!*	أَيْوَة، إنْتَ صحّ!
wrong (person)	*ɣalṭān*	غلْطان
I think you're wrong (about that).	*a3táqid ínnak ɣalṭān.*	أعْتِقِد إنّك غلْطان.
slow	*baṭīʔ (buṭāʔ)*	بطيء (بُطاء)
fast, quick	*sarī3 (surā3)*	سريع (سُراع)
hot	*suxn*	سُخْن
warm	*dāfi*	دافي
cool, cold	*sāʔi3*	ساقِع
famous	*mašhūr*	مشْهور
independent	*mustaqíll*	مُسْتقِلّ
busy	*mašɣūl*	مشْغول

empty; available, free (person)	*fāḍi*	فاضي
Are you free tomorrow?	*ínta fāḍi búkra?*	إنْتَ فاضي بُكْره؟
full	*malyān*	ملْيان
useful	*mufīd*	مُفيد
useless	*ma-lūš lázma* *min ɣēr fáyda*	ملوش لازْمة مِن غيْر فايْدة
careful, cautious	*ɧarīṣ (ɧuraṣā?)* *bi-htimām*	حريص (حُرصاء) بِاهْتِمام
careless	*múhmil*	مُهْمِل
absent-minded	*sarɧān*	سرْحان
open	*maftūɧ*	مفْتوح
closed	*maʔfūl*	مقْفول
wet	*mablūl*	مبْلول
dry	*nāšif*	ناشِف
quiet	*hādi*	هادي
noisy	*múz3ig*	مُزْعِج
rough	*xíšin*	خِشِن
smooth	*nā3im*	ناعِم
narrow; tight	*ḍáyyaʔ*	ضيّق
wide; loose	*wāsi3*	واسِع
dark	*ḍílim* *miḍállim*	ضِلْم مِضلِّم
bright, light	*mináwwar*	مِنوّر

sharp	*ḩādd*	حادّ
blunt	*miš ḩādd*	مِش حادّ
additional	*iḑāfi*	إضافي
the same __	*nafs il__*	نفْس الـ__
similar	*mušābih*	مْشابِه
different	*muxtálif*	مُخْتلِف
possible	*múmkin*	مُمْكِن
impossible	*mustaḩīl*	مُسْتحيل
probable, likely	*muḩtámal*	مُحْتمل

Index

boner **30**
bonnet **102**
bonus **73**
boob **28**
book **114**, **123**, **146**, **150**
bookcase **51**
bookmark **114**
bookstore **114**
boot (car boot) **103**
boots **37**
border **146**
born **1**
borrow **111**
bosom **28**
boss **72**
bottle **58**
bottom **30**
bowels **28**
bowl **47**
boxing **137**
boy **2**
boyfriend **11**
bra **34**
bracelet **40**
bracket **187**
braids **23**
brain **16**
brain sandwich **69**
brake **104**
branch **218**
Brazil **193**
bread **66**
break **72**, **81**, **90**, **263**
break (a bill) **158**
break in **155**
break someone's heart **11**
break the law **155**
break up **11**
break wind **31**
breakfast **57**
breast **28**
breastfeed **1**
breath **21**
breathe **21**
breathe in/out **142**
brick **110**
bride **12**
bridge **102**
briefcase **35**
bright **271**
bring **263**
broad bean **62**
broccoli **62**
brooch **41**
broom **44**
brother **7**
brow **16**
brown **220**
bruise **90**
brush **23**
brush one's teeth **20**, **52**
buckle **35**
Buddha **178**
Buddhism **178**
Buddhist **178**
buffalo **212**
bug **215**
build **109**
building **109**
Bulgaria **192**
bum **31**
bumper **106**
bun **23**
burial **5**
burn **90**, **263**
burp **21**
bury **4**
bus **98**, **149**
bus driver **75**, **98**
bus station **149**
bus stop **98**
bush **218**
business **160**
business class **147**
business trip **73**, **160**
businessman **160**
businesswoman **160**
busker **133**
busy **270**
but **254**
butcher **75**
butcher shop **107**
butt **31**
butter **59**
butterfly **215**
buttocks **30**
button **37**
buy **117**
by **261**
cabbage **62**
cabinet **47**, **151**
cactus **219**
Caesar salad **63**
café **108**
cafeteria **81**
cage **212**
Cairo **195**, **197**
Cairo Opera House **198**
Cairo Tower **198**
Cairo University **199**
cake **61**
calculate **229**
calculation **229**
calculator **229**
calendar **236**
calf **27**
call **14**, **96**
call to prayer **178**
call: be called **14**
calligraphy **183**
calories **141**
camel **163**
camera **127**
camp **145**
campus **84**
can **58**, **263**
Canada **193**
canal **202**
canary **214**
cancel **161**
canceled **147**
cancer **90**
candidate **71**
candle **45**
candy **61**
cap **36**
capital **153**
capital city **153**
capital punishment **157**
capsicum **62**
car **100**
car door **103**
car park **101**
car roof **106**
carbonated drink **57**
cardinal number **226**
cardio exercise **140**
cardiologist **87**
cards (game) **135**
care **263**
career **74**
careful **271**
careless **271**
carnation **218**
carpenter **75**
carpet **43**
carrot **62**
carry **263**
carton **69**
cartoon **124**
case **186**
cashier **75**, **119**
casserole dish **48**
cassette (tape) **125**
cast **90**
cat **212**
cataract **202**
catch **138**
cattle **162**
cauliflower **62**
cautious **271**
cavity **93**
CD **125**
CD player **125**
ceiling **43**
celery **62**
cell phone **96**
cemetary **5**
centimeter **223**
century **239**
cereals **163**
ceremony **176**

certain **173**
certificate **85**
chain **100**
chair **43**, **160**
chairman **160**
chalk **80**
champion **138**
change **263**
change (clothes) **38**
change (coins) **158**
change (money back) **117**
change money **146**
changing room **140**
channel **124**
charge (accusation) **157**
chase **264**
cheap **117**
cheat **13**, **264**
check **82**, **112**
check in **147**, **150**
check out **150**
check-up **88**
Check! (in chess) **135**
Checkmate! (in chess) **135**
cheddar cheese **60**
cheek **16**
cheer **264**
Cheers! **59**
cheese **60**
cheetah **213**
chef **75**, **121**
chemistry **86**
cherry **63**
chess **135**
chess piece **135**
chest **28**
chew **21**, **54**, **60**
chew gum **60**
chewing gum **60**
chick **162**
chicken **67**, **162**
chickpea **62**
chickpea salad **63**
child **43837**
childhood **3**
childish **2**
children's program **124**
Chile **193**
chili pepper **62**
chin **16**
China **192**
Chinese **181**
chipped tooth **93**
chives **65**
chocolate **60**
choir **180**
choke **55**
choke on **22**
choose **264**
chop **47**
chop wood **53**
Christ **178**
Christian **177**
Christianity **177**
Christmas **239**
chrysanthemum **219**
chubby **32**
church **179**
church service **179**
cigar **130**
cigarette **130**
cigarette butt **131**
cinema **128**
cinnamon **65**
circle **222**
circular **222**
circus **130**
Citadel **198**
citizen **152**
citizenship **188**
city **107**
city hall **107**
City of the Dead **199**
civil servant **71**
class **79**, **146**
Classical Arabic **182**
classical music **132**
classroom **80**
claw **216**
clean **44**, **270**
clean-shaven **24**
cleaner **75**
clear **269**
clear (a table) **46**
clever **167**
click on **94**
client **73**
cliff **201**
climate **211**
climb **264**
clinic **88**
clock **44**
close **94**, **264**
close one's eyes **17**
close one's mouth **20**
close to **259**
closed **271**
cloth **39**
clothesline **39**
clothing **34**
cloud **208**
clove **65**
clown **130**
clutch **104**
coach **147**
coal **131**
coast **143**
coat **36**
cobra **214**
Coca Cola **58**
cock **30**
cockroach **215**
coconut **64**
coffee **58**
coffee beans **59**
coffee maker **48**
coffee shop **108**
coffin **5**
coin **158**
Coke **58**
cola **57**
cold **270**
cold (illness) **89**
cold water **52**
coldness **207**
collar **34**
colleague **72**
college **79**
college student **85**
colloquial language **182**
Colombia **193**
colon **187**
color **220**
colorful **221**
column **114**
comb **23**
come **264**
comedy program **123**
comet **204**
comfortable **149**
comic book **123**
comma **187**
command **266**
commerce **160**
commercial **160**
commercial venture **160**
commit a crime **155**
committee **160**
company **72**, **160**
compare **264**
compartment **149**
compass **204**
complain **171**
complaint **171**
complete **265**
composition **82**
computer **94**
computer program **94**
concrete **110**
condiments **64**
condom **92**
condor **214**
conference **161**

congested (nose) **89**
conjugate **185**
conjugation **185**
consciousness **166**
consonant **187**
constipated **89**
constitution **153**
construction **109**
contact **264**
contact lenses **40**
contagious **91**
continent **201**
continue **264**, **266**
convict **156**
cook **47**, **75**, **121**
cookbook **48**
cooker **47**
cookie **61**
cooking **47**
cool **270**
coolness **207**
coop **162**
Coptic Cairo **199**
copy **80**
corn **163**
corner **107**
corpse **4**
corral **162**
correct **80**, **265**
correct (a test) **83**
cosmos **203**
cost **117**
cotton **39**
cotton candy **61**
couch **46**
cough **21**, **89**
council **160**
count **226**
counter **47**, **113**
country **188**
couple (dating) **11**
couple (of) **225**
coupon **118**
courgette **63**
courier bag **35**
course **83**
court **156**
courtyard **53**
cousin **44084**
cow **162**
coworker **72**
crab **68**
cracker **61**
craft **74**
crash **106**
crazy **167**
cream **60**
cream soup **69**
cremate **5**
cremation **5**
cricket **215**
crime **155**
criminal **155**
crisps **60**
criticism **171**
criticize **171**
crochet **126**
crocodile **214**
cross the street **101**
cross walk **101**
cross-eyed **18**
crow **214**
crowd **129**
cruel **170**
cry **18**, **168**
cubic meter **223**
cucumber **62**
culture **188**
cumin **65**
cup **58**
cupboard **47**
cure **91**
curly (hair) **22**
currency **158**
curriculum **80**
curry **65**
curtain **43**
cushion **49**
customer **119**
customs **146**
customs officer **146**
cut **47**, **90**
cut in half **47**
cute **33**
cuttlefish **68**
cyclist **100**
cyclone **210**
Czech Republic **191**
dad **6**
dairy products **59**
daisy **219**
Damanhur **194**
Damietta **194**
dance **134**
dancer **134**
dark **271**
dark (color) **221**
dark-skinned **24**
darkness **208**
darling **11**
darn **126**
dashboard **103**
date **63**
date (romantic) **11**
date palm **218**
date: go on a date with __ **11**
dating **11**
daughter **7**
dawn prayer **179**
day **234**
day off **122**
day shift **73**
dead **4**
deaf **20**
death **4**
death sentence **157**
debt **111**
decade **239**
deceased **4**
deceive **264**
December **236**
decide **166**
decision **166**
declare **146**
declare war on **164**
declension **185**
decline **185**, **264**
decrease **264**
deep **269**
deer **213**
defecate **31**
defend **164**
defense **157**, **164**
definite **187**
degree **85**
delayed **147**
delete **94**
delicious **55**
Delta (region) **194**
demand **264**
democracy **152**
democratic **152**
demolish **109**
demon **177**
demonstrate **153**
demonstration **153**
demonstrator **153**
Denmark **190**
dent **106**
dental floss **52**
dentist **75**, **93**
dentistry **86**
deny **264**
depart **149**
department **84**, **151**
departure **149**
deposit **112**
descend **264**
descendants **10**
describe **264**
desert **202**, **262**
design **264**
desire **175**
desk **51**, **80**
devil **177**
diabetes **90**
diabetic **90**
diagnose **88**
diagnosis **88**
dial **97**
dialect **182**
diamonds **41**
diaper **1**
diarrhea **89**
dice **47**, **136**
dick **30**
dictator **153**

dictatorship **153**
dictionary **185**
die **4**
diet **140**
Diet Coke **58**
Diet Pepsi **58**
differ **264**
different **272**
difficult **269**
dig **53**
diligent **170**
dining room **46**
dining table **46**
dinner **57**
diploma **85**
dirty **270**
disagree **173**
disappear **264**
discount **118**
discussion **173**
disease **87**
dish **46**
dishes **48**
dishwashing liquid **48**
dissertation **85**
distance **223**
dive **144**
divide **230**
divorce **13**
divorced **13**
divorcee **13**
dizziness **89**
dizzy **89**
do **264**
doctor **15**, **75**, **87**
doctor's office **88**
Doctorate **85**
documentary **124**
dog **212**
dog collar **212**
doll **135**
dollar **158**
dolphin **214**
donkey **162**
door **43**
doorman **43**
Doqqi (district) **199**
dormant **203**
dormitories **84**
dove **214**
download **95**, **126**
downstairs **253**
downtown **107**
doze off **50**
dragonfly **215**
drama **123**, **129**
draw **127**
drawer **51**
drawing **127**
dream **50**
dress **35**
dresser **51**
dressing gown **36**
drink **54**
drive **100**, **103**
driver **100**
driver's license **100**
drop **264**
drop off **102**
drought **211**
drowsy **50**
drum **133**
drunk **59**
dry **39**, **211**, **271**
dry herbs **64**
dry off **52**
dry skin **24**
dryer **39**
dual **186**
duck **163**
Duha prayer **179**
dumbbell **140**
dusk **204**
dust **44**
dust devil **210**
dust storm **210**
dustbin **49**
dustman **75**
dusty **44**
Dutch **181**
duvet **49**
dye **22**
eagle **214**
ear **19**
ear wax **20**
earlobe **19**
early **243**
earn **73**
earphones **126**
earring **40**
earth **201**
earthquake **203**
east **204**
Easter **239**
eastern **205**
Eastern Desert **196**
easy **269**
eat **54**
eat soup **68**
economics **86**
economy class **147**
edit **265**
editor **75**
educated **78**
education **78**
egg **66**
egg white **66**
eggplant **62**
Egypt **188**
Egyptian Arabic **182**
Egyptian Museum **197**
Egyptian pound **158**
Eid Al-Adha **238**
Eid Al-Fitr **238**
Eid prayers **179**
eight **227**
eighteen **227**
eighth **232**
eighty **228**
elbow **25**
elect **152**
elections **152**
electric razor **53**
electrical outlet **45**
electrician **75**
elementary school **78**
elephant **213**
elevator **109**
eleven **227**
elliptical trainer **141**
email **95**
embarrassed **169**
embroider **126**
emeralds **41**
emergency brake **103**
Emirates **190**
emotion **168**
emperor **152**
empire **152**
employ **72**
employed **71**
employee **72**
employer **72**
employment **72**
empress **152**
empty **271**
encourage **264**
end **265**
engaged **11**
engagement **11**
engagement ring **40**
engineer **75**
England **191**
English **181**, **191**
enjoy **171**
enjoyable **122**
enlist **164**
enough **251**
enroll **83**
enrollment **83**
entertain guests **126**
entrepreneur **160**
envelope **113**
envious **170**
Epiphany **239**
episode **124**
equal **230**
equal to **230**
equals **230**
equator **202**
era **239**
erase **115**
eraser **115**
erection **30**

erupt **203**
eruption **203**
escalator **109**
escape **157**
especially **249**
espresso **58**
essay **82**
Ethiopia **190**
euro **158**
Europe **201**
evade **159**
evangelical **180**
even **226**
evening **234**, **242**
evening prayer **179**
every **224**
everyone **244**
everything **245**
everywhere **249**
evil **177**
exam **81**
examination **88**
examine **88**
exchange **120**
exchange office **146**
exchange rate **146**
excited **169**
exciting **169**
exclamation mark **187**
excrement **31**
exercise **138**, **141**, **182**
expect **167**
expenses **159**
expensive **118**
experience **72**
expiration date **55**
expire **145**
explode **164**
explosion **164**
express **265**
express train **149**
expressway **102**
extension cord **45**
extinct **203**
extra-large (size) **38**
eye **16**
eye doctor **87**
eyebrow **17**
eyelash **17**
eyelid **17**
eyesight **18**
fabric **39**
face **16**
factory **161**
faculty **84**
fail (a test) **82**
faint **89**
fair **206**
fair-skinned **24**
fairy tale **114**
faith **176**
Faiyum **195**
falafel **69**
falcon **214**
fall **237**, **265**
fall asleep **49**
falling star **204**
family **6**
famous **270**
fantasy **129**
far from **259**
Farafra **196**
farm **162**
farmer **75**, **162**
Farsi **181**
fart **31**
fast **249**, **270**
fast food **60**, **121**
fat **32**, **68**
fateer **69**
father **6**
faucet **48**
fava bean **62**
fax **96**
fax machine **96**
fear **169**
Feast of the Sacrifice **238**
feathers **216**
February **236**
feces **31**
fed up with **168**
fee **118**
feed **212**
feel **168**
feeler **216**
feeling **168**
felucca (river sailboat) **122**
feminine **186**
fence **42**
fender **106**
fender-bender **106**
fertilize **219**
fever **89**
few **224**
fiancé(e) **12**
field **163**
fifteen **227**
fifth **231**, **233**
fifty **228**
fig **63**
file **94**
filling (tooth) **93**
film **123**, **128**
final exam **81**
finance **111**
financial **159**
finch **214**
find **265**
finger **26**
fingernail **26**
fingerprint **26**
fingertip **26**
finish **265**
Finland **190**
fire (make redundant) **74**
fire fighter **75**
fire station **107**
fired **74**
first **231**
first class **148**
fiscal **159**
fish **67**, **215**
fish bone **67**
fisherman **75**
fishing **127**
fishing pole **127**
fishing tackle **127**
fist **27**
fitness **138**
five **227**
fix **265**
fixed price **118**
flashcard **185**
flat **42**, **201**
flat tire **104**
flea **215**
flight **146**
flight attendant **75**, **148**
float **265**
flood **211**
floor **42**, **43**, **110**
floss **21**, **52**
flour **66**
flower **218**
flu **89**
fluently **184**
flush the toilet **52**
flute **133**
fly **146**, **215**
fog **209**
folder **94**
folk music **132**
follow a recipe **48**
food **54**
foot **27**, **223**
football (American) **137**
football (soccer) **136**
football pitch **137**
for **243**
for free **118**
forefathers **10**
forehead **16**
foreign **188**
foreign language **181**
foreigner **188**
forest **202**
forget **166**
forgetful **166**
fork **46**
forty **228**
forward **125**
fountain **107**
four **226**

fourteen **227**
fourth **231**, **232**
fox **213**
fraction **232**
France **191**
freckles **25**
free **118**, **154**
free (person) **271**
free weights **140**
freedom **154**
freeze **202**
freezer **47**
freight **98**
French **181**, **191**
fresh **56**
freshman **84**
Friday **235**
Friday prayer **178**
Friday sermon **178**
fried **69**
friend **122**
friendly **170**
fringe **23**
frog **215**
from **258**
front door **43**
front seat **103**
front teeth **21**
frown **16**, **168**
fruit **63**
fry **48**
fuck **13**
ful (refried fava beans) **69**
full **55**, **271**
full stop **187**
full-time **71**
fun **122**
funds **159**
funeral **4**
funny **170**
fur **216**
furnished **43**
furniture **43**
fuse **45**
fuse box **45**
fuchsia **220**
future **240**
future tense **186**
gain weight **140**
galabeya **35**
gallbladder **29**
game **135**
game show **124**
garbage **48**
garbage can **49**
garbage collector **75**
garden **53**
Garden City (district) **198**
gardener **42**, **75**
gargle **52**
garlic **62**
gas gauge **105**
gas pedal **104**
gas pump **105**
gasoline **105**
gate **42**, **147**
gazelle **213**
Gazira Island **198**
gear **104**
gender **186**
generous **170**
genie **177**
geography **86**
geology **86**
geometry **86**
German **181**
Germany **191**
get **263**, **265**
get dressed **38**
get in **98**
get off **98**
get off work **72**
get on **98**
get out of **98**
get up **51**
ghee **59**
ginger **65**
giraffe **213**
girl **2**
girlfriend **11**
give **265**
give birth **1**, **92**
Giza **195**, **199**
gland **29**
glass **58**, **110**
glass container (of shisha) **131**
glasses **40**
glove **36**
glove compartment **103**
go **265**, **268**
go down **264**
go online **95**
go past **266**
go up **262**
goal **136**
goat **162**
goatee **23**
god **176**
goddess **176**
gold **41**
golf **137**
good **206**, **269**
good at **86**
good luck **177**
good-looking **33**
goose **163**
gorge **201**
govern **151**
government **151**
grade **82**
grade (school year) **78**
graduate from **84**
grain **163**
gram **223**
grammar **185**
grammatical **185**
grandchildren **9**
granddaughter **9**
grandfather **9**
grandma **9**
grandmother **9**
grandpa **9**
grandson **9**
grape **63**
grapefruit **63**
graphic novel **123**
grasshopper **216**
grasslands **203**
grateful **169**
grave **5**
gravestone **5**
graveyard shift **73**
gravy **65**
gray **220**
graze **163**
greasy **68**
Great Britain **191**
great-grandfather **9**
Greater Cairo **197**
Greater Eid **238**
greedy **170**
Greek **181**
green **220**
green bean **62**
green light **101**
green onion **62**
greet **268**
grenade **164**
grilled **69**
grip **27**
grocery store **107**
groom **12**
ground **201**
ground floor **109**
group **132**
grow **219**
grow (a plant) **219**
grow old **3**
grow up **2**
grown-up **2**
guess **167**
guitar **133**
guitar strings **133**
gulf **202**
Gulf Arabic **182**
Gulf of Aqaba **195**
Gulf of Suez **195**
gums **20**
gym **139**
gym clothes **140**
gymnasium **81**
Hadith **179**
haggle **118**
hail **209**
hail (a taxi) **99**
hair **22**
hair clip **36**
hair dryer **52**
haircut **23**

hairdresser **76**
half **232**
half-brother **8**
half-sister **8**
Halloween **237**
ham **67**
hamburger **60**
hammer **53**
hand **26**
hand brake **103**
handbag **35**
handicapped **87**
handsome **33**
handwriting **183**
hang **44**
hang (execution) **157**
hang out (laundry) **39**
hang out (with friends) **122**
hang up (the phone) **97**
hanger **51**
happen **265**
happy **168**
hard **269**
hard of hearing **19**
hard-on **30**
hard-working **170**
harsh **170**
harvest **163**
hat **36**
hate **171**
have **265**
have (a child) **7**
have nasal congestion **89**
hawk **214**
hay **163**
hazelnut **64**
he **244**
head **16**
head office **161**
headache **89**
headboard **49**
headlight **106**
headline **114**
headphones **126**
headquarters **161**
headscarf **35**
headstone **5**
heal **91**
healing **91**
health **87**
health club **139**
healthful **56**
healthy **56**, **87**
hear **19**
hearing aid **20**
heart **28**
heartbeat **28**
heat **207**
heat up **47**
heater **45**
heatwave **207**
heaven **176**
heavy **270**
Hebrew **181**
heel **27**
height **32**, **222**
Heliopolis (district) **199**
hell **177**
helmet **100**
help **265**
Helwan **197**
hen **162**
herbs **64**
here **249**
high **206**
high heels **37**
high school **78**
high-rise (building) **109**
highway **102**
hijab **35**
hiking **145**
hill **201**
hilly **201**
Hindi **181**
Hindu **178**
Hinduism **178**
hippopotamus **213**
hips **28**
history **86**
hit **138**, **265**
hitchhike **149**
HIV **90**
hobby **171**
hockey **137**
hold **27**
holiday **143**, **237**
Holland **191**
home loan **111**
homework **82**
honey **66**
honeymoon **12**
hood (car) **102**
hook **127**
hookah **131**
hoop (basketball) **137**
hope **175**
horn **216**
horror movie **129**
horse **163**
hose **53**
hose (of shisha) **131**
hospital **88**
hot **270**
hot dog **67**
hot water **52**
hotel **150**
hour **240**
house **42**
house painter **76**
housekeeper **43**
housework **44**
how **246**
how long **247**
how many **247**
how much **247**
how often **248**
humid **211**
hundred **228**
Hungary **191**
hunger **55**
hungry **55**
hunt **127**
hunter **127**
hunting **127**
Hurghada **196**
hurricane **210**
husband **8**
I **244**
ice **57**
ice cream **59**
idiocy **167**
if **254**, **256**
ill **87**
illegal **156**
illegible **183**
illiteracy **78**
illiterate **78**
illness **87**
imagination **167**
imagine **167**, **266**
imam **76**, **178**
immature **2**
important **269**
impossible **272**
imprisoned **157**
in **258**
in front of **259**
in good health **87**
in love **11**
in order to **254**
in the box **258**
incentive **73**
inch **223**
income **159**
incorrect **80**
indefinite **187**
Independence Day **237**
independent **270**
India **192**
Indian Ocean **202**
indigestion **89**
Indonesia **192**
industry **161**
infant **1**
infection **91**
inflect **185**
inflection **186**
injection **91**
injured **90**
ink **115**
insane **167**
insect **215**
inside **252**, **258**
insomnia **50**
installment **111**
installments **111**

instant coffee **59**
insurance **102**
intelligence **166, 167**
intelligent **167**
intend **266**
intention **175**
interest **111**
interested **171**
intermediate **182**
intermission **129**
international **188**
Internet **95**
interrogate **156**
intersection **102**
interview **72**
intestines **28**
into **258**
Iran **192**
Iraq **189**
Ireland **191**
iris **17**
iron **39, 110**
ironing board **39**
irrigate **163**
Islam **177**
Islamic **177**
Islamic Cairo **198**
island **201**
Ismaïlia **194**
issue (a visa) **145**
it **244**
Italian **181**
Italy **191**
jacket **36**
jam **66**
January **236**
Japan **192**
Japanese **181**
jar **69**
jaw **16**
jazz **132**
jealous **170**
jeans **35**
jellyfish **215**
Jesus **178**
Jew **178**
jewelry **40**
Jewish **178**
jinn **177**
job **71**
job interview **72**
jobless **74**
jog **141**
jogging **141**
Jordan **189**
journey **143**
jovial **170**
Judaism **178**
judge **76, 156**
judgment **156**
juice **57**
July **236**
jump **266**
jump rope **142**
June **236**
jungle **202**
junior **84**
junk food **60**
just **240, 252**
just now **240**
just right **39**
justice **156**
kangaroo **213**
keep **266**
kennel **212**
ketchup **65**
kettle **48**
key **43**
keyboard **94**
khamsin **209**
Khan el-Khalili **199**
kick (a ball) **137**
kidney **28**
kill **155**
kilogram **223**
kilometer **223**
kind **170**
kindergarten **78**
king **151**
king (in chess) **135**
kingdom **151**
kiss **13**
kitchen **47**
kite **122**
knee **27**
knife **46**
knight (in chess) **135**
knit **126**
knit one's brow **16**
knitting needle **126**
know **166**
knowledge **166**
knuckles **26**
koala **213**
Korea **192**
Korean **181**
koshary **69**
Kuwait **189**
Labor Day **238**
laboratory **81**
laborer **76**
lake **202**
lamb **67**
lamp **45**
land **201**
land (plane) **148**
landlady **42**
landlord **42**
lane **102**
language **181**
language academy **79**
laptop **94**
large **222**
large (size) **38**
larynx **21**
last **232**
last night **234**
late **243**
later **240**
laugh **168**
laughter **168**
laundry **39**
laundry basket **39**
lava **203**
law **86, 156**
lawn **53**
lawyer **76, 156**
lay an egg **163**
lay off **74**
layover **148**
lazy **170**
leaf **218**
learn **78, 182**
leash **212**
leather **40**
leave **266, 268**
Lebanon **189**
lecture **79**
lecture hall **80**
lecturer **82**
left **99**
leg **27, 216**
legal **156**
legible **183**
lemon **63**
lemon-yellow **220**
lend **111**
length **222**
leopard **213**
Lesser Eid **238**
lesson **79**
letter **113, 183**
letter box **113**
Levantine Arabic **182**
level **182**
liberate **165**
liberation **165**
library **81, 114**
Libya **189**
lice **216**
license plate **102**
lie **266**
life **1**
life span **3**
lift **109, 142, 263**
light **45, 270, 271**
light (a cigarette) **130**
light (color) **221**
light blue **220**
light switch **45**
lighter **130**
lightning **210**
like **171**
likeable **170**
likely **272**
line **96**
linen **40**
linguistics **86**
lion **213**
lip **20**

liquor **59**
listen to **132**, **185**
listening **185**
literate **78**
literature **86**
little **222**
little: a little (bit) **224**
live **1**, **266**
lively **170**
liver **28**
liver sandwich **69**
living room **46**
lizard **215**
loan **111**
lobby **150**
lobster **68**
lock **264**
locker **140**
locker room **140**
locust **216**
long **222**, **269**
long johns **34**
loofah **52**
look **266**
look forward to **175**
look up (a word) **185**
looks **33**
loose **38**, **271**
lorry **98**
lose **266**
lose (a game) **138**
lose weight **140**
lot: a lot (of) **224**
lotion **24**
louse **216**
love **11**, **171**
lover **11**
low **206**
lower **142**
luck **177**
lunch **57**
lunch break **81**
lung **28**
lute **133**
Luxor **195**
ma'am **15**
Maadi (district) **199**
mad **166**
madam **15**
magazine **123**
maid **43**, **76**
mail **113**
mail carrier **113**
mailbox **113**
major **84**
majority **152**
make **264**
Malaysia **192**
mall **119**
man **2**
manager **72**
mango **64**
Mansoura **194**
manual **104**
manufacture **161**
map **81**, **204**
march **153**
March **236**
margarine **60**
market **119**
marriage **12**
married **12**
marry **12**
masculine **186**
masjid **178**
master's degree **85**
matches **130**
mathematics **86**
mattress **49**
mature **2**
Mawlid **238**
May **236**
mayonnaise **65**
meal **56**
mean **266**
measure **222**
measurement **222**
meat **67**
mechanic **76**
medicine **86**, **91**
Mediterranean Sea **194**
medium (size) **38**
meet **161**
meet up with **122**
meeting **73**, **161**
melt **202**
member **139**
member of parliament **151**
membership **139**
memory **166**
merchant **160**
merry **170**
Mersa Matruh **194**
messenger **176**
metal **110**
meteorite **204**
meter **223**
metro **99**
metro station **99**
Mexico **193**
microwave **47**
mid-term (exam) **81**
middle class **159**
middle school **78**
middle-aged **2**
midnight **234**
migraine **89**
mile **223**
military **164**
milk **59**, **162**
millennium **239**
millimeter **223**
million **229**
minced meat **67**
mind **16**, **166**
mine **164**
mineral water **57**
minister **151**, **179**
ministry **151**
minor **84**
minority **152**
minus **231**
minute **240**
Minya **195**
mirror **52**
mischievous **2**
miserable **206**
miss (the bus) **98**
miss (unmarried woman) **15**
missile **165**
mistake **80**
mister **15**
mixer **48**
mizmar (wooden flute) **133**
Modern Standard Arabic **182**
modest **170**
Mogamma **197**
Mohandessin (district) **199**
molar **21**
mole **25**
mom **6**
monarchy **151**
Monday **235**
monetary **159**
money **158**
monitor **94**
month **236**
moon **203**
mop **44**
morning **234**, **242**
Moroccan Arabic **182**
Morocco **189**
mortgage **111**
mosque **178**
Mosque of Muhammad Ali **199**
mosquito **216**
mosquito bite **216**
moss **219**
most **224**
moth **216**
mother **6**
Mother's Day **238**
motorcycle **100**
motorway **102**
mountain **201**
mountain range **201**
mountainous **201**
mourn **5**
mourning **5**

mouse **94**
mouse; rat **213**
mouth **20**
mouth wash **52**
mouthpiece (of shisha) **131**
mouthful **54**
move **135**, **266**
movie **123**, **128**
movie theater **128**
movie ticket **128**
mow **53**
MP **151**
MP3 **126**
MP3 player **126**
mug **58**
mule **162**
multi-colored **222**
multiply **230**
mum **6**, **219**
murder **155**
murderer **155**
muscle **29**
museum **107**
mushroom **62**
music **132**
musical instrument **133**
musician **76**, **133**
Muslim **177**
mussel **68**
mustache **23**
mustard **65**
my grandparents **9**
nail **53**
naked **30**
name **14**
nap **50**
nape of the neck **21**
napkin **47**
narrow **271**
narrow street **107**
Nasr City (district) **199**
nation **152**, **188**
National Police Day **237**
nationality **188**
native language **181**
naughty **2**
nausea **89**
nauseous **89**
navel **28**
navy **164**
navy blue **220**
near **259**
nearly **249**
necessary **269**
neck **21**
necktie **35**
necklace **41**
negotiate **99**
nerve **29**
Netherlands **191**
neuter **186**
never **250**
new **269**
New Testament **180**
New Year's Day **237**
New Year's Eve **237**
New Zealand **192**
newborn **1**
newlyweds **12**
news **124**
newspaper **114**, **122**
next to **259**
ney (reed flute) **133**
nice **170**, **206**
nickname **14**
Nigeria **190**
night **242**
night shift **73**
nightgown **36**
nightmare **50**
Nile **198**
Nile Corniche **198**
nine **227**
nineteen **227**
ninety **228**
ninth **232**
nipple **28**
niqab **35**
no **224**
no one **245**
noisy **271**
nominate **152**
nomination **152**
non-smoker **130**
none of **224**
none of the students **224**
noon **234**
noon prayer **179**
north **204**
North America **201**
north pole **205**
northeast **204**
northern **205**
northwest **204**
Norway **190**
nose **18**
nostril **18**
notebook **80**
notes **80**
nothing **245**
noun **186**
novel **114**, **123**
November **236**
now **240**
nowhere **249**
number **226**
number plate **102**
numeral **226**
nun **180**
nurse **76**, **88**
nut **64**
nutmeg **65**
nuts **64**
nylon **40**
o'clock **242**
oak tree **218**
oasis **203**
object **187**
Obour City **197**
obtain **265**
obvious **269**
occupation **165**
occupy **165**
ocean **202**
October **236**
octopus **68**
odd **226**
off **260**
off work **73**
office **73**, **161**
office building **109**
office worker **73**
often **251**
oil (vegetable) **69**
oily **68**
okay **173**
okra **62**
old **2**, **269**
old age **3**
Old Cairo **199**
old man **3**
old woman **3**
olive **62**, **221**
olive complexion **24**
Oman **190**
omelet **67**
on **258**
one **226**
one-way ticket **148**
onion **62**
online **95**
onto **258**
open **266**, **271**
open one's eyes **17**
open one's mouth **20**
operate on **92**
operation **92**
ophthalmologist **87**
opinion **173**
opposite **259**
or **254**
orange **64**, **221**
orange juice **57**
orchard **163**
orchestra **134**
order **266**
ordinal number **231**
oregano **65**
organize **262**
organs **28**

orphan **10**
orphanage **10**
orzo soup **69**
ostrich **214**
oud **133**
ounce **223**
out of **258**
outer space **204**
outside **253**
outside of **258**
oval **222**
oven **47**
over **258**
overpass **102**
overseas **253**
overtake **101**
overtime **72**
overweight **32**
oyster **68**
Pacific Ocean **202**
pack **145**
pack of cigarettes **131**
package **113**
pagan **177**
paganism **177**
page **114**
page number **114**
paid **73**
pain **88**
paint **127**
painter **76**
painting **44**, **127**
pajamas **36**
Pakistan **192**
Palestine **189**
palm **26**
palm tree **218**
palpitate **28**
pan **48**
pant leg **35**
panties **34**
pants **34**, **35**
panty hose **34**
paper **82**, **115**
paperclip **115**
Paradise **176**
paragraph **187**
parcel **113**
parentheses **187**
parents **6**
park **107**
park (a car) **101**
parking garage **101**
parking lot **101**
parliament **151**
parrot **214**
parsley **65**
part-time **71**
party (political) **152**
pass **101**, **266**
pass (a test) **81**
pass away **4**
passenger **100**
passing **4**
passion **11**
passport **145**
passport photo **145**
password **95**
past **240**, **260**
past tense **186**
pasta **66**
pastor **179**
pastrami **67**
pastries **60**
patch **126**
patient **88**
pause **126**
pavement **101**
paw **216**
pawn (in chess) **135**
pay **73**, **117**
pay off (a debt) **111**
pay raise **73**
pay the bill **121**
payday **73**
payment **111**
pea **62**
peace **164**
peach **64**
peacock **214**
peanut **64**
peanut butter **64**
pear **64**
pedal **100**, **104**
pedestrian crossing **101**
pedestrians **101**
pee **31**
pen **115**, **162**
pencil **115**
penguin **214**
peninsula **201**
penis **30**
penmanship **183**
pension **74**
penthouse **42**
people **2**, **152**
peppermint **65**
Pepsi **58**
percent **233**
percentage **233**
period **79**, **187**, **239**
period piece **129**
person **2**
personal trainer **139**
personality **170**
pet **212**
petal **218**
petrol **105**
pharmacist **76**
Philippines **192**
philosophy **86**
phone **96**
phone call **96**
phone number **96**
photo(graph) **127**
photocopy **116**
photocopy machine **116**
photographer **127**
photography **127**
physical education **86**
physics **86**
piano **133**
piano keys **133**
piastre **158**
pick one's nose **19**
pick up **102**, **263**
pick-up (truck) **98**
pickled vegetables **70**
pickpocket **155**
picture **44**
pie **61**
pierced ears **20**
pig **162**
pigeon **214**
pill **91**
pillow **49**
pillowcase **49**
pilot **76**, **148**
pimple **24**
pin **115**
pine tree **218**
pineapple **64**
pink **221**
pinky **26**
pipe **130**
piss **31**
pita bread **66**
pizza **60**
plains **203**
plan **166**
plan on **166**
planet **203**
plant **163**, **218**
plant (a seed) **219**
plant pot **219**
plaster **90**
plastic bag **119**
plastic surgeon **92**
plastic surgery **92**
plate **46**
plateau **201**
platform **148**
play **128**, **135**
play (an instrument) **133**
player **138**
playground **81**
plead **263**
pleasant **170**
plow **163**
plug **45**
plum **64**
plumber **76**
plump **33**
plural **186**

plus **230**
pocket **37**
poem **114**
poet **114**
poetry **114**
point to **27**
Poland **191**
polar bear **213**
police officer **76**
police station **108**
polish **37**
political **153**
political science **86**
politician **76**, **153**
politics **153**
polo shirt **34**
pomegranate **64**
ponytail **23**
poo **31**
poop **31**
poor **159**
pop music **132**
popcorn **129**
pope **180**
poppy **219**
popular music **132**
pork **67**
Port Said **194**
porter **150**
Portugal **191**
Portuguese **181**
possible **272**
post **113**
post office **108**, **113**
postcard **113**
poster **44**
posterior **30**
postman **113**
postpone **161**
pot **48**
potato **62**
potato chips **60**
pound **223**
pound sterling **158**
poverty **159**
practice **182**
praise **171**
pray **176**
prayer **176**, **179**
preach **178**, **180**
predict **167**
prefer **172**
prefix **186**
pregnancy **92**
pregnant **92**
prepare **266**
preposition **186**
preschool **78**
prescribe **91**
prescription **91**
present **240**
present tense **186**
president **151**
presidential term **152**
pretty **33**
price **117**
priest **76**, **180**
primary school **78**
prime minister **151**
prince **151**
princess **151**
principal **83**
print **96**, **115**
printer **96**
prison **156**
prisoner **157**
private parts **29**
private sector **71**
probable **272**
problem **88**
professor **76**, **83**
prohibit **266**
promotion **74**
pronounce **184**
pronunciation **184**
prophet **176**
proposal **161**
propose **267**
prose **114**
prosecutor **156**
protein **66**
protest **153**
protester **153**
proud **169**
province **153**
pseudonym **14**
psychology **86**
public sector **71**
publish **115**
pull **142**
pull-ups **141**
pulpit **180**
pulse **28**
punctuation **187**
punctuation mark **187**
pungent **56**, **60**
punish **267**
punishment **156**
pupil **17**
puppet **135**
purple **221**
purse **35**
pursue **264**
push **141**
push-ups **141**
pushpin **115**
pussy **30**
put **267**
put aside **112**
put on **38**
pyjamas **36**
Pyramids (of Giza) **200**
Qasr Al-Nil Bridge **198**
Qatar **189**
Qena **195**
quarter **232**
queen **151**
queen (in chess) **135**
question **80**
question mark **187**
quick **270**
quickly **249**
quiet **271**
quilt **49**
quit **74**, **266**
quit smoking **130**
quotation mark **187**
Quran **179**
rabbit **213**
radio **125**
radio station **125**
radish **62**
railroad **148**
rails **148**
railway **148**
rain **208**
rainbow **209**
raise (one's hand) **80**
Ramadan **238**
rap **132**
rape **155**
rash (skin) **89**
raspberry **64**
raven **214**
ravine **201**
razor blade **53**
read **122**, **183**
reading **183**
ready **270**
real estate agent **76**
reality TV show **124**
rear view mirror **103**
receipt **117**
receive **265**
receiver **97**
recess **81**
recipe **48**
recite (the Quran) **179**
recommend **262**
record (vinyl) **125**
recovery **91**
recruit **164**
rectangle **222**
red **220**
red light **101**
Red Sea **196**
reduce **264**
reference book **114**
reform **153**
refrigerator **47**
refund **120**
related to **6**
relationship **11**

relative **6**
relax **122**
relaxation **122**
religion **176**
religious **176**
remarry **13**
remember **166**
remind **166**
rent **42**
renter **42**
rep (in a set) **141**
repairman **76**
repeat **185**
repetition **185**
reply **262**
report card **82**
representative **75**
reptiles **214**
republic **151**
request **266**
reservation **150**
reserve, book **150**
residence permit **145**
resign **74**
respond **262**
rest **122**
restaurant **108**, **121**
results **82**
retire **74**
retirement **74**
return **119**
return ticket **148**
reverse (gear) **104**
review **82**
revise **82**
revolution **153**
Revolution Day **238**
rewind **125**
rhinoceros **213**
rib **29**
ribbon **36**
rice **66**
rice pudding **61**
rich **159**
ride **100**
rifle **127**
right **80**, **99**, **270**
right away **240**
right now **240**
right of way **101**
ring **40**, **96**
ringtone **96**
river **202**
roast **69**
rob **155**
rock music **132**
role **129**
romance **11**
Romania **191**
romantic comedy **129**
roof **42**
rook (in chess) **135**
room **43**, **150**
rooster **162**
rose **219**
rosemary **65**
rot **56**
rough **271**
round-about **102**
round-trip ticket **148**
rouse **50**
Royal Poinciana tree **218**
royalty **151**
rubber **115**
rubbish **48**
ruby **41**
rule (grammar) **185**
rule over **151**
ruler **115**
run **141**
run a red light **101**
running machine **141**
rush hour **101**
Russia **192**
Russian **181**
sad **168**
sage **65**
sailor **76**, **164**
salad **63**
salad dressing **63**
salary **73**
sale **118**
sales tax **159**
salesperson **76**
saliva **21**
salmon **68**
salsa **65**
salt **65**
salty **56**
same **272**
sand **143**
sand dunes **203**
sandals **37**
sandcastle **143**
sandstorm **210**
sandwich roll **66**
Saqqara **195**
Satan **177**
satellite dish **125**
satiated **55**
Saturday **235**
sauce **65**
Saudi Arabia **190**
sausage **67**
save **94**, **112**
savings **112**
savings account **111**
saw **53**
say **267**
scale **142**
scan **96**
scanner **96**
scar **25**
scarf **35**, **36**
scholarship **83**
school **78**
school bus **81**
school yard **81**
school year **83**
science **86**
science fiction **129**
scissors **115**
sclera **17**
score **136**, **138**
scorpion **216**
Scotland **191**
scowl **16**
screen **94**, **128**
screening room **128**
screw **53**
screwdriver **53**
scrotum **30**
scuba diving **144**
sea **202**
seafood **68**
seagull **214**
seal **213**
sealion **213**
seaside **143**
seaside resort **143**
season **124**, **237**
seat **128**
seat belt **105**
seatbelt **105**
second **231**, **240**
second class **148**
secondary school **78**
secretary **76**, **151**
secular **176**
see **18**
seed **219**
selfie **127**
sell **117**
semester **83**
seminar **161**
send **113**
senior **85**
sentence **156**, **187**
sentence, judge **156**
September **236**
series **124**
serious **170**
sermon **180**
servant **76**
service **121**
set (a table) **46**
set (of reps) **141**
set down **267**
settle **111**
seven **227**
seventeen **227**
seventh **232**
seventy **228**

several **225**
sew **126**
sewing machine **126**
sewing needle **126**
sex **13**
sexual organs **29**
shade **221**
shallow **269**
Sham el-Nessim **238**
shampoo **52**
shape **222**
shark **68**, **215**
Sharm el-Sheikh **195**
sharp **60**, **272**
sharpen a pencil **115**
shave **24**, **53**
shaving cream **53**
she **244**
sheep **162**
sheet (of paper) **115**
shelf **43**
shellfish **68**
shepherd **162**
shift (work) **73**
shin **27**
ship **98**
shipping **98**
shirt **34**
shisha **131**
shit **31**
shoe **37**
shoe polish **37**
shoe size **38**
shoelaces **37**
shoes **37**
shop **119**, **160**
shop assistant **77**, **119**
shop keeper **119**
shopkeeper **77**
shopping **117**
shopping area **119**
shopping bag **119**
shopping center **119**
short **32**, **222**, **269**
shorts **35**
shot **91**
shot (injection) **91**
shoulder **27**
shoulder-length **22**
shovel **53**
show **267**
show (a movie) **128**
shower **51**
shrimp **68**
shrub **218**
Shubra El-Kheima **197**
shutters **43**
shy **170**
siblings **7**
sick **87**
sickness **87**
side view mirror **103**
sideburns **23**
sidewalk **101**
sign **112**
signature **112**
silent mode **96**
silk **40**
silver **41**
similar **272**
sin **177**
Sinai (region and peninsula) **195**
since **243**
sing **132**
singer **132**
singing **132**
single **12**
singular **186**
sink **48**, **52**, **267**
sip **54**, **68**
sir **15**
sister **7**
sit-ups **141**
sitcom **124**
sitting room **46**
Siwa **196**
six **227**
sixteen **227**
sixth **232**
sixty **228**
size **222**
size (clothing) **38**
skeleton **29**
sketch **127**
ski **137**
skin **24**
skinny **33**
skirt **35**
skull **16**
skull cap **36**
skunk **213**
sky **203**, **208**
skyscraper **109**
sleep **49**
sleep with **13**
sleepwalk **50**
sleepy **50**
sleeve **34**
slice **47**
slippers **37**
Slovakia **191**
slow **270**
slow down **104**
slowly **249**
slurp **68**
small **222**
small (size) **38**
smell **19**
smile **20**, **168**
smoke **130**
smoker **130**
smoking **130**
smooth **271**
smuggle **146**
snack **57**
snail **216**
snake **215**
snake eyes **136**
sneeze **19**
snore **50**
snorkel **144**
snot **19**
snow **209**
so **254**
so that **254**
soap **52**
soccer **136**
soccer field **137**
soccer jersey **34**
soccer match **123**
sociable **170**
social **154**
social studies **86**
society **154**
socket **45**
socks **38**
soda **57**
sofa **46**
soft **269**
Sohag **195**
soil **201**
soldier **77**, **164**
sole **27**
solicitor **156**
Somalia **190**
some **224**
someday **240**
somehow **251**
someone **244**
something **245**
sometime **250**
sometimes **250**
somewhere **249**
son **7**
song **125**, **132**
soon **240**
sophomore **84**
sore throat **89**
soul **176**
soup **68**
sour **56**
south **204**
South Africa **190**
South America **201**
South Korea **192**
south pole **205**
southeast **204**
southern **205**
southwest **204**
soy sauce **65**
space **204**
Spain **191**
Spanish **181**, **191**

spanner **53**
spare tire **104**
sparrow **214**
speak **184**
speakers **125**
speaking **183**
spearmint **65**
specialist **87**
spectator **129**
speech **183**
speed **105**
speed limit **102**, **105**
speed up **104**
speedometer **105**
spell **183**
spelling **183**
Sphinx **200**
Sphinx Square **200**
spices **64**
spicy **56**
spider **216**
spider web **216**
spinach **62**
spine **29**
spit **21**
spittle **21**
sponge **52**
spoon **46**
sport **136**
sporting event **123**
sports program **123**
spot **24**
sprained ankle **90**
spring **237**
square **107**, **222**
square meter **223**
squid **68**
squirrel **213**
stable **163**
stage **129**
staircase **109**
stairs **109**
stale **56**
stalk **218**
stamp **113**
staple **115**
stapler **115**
star **203**
star (movie) **129**
start **263**
start university **83**
state **153**
stationary bicycle **141**
stationery **115**
stay **267**
stay up **50**
steak **67**
steal **155**
steel **110**
steer **103**
steering wheel **103**
stem **218**
stepbrother **8**
stepdaughter **9**
stepfather **8**
stepmother **8**
stepsister **8**
stepson **9**
stereo **125**
stick shift **104**
still **252**
stitch **90**
stitches **90**
stomach **28**
stomachache **89**
stop **101**, **126**
store **119**, **160**
stork **214**
storm **209**
story (floor) **42**
story (tale) **110**, **114**
stout **33**
stove **47**
straight **99**
straight (hair) **22**
strange **170**
strawberry **64**
stream **202**
street **107**
street musician **133**
strong **269**
structure **109**
stubble **24**
student **78**
student loan **83**
studies **80**
study **79**, **82**
stupid **167**
stupidity **167**
subject **85**, **186**
subtract **230**
subway **99**
succeed **267**
suckle **1**
Sudan **188**
Suez **194**
Suez Canal **195**
suffix **186**
sugar **65**
suggest **267**
suit **35**
suit jacket **35**
suitcase **145**
summer **237**
summer vacation **81**
summit **153**
sun **203**, **208**
sun umbrella **144**
sunbathe **144**
sunblock **144**
sunburn **144**
Sunday **235**
sunflower **219**
sunglasses **40**
sunlight **204**
Sunnah **179**
sunrise **204**
sunscreen **25**
sunset **204**
sunset prayer **179**
supermarket **108**, **119**
superstition **177**
superstitious **177**
sura **179**
sure **173**
surface area **222**
surgeon **92**
surgery **92**
surprise **169**
surprised **169**
surprising **169**
surrounding **259**
swallow **21**, **54**, **214**
swamp **202**
swan **214**
sweat **25**
sweater **36**
sweatshirt **36**
sweaty **25**
Sweden **190**
sweep **44**
sweet **56**, **58**, **170**
sweet pepper **62**
sweet potato **63**
sweets **60**, **61**
swim **144**
swimming **144**
swimming pool **144**
swimsuit **36**
Switzerland **191**
sycamore tree **218**
syllable **187**
Syria **189**
T-shirt **34**
table **43**
table manners **70**
tahini **63**
Tahrir Square **197**
tail **217**
Taiwan **192**
take **102**, **265**, **267**
take (transportation) **98**
take a sip of **54**
take a test **81**
take off **38**
take off (plane) **147**
Talaat Harb Square **198**
talk show **124**
tall **32**, **222**, **269**
talon **216**
tan **144**
tangerine **64**

tank **165**
tanned **144**
Tanta **194**
tap **48**
tape **115**
task **71**
taste **20**, **55**
tasty **55**
tattoo **25**
tax **158**
taxi **99**
taxi driver **77**, **99**
taxi meter **99**
tea **59**
teach **83**
teacher **77**, **82**
team **138**
tear **267**
tear(drop) **18**
teats **217**
technician **77**
technology **94**
teddy **36**
teddy bear **135**
teenager **2**
teknonym **14**
telephone **96**
television **46**, **123**
tell **267**
temperature **206**
ten **227**
tenant **42**
tennis **137**
tense **186**
tent **145**
tenth **232**
test **81**
testicle **30**
testicles **30**
text book **80**
text message **96**
Thailand **192**
thank **267**
thankful **169**
Thanksgiving **237**
that **244**, **254**
theater **81**, **129**
theft **155**
there **249**
these **244**
thesis **85**
they **244**
thief **155**
thigh **27**
thimble **126**
thin **33**
think about **166**
third **231**, **232**
third class **148**
thirst **55**
thirsty **55**
thirteen **227**
thirty **228**
this **244**
those **244**
thousand **229**
thread **126**
three **226**
thriller **129**
throat **21**
through **260**
throw **138**
throw away **49**
throw up **89**
thumb **26**
thunder **210**
Thursday **235**
thyme **65**
thyroid gland **29**
ticket **146**
tidy up **44**
tie **35**, **37**, **267**
tiger **213**
tight **38**, **271**
tights **34**
tiles **43**
time **234**
times **231**
tip **121**
tipsy **59**
tire (wheel) **103**
tire pressure **104**
tired **169**
tiring **149**, **169**
title **14**
to **258**
toast **66**
toaster **48**
tobacco **130**
today **234**
toddler **1**
toe **27**
toilet (bowl) **52**
toilet paper **52**
toilet seat **52**
tomato **63**
tomato puree **65**
tomato sauce **65**
tomato soup **69**
tomorrow **234**
ton **223**
tongue **20**
tonight **234**
tonsils **21**
too **249**, **251**
too many **251**
tool **53**
tooth **20**
tooth paste **52**
toothache **93**
toothbrush **52**
top floor **109**
topaz **41**
tornado **210**
tortoise **215**
touch **267**
toupee **23**
tour **143**
tour guide **143**
tourism **143**
tourist **143**
tourist police **143**
tourist visa **145**
toward **261**
towel **52**
towel rack **52**
tower **109**
town **107**
toy **135**
track **125**, **148**
tractor **163**
trade **74**
trade; business **160**
traffic **100**
traffic jam **100**
traffic light **101**
train **148**, **212**
train car **149**
train station **148**
training session **139**
transit **148**
transportation **98**
travel **143**, **145**
travel agent **77**
traveling **143**
tray **48**
treadmill **141**
treat **91**
treatment **91**
tree **218**
trek **145**
triangle **222**
trim **23**
trip **143**
tropical **211**
tropics **202**
trousers **35**
truck **98**
trumpet **133**
trunk **218**
trunk (car) **103**
try **267**
try out **267**
Tuesday **235**
tuition **83**
tuk-tuk **100**
tulip **219**
tuna **68**
tune (a guitar) **133**
Tunisia **189**
tunnel **201**
turban **36**
turkey **163**, **192**
Turkish **181**
Turkish coffee **58**
turn **135**
turn __ years old **4**
turn down (volume) **125**
turn off **45**
turn off (a computer) **94**
turn on **45**

turn on (a computer) **94**
turn signal **103**
turn up (volume) **125**
turnip **63**
turquoise **221**
turtle **215**
TV program **123**
TV show **123**
twelve **227**
twenty **227**
twilight **204**
twin **7**
two **226**
typewriter **115**
typhoon **210**
tyre **103**
udder **217**
ugly **33**
Ukraine **192**
unbutton **37**
uncle **9**
unclear **270**
uncomfortable **149**
under **259**
undergraduate **85**
underground **99**
undershirt **34**
understand **166**
underwear **34**
undress **38**
unemployed **74**
unemployment **74**
unhealthy **56**
uniform **35**
United States **193**
universe **203**
university **79**, **83**
unmarried **12**
unpack **145**
unplug **45**
untie **37**
until **243**, **255**
unzip **37**
upload **95**
upper class **159**
Upper Egypt **195**
upset **168**
upstairs **253**
urinate **31**
urine **31**
use **267**
useful **271**
useless **271**
username **95**
usually **250**
vacation **143**
vacuum **44**
vagina **30**
Valentine's Day **237**
valid **145**
valley **201**
Valley of the Kings **195**
vandalism **155**
vandalize **155**
vanilla **65**
vase **46**
VAT **159**
vegetable **62**
vegetable soup **69**
vein **29**
Venezuela **193**
verb **186**
verse **179**
very **251**
vest **34**
veterinarian **77**
vibration **96**
vice president **151**
Vietnam **192**
village **107**
vine **219**
vinegar **65**
violet **219**, **221**
violin **133**
visa **145**
vision **18**
visit **126**
vocabulary **185**
volcano **203**
volleyball **137**
volume **124**, **222**
vomit **89**
vote **152**
voter **152**
vowel **187**
vulture **214**
wafer **61**
wage **73**
waist **28**
wait **267**
waiter **77**, **121**
waiting room **148**
waitress **77**, **121**
wake up **51**
Wales **191**
walk **268**
wall **44**
wallet **35**
walnut **64**
want **175**
war **164**
wardrobe **51**
warm **270**
warmth **207**
wash one's face **16**, **52**
washing machine **39**
wasp **216**
watch **35**
watch TV **123**
water **57**, **202**
water (a plant) **219**
water heater **52**
water-pipe **131**
waterfall **202**
wave **144**
wavy (hair) **22**
we **244**
weak **269**
wealth **159**
wear **38**
weather **206**
weather forecast **210**
weather report **124**
web page **95**
web site **95**
wed **12**
wedding **12**
wedding ring **40**
Wednesday **235**
weed (a garden) **219**
week **235**
weekday **235**
weekend **235**
weigh **223**
weigh oneself **142**
weight **32**, **223**
weight machine **140**
weights **140**
welcome **268**
well **251**
well-behaved **2**
west **204**
western **205**
Western Desert **196**
wet **271**
whale **214**
what **246**, **257**
What a nice day! **206**
wheat **163**
wheelchair **87**
when **242**, **246**, **256**
where **246**, **256**
whether **254**
which **246**
while **256**
white **60**, **220**
White Desert **196**
white of one's eyes **17**
whiteboard **80**
who **246**, **257**
whole **232**
why **246**, **257**
wide **271**
widow **13**
widowed **13**
widower **13**
width **222**
wife **8**
WIFI **95**
wig **23**
willow tree **218**
win (a game) **138**

wind **209**
window **43**, **103**, **113**
window seat **147**
windscreen **102**
windshield **102**
wine **59**
wing **217**
wink **17**
winter **237**
winter vacation **81**
wish **175**
with **261**
withdraw **112**
without **261**
wolf **213**
woman **2**
wood **110**
wool **39**
word **185**
word order **187**work **71**
workday **235**
work out **139**, **229**
work permit **145**
working class **159**
working hours **72**
workout **139**
workout clothes **140**
worldwide **188**
worm **216**
wound **90**
wrap **119**
wrench **53**
wrinkled **39**
wrinkles **25**
wrist **26**, **27**
write **183**
writer **77**, **114**
writing **183**wrong **80**, **270**
x-ray **91**
yard **53**
yawn **21**
year **4**, **239**
yeast **66**
yellow **220**
yellow light **101**
Yemen **190**
yesterday **234**
yet **252**
yield to **101**
yoga **141**
yoghurt **59**
yolk **66**
you **244**
young **2**
young man **2**
young people **2**
young woman **2**
youth **2**, **3**
Zagazig **194**
Zamalek (district) **198**
zebra crossing **101**
zero **226**
zip up **37**
zipper **37**
zucchini **63**

Made in the USA
Monee, IL
24 June 2024

60603414R00167